Personality: Making The Most Of It

Personality: Making The Most Of It

Ken Chapman, Ph.D.

Writers Club Press

San Jose New York Lincoln Shanghai

Personality: Making The Most Of It

Writers Club Press
an imprint of iUniverse, Inc.

For information address:
iUniverse, Inc.
5220 S. 16th St., Suite 200
Lincoln, NE 68512
www.iuniverse.com

ISBN: 0-595-22239-0

Printed in the United States of America

For
Jeremiah George Chapman

Contents

Acknowledgments

As is true of most of life's endeavors, what follows is the product of many. It is true that the words and ideas are mine. It is also true that this book is possible only because of the knowledge, skill, and encouragement of others.

My thanks to Jean Graham, who typed and retyped the manuscript; to Jean Graham and Rick Mitchell for their reading and critique of the initial draft; and to my wife, Rhonda Pruitt Chapman, for her tireless and invaluable editorial contributions; and to my teachers, associates and mentors, from grade school on who provided encouragement.

Ken Chapman
Spring 2002

Author's Preface

In nearly thirty years of studying the human experience, I have learned that "people are people," no matter where you find them. Almost all of us are capable of enormously good behavior, as well as tragically self-destructive behavior. At our best, we are nothing short of heroic in the face of disappointment or danger. At our worst, we are equally capable of cowardly behaviors which harm even the innocent. People from both ends of the continuum can be found in every setting where people gather—the workplace, schools, government, and yes, even in religious institutions, and the home. In my experience, three things separate the emotionally healthy from the self-destructive.

1. Emotionally healthy people know they are imperfect and, therefore, capable of committing self-destructive acts. Thus, they guard against such behavior. By contrast, self-destructive people cannot tolerate the thought of their imperfection and go to extraordinary measures to avoid facing their own fallibility—lying to themselves, blaming others, and even harming those who will not turn a blind eye to their pretense of perfection.

2. Emotionally healthy people self-critique. They tend to explain the world in terms of their own behavior, not in terms of other people's faults. They refuse to be victims and they refuse to victimize others. Emotionally healthy people focus the bulk of their energy in managing their own words and behavior. We recognize them by how well they lead themselves.

3. Emotionally healthy people consider self-knowledge the starting point for all wisdom. They believe that accepting the capacity for wrong is the best way to guard against doing wrong. They believe the wise will assume responsibility for themselves, because it is impossible to control or be responsible for others. Therefore, the emotionally

healthy view personal insight as a painful, but valuable road to greater wisdom, happiness, and professional effectiveness.

In **Personality: Making the Most of It**, I attempt to make a contribution to the effectiveness of the emotionally healthy, no matter where they are found.

1

Your Unique Life Pattern

Your personality style is your organizing theme; that which defines your life path. It represents the orderly arrangement of all your attributes, thoughts, feelings, attitudes, behaviors, and coping mechanisms. It is the distinctive pattern of your psychological functioning—the way you think, feel, and behave that makes you definitely you.

After you have gained 30 pounds, started to turn gray, and begun wearing glasses, your personality style is what causes your classmates at your 25th high school reunion to exclaim, "Why, you haven't changed a bit." What has stayed the same and is so easily recognizable is the way you react to others, your emotional style, your way of reasoning and expressing yourself, your body language, the outward effects of the core traits that have consistently marked your style since your earliest years.

Scientific exploration of human personality is on the cutting edge of modern psychiatry. In the fields of neuropsychiatry and behavioral genetics, we are beginning to prove that the foundations of personality are largely inherited. In other words, biologically determined. To psychiatrists, the inborn, genetic aspect of your personality is called your temperament. Your natural activity level, your characteristic mood ranges—cheerful or not, and your reaction ranges, are among the many features of your temperament or biological style with which you emerged preprogrammed from the womb. We are even beginning to mark each personality style with the underlying chemical communication patterns among brain cells. Things are truly changing at a dramatic rate. In the next ten years, we expect to learn more about personality and brain function than we have learned in all the previous history of medical research.

As with a number of physical traits such as height, genes confer a range of personality predispositions. Environment and life experience, parents, family, life events, culture and peers, sculpt the final "you" from the possibilities. Adverse experience can alter the possibilities for the worse. For example, you may have grown taller were it not for poor nutrition or illness during your childhood. By the same token, had your parents abused you instead of appreciating and responding sufficiently to your needs, your powerful aggressiveness might have landed you in jail instead of fueling your brilliant maneuvers in the court room.

Personality is like a deck of cards. You are dealt a hand at conception, and life experiences determine which genetic cards will be turned up and, therefore, what the nature of your normal experience will be. Your hand, that is your personality style, will be fairly set by the end of childhood and you will be playing the "game of life" in your distinctive way for the remainder of your years. Although psychiatrists or psychologists have not invented a crystal ball that can predict what "move" you or anyone else will make in response to any single situation, research shows that much of the time we can count on people playing the game true to their personalities well into old age.

Style versus disorder

You do, of course, grow and change throughout your lifetime, but you do so in your consistent, characteristic manner. Your personality style is your way of being, of becoming, and of meeting life's challenges. Most people's styles have a built-in flexibility factor that allows them to deal with the hurdles thrown in their path. They can adapt to change which makes a variety of experiences possible. Other people, however, find themselves up against the same old walls. They are locked into rigid, inflexible personality disorders. These are personality disorders which can cause them to have the same troubled, bored, empty, lonely, or disruptive experiences over and over again through-out their lives.

The Personality Style—Personality Disorder Continuum

Style	—>	Disorder
Conscientious		Obsessive-Compulsive
Self-Confident		Narcissistic
Dramatic		Histrionic
Vigilant		Paranoid
Mercurial		Borderline
Devoted		Dependent
Solitary		Schizoid
Leisurely		Passive-Aggressive
Sensitive		Avoidant
Idiosyncratic		Schizotypal
Adventurous		Antisocial
Self-Sacrificing		Self-Defeating
Aggressive		Sadistic
Serious		Depressive

Case of Sam Gant

A man goes to a psychiatrist because his wife has threatened to leave him, "If you don't get your act together Sam, I mean it this time, I'll take the kids and go to mother's." Sam is 44 years old and has just been put on three months probation at his job because he mistakenly erased from the computer and somehow managed to destroy the backup copies of the key documentation for a project. His department consequently failed to meet an extremely important deadline and the company nearly lost a major contract.

Sam is an industrial engineer in an auto parts manufacturing company. He has lost three jobs in the last ten years. He says to the psychiatrist that there is nothing wrong with him. He has had a run of bad luck with rotten bosses. It is not his fault if the losers get promoted and management then asks him to do the impossible, says Sam. Sam concedes that all his "bad" bosses accused him of being forgetful, slow, stubborn, and uncooperative. The same complaints he admits, when pressed, that his wife has against him. She is always on his back to help around the house, which he refuses to do. She also annoys him by complaining about his constant grouchiness and his drinking, which Sam is sure he has under control. Sam says that his wife does not understand him—that's his problem, he tells the psychiatrist.

Nearly everybody delays and procrastinates and passively resists authority once in a while and some people are simply more relaxed and easy going than others about deadlines and assignments. They put them off while they attend to other more interesting things, but they do them eventually. These folks have a strong streak of the leisurely personality style. They get along fine in life as long as they steer clear of rush deadlines, high demand careers, and do not pair up with perfectionists. They will reward you with love and appreciation if you accept them as they are and take good care of them.

But Sam has more than a healthy share of these traits. For him, passive resistance to the demands of authority has become his only way of life. At home, he avoids everything his wife or teenage kids expect of him. At work, he continually sabotages his efforts to the point of jeopardizing his livelihood and his family's welfare. He has been this way at least since adolescence, when although intellectually gifted, he flunked out of two colleges before finally receiving his degree. Now, he is about to lose his marriage and his job.

Sam misses his second appointment with the therapist. "I forgot" he explains. But by the end of their next visit, the psychiatrist believes he has heard enough to make a preliminary diagnosis. Sam has a personality disorder. His personality style has become rigid and inflexible. Instead of providing a way of coping and adapting to the demands of life, his personality pattern has thrown him into one vicious cycle after another. He does not recognize that his repetitive patterns of behavior have made his life miserable. All he knows how to do is blame and envy others and say "no" so nothing good ever happens to Sam anymore.

Sam needs help. Specifically, Sam is suffering from passive-aggressive personality disorder. It is one of many disorders which represent a dysfunctional personality pattern.

Difficult People

In the following pages, I will take care to distinguish between personality disorders, and acute, painfully symptomatic conditions such as depression, schizophrenia, eating disorders, sexual disorders, and panic disorders. The latter are considered clinical symptoms syndromes. Their dramatic symptoms tend to flare up periodically. Often they have a powerful biological component and can be treated with medication.

Personality disorders, on the other hand, are long-term patterns of inflexible and maladaptive behavior that are manifest from adolescence. Without treatment, they last a lifetime, although they may lessen in intensity in middle and old age. This does not mean that people with problems stemming from their personalities do not also get depressed or develop problems such as panic attacks, addictions to drugs or other substances, or suffer severe mental anguish. Very often, as we will see in the chapters that follow, certain personality disorders create vulnerability to specific clinical symptom syndromes. The acute conditions erupt under particular kinds of stress such as the breakup of a relationship.

Personality Style—the Good Thing

Psychiatry concerns itself with disorder. Our primary concern in this book is to talk about the normal adaptive personality styles that the disorders take to an extreme. We will return to passive-aggressive Sam later. There, in addition to leisurely styles and to the artistic style, we will find what are often intriguing and highly creative people. Sam can be stubborn and resist his wife's demands, but not under every circumstance. He will feel guilty about his behavior and eventually he will end up doing something about it, although perhaps not right away. Fortunately, Sam's wife knows how to deal with him and often can coax him to do more than any boss would ever succeed in doing.

The Flexibility/Variety/Adaptability Standard

No one can say exactly where style ends and disorder begins. The difference between Sam and someone who fits into society more easily, therefore, leading a productive and satisfying life, involves flexibility, variety, and adaptability. Establishing a diagnosis is the responsibility of mental health professionals. But you can think about your behavior and life experience or your level of frustration with another person in terms of these standards:

1. Flexibility and inflexibility. Sam is stuck with one principle way of behaving in response to demanding people and situations in his life. What he needs is a larger repertoire of behaviors. For instance, he needs to be able to negotiate with his wife and to see her particular point of view. He also needs to be able to put himself in his boss's position, and understand how to meet his boss's needs in order to succeed in the workplace. But looking at the world from the rigid perspective that is characteristic of Sam, he finds this very difficult to do.

2. Variety and repetition. Sam lives a life of repetitions. He is always in trouble at work, his marriage is often in crisis, he has few rewarding experiences, and he makes no progress. His life is the same old story day after day. What he needs, however, is to be less a creature of habit.

He needs to find a way to be a bit more spontaneous and find a way to have fun with his family and even with his work. In other words, he needs to find a way to be happy as opposed to simply rebelling against the authority figures in his life.

3. Adaptability and inability to cope with stress. It is not unusual to find a person who has a tendency to withdraw and to become obstinate when faced with stressful demands from other people. But it is also common to find that such people usually find a way to deal with the issues they are confronted with, often dealing with them in ways that produce satisfying results. Sam, on the other hand, cannot master the slightest stress. When he was under the pressure of a departmental deadline, instead of tolerating the extra demands on him and demonstrating the ability he possessed, he consciously erased from the computer months of painstaking work. When an individual displays an ability to cope with the environment in a flexible manner, and his or her typical perceptions and behaviors foster personal satisfaction, then the person may be said to possess a "normal or healthy personality," writes psychologist, Theodore Millon. "Conversely, when average or everyday responsibilities are responded to inflexibly or defectively, or when the individual's perceptions and behaviors result in personal discomfort or curtail opportunities to learn and to grow, then we may speak of a pathological or maladaptive pattern."

The Six Domains of Functioning

Flexible or otherwise, your personality etches its distinctive imprint on six key areas of life—your self, your relationships, your work, your emotions, your self-control, and your notions about the real world. Modern psychiatric thinking has determined that these six domains are fundamental to the assessment of your personality pattern. As we will demonstrate, each of the personality styles portrays a characteristically normal pattern of thinking, feeling, and behaving in each of these six domains. Also, for each personality style, one or two, and in one case, three of these domains dominate the entire style and determine functioning in all the domains. For example: work is clearly the ruling domain for people of the conscientious style. It dominates their emotional life and they are miserable when there is no work to accomplish. For the leisurely style, the domain is the self. Here the need to be independent, and to pursue their own meaning in life is essential to them, even more important even than their relationships.

Self

This domain includes your sense of self, your self-esteem, your self-image, the way you see, think, and feel about yourself. Your place in the universe and your place in other people's estimation. Self-confident types, for example, have a sense of entitlement and a real feeling of personal destiny. For them, the self domain is key which helps to explain their sureness of purpose, their drive, and their ability to succeed despite obstacles. Idiosyncratic types are sustained by the rich inner worlds of their selves. They may or may not be successful by other people's standards, or fit comfortably into the social order. But no matter what others say or convention dictates, they continue to march to their own drummer. For those with dramatic style, the self shines brightest when others appreciate their qualities. They rise to the occasion when all eyes are on them.

Your style of functioning in the self domain influences many important aspects of your behavior, for instance, how you perform at a job interview. Adventurous types may have such power in the self domain that they can talk people into giving them jobs for which they are really not qualified. Those with self-sacrificing style, who, as the name of the style suggests, come into their own when they are giving of themselves to others, commonly will play down their very real capabilities rather than appear to be boastful.

How do you think and feel about yourself? What do you think about your body? Where do you place yourself in the universe or in other people's estimation? Who comes first, you or them? What are your dreams for yourself? Questions such as these reveal what is normal for you in the self domain.

Relationships

This domain is a dominate factor in more than half of all personality styles. It defines how important other people are to us and how we lead our lives. Besides being individuals, we are members of families, couples, friendships, school classes, communities, business organizations, even crowds of strangers. The nature and style of our reactions and involvements with these other people reveal a great deal. Solitary people, for example, need to keep others at a distance. They can connect with others as long as they can then step away. Dramatic men and women often function poorly when they are alone. They need to be surrounded, admired, applauded. Vigilant types are very cautious of others. They take their time getting to know you before they move close. They are at their best with people when they feel in control in their relationships. For devoted types, other people are their reason for being. They feel incomplete unless they are committed to or even merged with someone. Sensitive people flourish in the company of a small group of friends or within their families, but they are uneasy and definitely "not themselves" in large groups or among strangers. Aggressive types have to be one step ahead in all relationships.

Work

This domain encompasses your style of "doing" and through play, school, career, housework, child care, chores, and hobbies, you have been spending your day working at something virtually all your life. Your personality style reveals itself in how you complete tasks, take and/or give orders, make decisions, plan, handle external and internal demands, take or give criticism, obey rules, take and delegate responsibility, and operate with other people.

For the conscientious style person, work is the ruling domain. People within this domain are always busy doing something even in their leisure time. It is their work and how well they do it that defines them and makes them comfortable in life. Work is a key domain for the aggressive style too. Clinical success at work is essential for this "take charge, top dog" style. Work also directs the serious style person. Life is work and work is life for this sober, no nonsense individual.

Although for conscientious and aggressive styles, work and fun are often synonymous, leisurely types usually think otherwise. They do what is required of them and no more so that they can escape their labors and relax and have a good time. Adventurous types are notoriously unresponsive to authority. They love a challenge, though, and as long as their work, meaning also sports and hobbies, include conquering some risk, they will stick with it.

What you choose to do in your life, how you choose it, and how you deal with work domain difficulties, including being out of work, and having to work two jobs to make ends meet, are also revealing of your personality style. For example: devoted styles will often go into the family business because it is expected of them. It may never occur to them to ask themselves what they would rather do and if they feel empty and dissatisfied, they will simply assume that they will have to stick it out and meet their responsibilities.

Emotions

The emotions or feelings domain include your usual moods and emotional states such as happiness, sadness, sexual feelings, anger, irritability, fear, anxiety, and sensitivity to praise and to criticism. What weight does this domain play in your personality pattern? People with dramatic style are ruled by their feelings. They judge and experience not by what they think about it, but how they feel about it. They are sensuous, often seductive, sexy. Their emotional style can serve them well in their work if they choose careers or environments in which they are encouraged to be intuitive and creative. Conscientious style individuals, on the other hand, give little weight to their feelings. To them, logic counts. They have strong feelings, but they prefer to submerge them under a cool, controlled veneer.

Level of emotional intensity from hot and high pitched to cool and unperturbable is a feature of this domain as well. The mercurial style is emotionally "hot." These individuals experience the lightest range of moods and feelings with deepest intensity, anger included. Their intense and changeable moods may facilitate creative experiences in accomplishments, but they will be less of an asset in the corporate board room. Solitary types tend to be cool, calm, and relatively unmoved by others' opinions of them. They often make gifted, rational observers of other people and of the natural world. But when others insist that they experience and express their feelings, they feel a great deal of anxiety. Serious types dwell in a solemn, emotional world. Not given to levity in the best of times, they prove better able to handle sobering experience than those with most other personality styles.

Sensitive types have very tender feelings. They are easily made anxious and self-conscious so they build their personal and career lives around people they know well and situations with which they are familiar. As a result, they tend to form deeply, meaningful relationships and to become expert at what they do.

Self-Control

Do you have an "executive director" in your head who considers each temptation and determines whether you should indulge your appetites or passions? And passions, to what degree? And for how long? Or does nothing intervene between desire and surrender? This domain, your control or your impulsiveness, rules your level of spontaneity and ability to act on impulse. This determines your risk taking behavior, your ability to forestall rewards and fulfillment, your planning skill, your self-discipline, your frustration, tolerance, and your ability to stop and think before you act.

Issues of self-control are key for the adventurous and the mercurial styles. Adventurous types love to act on the moment. They could not live any other way. They do not plan for the future or spend much time worrying about the consequence of their actions. Their personalities thrive on excitement, thrills, gambles, and risks. Their spontaneity gives their lives meaning and fuels their daring accomplishments. Mercurial men and women are similarly spontaneous, often in creative fields. When a passion comes upon them, they give in to it completely. They are thoroughly responsive to pleasure and sensation, hungry for sensuous experiences. They are remarkable in many aspects, not the least of which is as romantic lovers.

On the other side of the self-control continuum are the aggressive, conscientious, vigilant, and sensitive styles. In varying ways and for differing reasons, these personality styles emphasize control. They are all plan ahead, goal directed types who are focused either on future rewards or present safety. Aggressive and self-confident types are masters of the calculated risk. Serious style people seek predictable regularity.

In this, as in all other of the six domains, there is no "right" or "wrong" way of behaving unless the style of functioning brings harm to oneself or others. Nonetheless, in this era of eating disorders, sexually transmitted diseases, drug and alcohol abuse, violent crimes, and suicide, and controversy over abortion, our culture demonstrates strongly mixed feelings about how a person "should" function in the domain of self-control. Culture influences the expression of personality traits and styles and, like the pendulum will shift from generation to generation and culture to culture.

Real World

Do you live in a world of concrete objects such as people and buildings where things are basically what they seem? Or, when you walk through a forest, are you listening for the spiritual things that inhabit the trees? Philosophers have disagreed about the nature of reality since earliest times. In personality assessment, psychiatrists are less interested in what is "true" than in the degree to which your ideas vary from the prevailing standard and how these notions influences your behavior.

What is your reality—your spirituality? If you are an idiosyncratic type, the only style in which this domain is key, the conventional explanations, religion, institutions, and scientific understandings do not hold great weight with you. If you believe in extrasensory perception, it exists. You are not swayed by doubters. Your mind might be open to the existence of ghosts, extraterrestrials or past lives. On the other side of the spectrum, conscientious individuals are perhaps the most accepting and respecting of conventional shared realities, be they scientific, religious, political, or philosophic.

In the chapters ahead, we will discuss how each personality style shapes a person's approach to his or her self-styled reality in a more metaphoric sense. For example: sensitive types perceive the real world to be full of danger, therefore, they create safe harbors for themselves—they stick close to family and they embrace the known. Vigilant types may approach the real world as if they are the only sane ones in a sea of madmen. Self-confident folks strut around their planet as if it belonged to them personally. Whereas, devoted types may react to a real world in which they perceive themselves to be less important or to carry less weight than other more important people.

A Changeable Fate

By ordering your experiences and reactions in a systematic way throughout all the domains of functioning, your personality style directs your life and becomes a kind of fate, but it is a changeable fate. Even for those with personality disorders, the potential for change always exists. Intense life pressures and experiences such as the horrors of war, the birth of a child, or the rigors of psychotherapy can exert tremendous force on the personality. To adapt, your personality restructures itself. You can also learn to make certain small changes and adjustments. First, by understanding how your personality is structured and then by knowing how to enter the system and fine tune it.

This capacity for change, like the foundations of personality, is an inborn, biological reality. Researchers in neuropsychiatric laboratories are daring to speculate that learning and significant experience can trigger previously unexpressed potentials that have been encoded in our genes from the start. The elegant work of neuroscientist, Eric Kandel, implies that no matter how rigid or how limited your personality, biologically your fate is never really sealed. Through experience, learning, or psychotherapy, you can turn up long-covered cards and expand your hand at any age. The bottom line is that you and I can change, but we must not forget that the most important prerequisite for change is our having decided that we need to change. Until we decide to change, we simply do not change.

2

The Conscientious Style

You can call them the backbone of America. Conscientious style people are men and women of strong moral principles and absolute certainty and they won't rest until the job is done and done right. They are loyal to their families, their causes, and their superiors. Hard work is a hallmark of this personality style. Conscientious types achieve. No accomplished doctor, lawyer, scientist, or business executive could get far without a substantial amount of conscientious style in his or her personality pattern. Neither could a computer whiz, an efficient housekeeper, an accountant, a straight-A student, a good secretary, or anyone else who works hard in order to do well.

The conscientious personality style flourishes within cultures in which the work ethic thrives. Conscientious traits—hard work, prudence, conventionality may even confer a longevity advantage. We address this style first among the 14 because the conscientious style is adaptable, common, and thus likely to be a principle component of many personality profiles. Indeed, within our society, so wide a range of conscientious behaviors is considered normal, even admirable, that it may be hard to draw the line between the conscientious personality style and the obsessive-compulsive personality disorder that marks its extreme.

What are we to say about the man or woman who always takes a briefcase full of work along on vacation? Is he or she a work-aholic who cannot relax and is headed for an early heart attack? Or, is this a person who loves to work, thrives on challenge, and is bound for great things in his or her career? That depends on whether the style enriches the six domains of this person's life or controls and distorts them.

The Eight Characteristics

The following eight traits and behaviors are clues to the presence of the conscientious style. A person who has a strong conscientious tendency will demonstrate more of these behaviors more intensely than someone who has less of this style.

1. Hard work. The conscientious person is dedicated to work, is a hard worker, and is capable of intense single-minded effort.

2. The right thing. To be conscientious is to be a person of conscience. These are men and women of strong moral principles and values, whose opinions and beliefs on any subject are rarely held lightly. Conscientious individuals want to do the right thing.

3. The right way. Everything must be done right and the conscientious person has a clear understanding of what that means, from the correct way to balance the checkbook to the best strategy to achieve the boss's objectives to how to fit every single dirty dish into the dishwasher.

4. Perfectionism. The conscientious person likes all tasks and projects to be complete to the final detail without even minor flaws.

5. Perseverance. They stick to their convictions and opinions. Opposition only serves to strengthen the conscientious person's dogged determination.

6. Order and detail. Conscientious people like the appearance of orderliness and tidiness. They are good organizers, catalogers, and list makers. No detail is too small for conscientious consideration.

7. Prudence. Thrifty, careful, and cautious in all areas of their lives, conscientious individuals do not give in to reckless abandonment or wild excess.

8. Accumulation. A pack rat—the conscientious person saves and collects things, reluctant to discard anything that has, formerly had, or someday may have value.

The Six Domains of Conscientious Functioning
Work—the Key Domain

Most of the key behaviors that identify the conscientious style occur in the area of work. And work, whether it is housework, career, or leisure time projects, is where this style shines. Work is the key domain of functioning for the conscientious style and it dominates all others.

Conscientious individuals are competent, organized, good with detail, thorough, determined, and loyal. This is the employee whom every boss dreams of finding, the student who makes a teacher's work worthwhile, the homemaker who keeps the family functioning like clockwork. They are doers and "doing" extends to all hours of the day. Even during their leisure time, conscientious people are busy with projects and activities. Conscientious is the man who retires finally at age seventy-five and is delighted to spend all day at his workbench. Conscientious is the executive who spends lunch hours at her health club doing situps. Conscientious is the person who takes up gardening as a hobby and with only evenings and weekends to devote to it, in just one season manages to create a gorgeous bed of annuals and perennials, all fertilized, mulched, staked, and free of weeds. Conscientious are all those people who work the daily crossword puzzles until every square is complete.

Conscientious people enjoy intense, focused, detailed activity and try hard at everything they do. Elbow grease is their stock in trade and they would rather try hard than have it easy. The effort is part of what makes the undertaking worthwhile.

Do not feel sorry that the conscientious person has to work so hard. He or she needs the challenge of working to perfection and thrives on the sheer drive toward accomplishment. It does not matter how much time it takes. Diana Weston asked Ken Carlton, her extremely conscientious assistant, to run her all-important 175-page document through the copying machine. Ken chose to stay late to hand-feed every page, checking to make sure the printing was uniformly dark and centered perfectly on each page and discarding pages that were even slightly unacceptable. If she had had to do it herself, Diana would have run the document off automatically and then spent the evening at the theater. But that is the difference between Diana and Ken. She would settle for good enough. To a conscientious person like Ken, no task is work doing unless it is done just right.

Ken's typically conscientious perseverance is both a plus and a minus at his job. Self-confident Diana is delighted to have an assistant who devotes himself to the details for which she has no patience, who does not demand special treatment for investing extra time in the pursuit of perfection. That is why she hired him. But when Diana wants Ken to go on to something else before he feels that he has completed a job to his personal standards, or to do something a different way, she grows frustrated and impatient with his inflexibility. Ken, for all his conscientiousness, cannot change courses midway or defer to someone else's methodology. He cannot eliminate steps in a process or skip over details. Indeed, reports he writes for Diana are, to her mind, drowning in minutiae. But Diana's self-confident style makes her good at delegating. Most of the time she accepts that he simply cannot, "cut to the chase," but since she can, she edits his reports down to the essential.

The Conscientious Leader

Because they are willing to devote much time and hard work, people with a substantial amount of conscientious style tend to move toward the top of many professions. While people with personality styles such as self-confident and aggressive can rise through the ranks through sheer political acumen and/or manipulation of power, conscientious individuals become successful through good, old-fashioned hard work. They are loyal, they respect authority, and they often do their best work when they are accountable to someone for it. For these reasons, a conscientious man or woman will often make an extraordinary second in command, the behind the scenes individual whom you can count on to implement your policies and projects.

The top managerial positions, however, may require skills that go against the conscientious grain such as making quick decisions, setting priorities, and delegating responsibility. Conscientious types set a high standard for themselves. They check and recheck every detail before coming to any conclusion, but they can be exasperatingly slow to make up their minds, even on minor matters.

Conscientious individuals tend to expect the same above and beyond the call of duty thoroughness, devotion, and accomplishment from others, which may not always be appropriate. Successful leadership requires greater flexibility in standards, ability to set priorities, and respect for differing work styles in other people than the "unadulterated" conscientious personality style may permit. Still, even extremely conscientious people tend to rise fairly high. If you work for someone who has more than his or her share of this personality style, you might want to consider the survival tips at the end of this chapter.

Careers for the Conscientious

The conscientious personality style goes hand-in-hand with a mind for facts, categories, and technical details. Thus, conscientious types tend to gravitate toward work in science, medicine, research, mathematics, business, accounting, law, engineering, computers, and data processing. In many skilled crafts, or to the technical organizing side of any profession, the conscientious style brings with it greater appreciation for, and ability to deal with the finer points than the big picture. Individuals with this personality style can often function well as right-hand assistants for leaders or supervisors who have strong conceptual skills and good hunches, but who need someone to research the background and fill in the details.

Self, the Hard-Working Conscientious

The conscientious person is quick to ask, "What do you do?" A person's occupation is the most important information a conscientious person can seek, because to a conscientious person, self is work. "I am a psychiatrist." "I am a writer." Conscientious individuals who do not have or believe they do not have important enough work by which to define themselves, may squirm at the "What do you do" question like some modern-day homemakers who, although they may be extraordinarily competent at that multi-skilled job and put in ceaseless overtime, may believe that they should be out in the workplace as well. Conscientious men and women set a high standard of responsibility for themselves. They believe that they must produce to the best of their abilities in social or culturally approved ways at all times. The conscientious person must never under perform and they must never have it easy.

Emotions, Self-Control, and the Real World— the Voice of Reason

The voice of authority, inner or outer that the conscientious person heeds, provides the basis for excellent self-discipline. Bobby Davidson made it to the major leagues by following a daily baseball training schedule for seven years in the minors and by refusing, even to consider, trying the recreational and supposedly performance enhancing drugs that some of his teammates were using. Conscientious young musicians practice their instruments while other kids take off on their skateboards. Conscientious adults stay within the credit card limits. When they finally decide to go to weight watchers, they can follow the regime without veering into the ice cream store.

Conscientious individuals are ruled by their heads. Emotions, urges, whims, or hungers do not often get the best of them. You could call them "left-brained" and there is some physiological evidence that people with conscientious personality styles are dominated by the left hemisphere of their brains, which is associated with reason and analytic thinking styles. If the conscientious person fails to meet some obligation, if they wake up late and, therefore, arrive late to work, they find it very difficult to forgive themselves. The stronger the conscientious bent, the harder it is to forgive oneself for ordinary human lapses.

When one's behavior does not measure up to high expectations—the "should's"—guilt results. Thus, guilt and worry are frequent companions to the conscientious personality style.

Reserve generally marks the emotional behavior of the conscientious style. If this is your dominant style, you are not sentimental or gushy. You play your feelings close to the vest. You prefer to act on reason and to react coolly. Conscientious men and women do not operate at their best in the "emotional mode." They do not express feelings easily or comfortably and often come across as dry, formal, and intellectual. Although they find it easier to express anger when they are with people whom they consider subordinate, in response to a conflict with someone in authority, they prefer to reason their way back into the boss's good graces.

This rational focus can sometimes turn the real world of the conscientious individual into a place devoid of nuance. The music of a conscientious virtuoso pianist may be a technical tour de force, that to those with an ear for it lacks feeling. Failing to perceive the world's subtle, emotional grays, conscientious individuals tend to perceive everything as clearly black and white. Fanatics, religious or otherwise, often are conscientious to an extreme. They know that they and their followers are right and that everyone else is wrong. To exceedingly conscientious and obsessive-compulsive people, the world may consist of two extremes with no question marks in between.

Decisions

Individuals dominated by this conscientious, rational/intellectual orientation may easily discern the differences between good and bad or right and wrong. However, they may run into trouble in deciding between two good or right things. For instance, Martha Daily is trying to figure out what is the best activity for her family for the summer. She has used her conscientious abilities to put together a list of possibilities that are all interesting and appealing: 1) They could spend a month on a working farm. 2) Martha and her husband could stay in town and have some time to themselves while the children go away to baseball camp. 3) They could all stay in town for the summer and plan different outings every weekend. 4) They could rent a house at the beach.

It is now mid May and Martha is not close to a decision. Martha's husband says anything is fine with him, but the kids change their minds from week to week. And Martha is beginning to wake up at 4:00 in the morning agonizing over which activity to choose.

"Well, Martha, what do you really want to do?" asked her inner conscience. "I want to do what is best for my family," she answers conscientiously. She is searching for the perfect activity as if there were such a thing and "head" oriented as she is, she cannot trust her feelings to help her decide. Conscientious people cannot operate comfortably on hunches, inspirations, or emotions. This protects them from acting on ill-considered impulses, but it also keeps them stuck weighing and reweighing all sides of the issue.

In fact, down deep, Martha dreams of plopping herself and her family at the beach for the summer and having a loose, free, spontaneous good time which makes her feel guilty. She worries. Conscientious people always worry. But this desire to take it easy conflicts with her duty to provide appropriate, constructive learning experiences for her family. In part, because she waited so long that some of the options became unavailable, (which is one way to make a decision) Martha and her family ended up going to the beach. Martha need not have worried. Her family did not grow lazy, fat, or lethargic in the sand. With Martha's unfailing focus and direction, they were assured of having projects and activities to occupy them throughout the month they spent at the beach. Nor did they get sun burned because Martha had them all slathered with just the right degree of sun block at all times.

Stress

Conscientious is a high-stress personality style prone to Type A health risks when the style becomes extreme. For all their enviable self-control and direction, many conscientious people find it difficult to relax, let stress drift away, calm their thoughts and worries, and experience pleasure.

To a conscientious person, unstructured free time could be more stressful than a briefcase full of work. So the conscientious individual will bring work home or take it along on vacation and plan structured activities to occupy their leisure time. When Carolyn lost her job following the corporate take-over, she plummeted briefly into panic and despair because she had time on her hands. It did not take her long, however, to master her crisis using the typical conscientious mechanism—roll up your sleeves and get to work at something. To some non-conscientious individuals, a work, work, work world like Carolyn's may seem an endless treadmill. But to Carolyn and her many comrades in the conscientious style, even running in circles beats sitting around doing nothing.

Stuff

Walk into a conscientious person's basement or attic and take a look at the piles of things stored there that may never be used again. You will never convince him or her of that.

Conscientious types are the prototypical pack rats. They save and collect anything and everything—string, books, magazines, tools, cosmetics, records, tapes, stationary supplies, antiques, and just plain junk. They keep all the letters they ever received, pictures they ever took, even the lousy duplicate shots, and clothes that have never been worn. This stuff may be a major source of stress to their spouses, but conscientious people want to know it is all there where they can find it.

Relationships: Steadiness, and Distance

Conscientious people can make great husbands or wives and good and lasting friends. These folks value their relationships and families and are not quick to give them up. They are loyal, faithful, responsible, and will take extremely good care of their mates, but they are unemotional and unromantic about it. You may not get silk lingerie from your conscientious husband or a dozen roses on your anniversary, but your house will have the most efficient new furnace on the block. The bills will be paid and the life insurance policy will have all the provisions you could ever need. The conscientious homemaker will take pains to have her husband's meals on the table, his shirts ironed, and the house cleaned spick and span, even if she works outside the home. But intimacy is hard for a conscientious person. For all their certainty about who they are and what they do, they are less secure with the emotional side of life. Conscientious people like to be around people, but they keep their emotional distance. Because they are task oriented, conscientious individuals are most at ease with people when they are doing something together—say fishing, playing tennis, or visiting a museum. They can discuss computers, cars, recipes, gardening, tools, and baseball statistics with great enthusiasm. And they can tell you what they think about politics and world events, but please do not ask them to share their feelings.

This does not mean that conscientious people have no feelings or emotional needs. They simply find it anxiety provoking to express their feelings or even sometimes to recognize them. A common source of stress in their love relationships is that conscientious men and women can't, don't, and won't say "I love you," or otherwise emotionally reassure their mates to whom they may, none the less, be deeply attached.

Other relationship difficulties arise from the conscientious person's stubbornness and need for perfection. Conscientious men and women may have a hard time letting others do things their own way. Problem solving may be difficult because conscientious people may need to be "right" and "win." To the person with a lot of conscientious style in his or her personality pattern, to compromise means "to give in."

Conscientious people can appear stingy, over cautious, and ungenerous. But beneath these habits is often a devoted, emotionally steady person who can be relied and depended upon, who is a good provider, and who will always come through for the people who stay close to him or her. During times of stress, conscientious people may bury all suggestion of emotion as they dive deep into their work, but they won't run away from you unless you push them. A healthy degree of conscientious personality style in either partner is good glue for a lasting relationship.

The Good Conscientious Parent

Conscientious parents teach their kids strong moral values and instill an appreciation for hard work and ambition. Their families are very important to them and they take care of them well. As with their direct reports and co-workers, conscientious mates tend to demand an across the board high level of competence from the members of their families. They must take care, though, not to take all the fun out of learning experiences by turning them into strict lessons on how things should be done. They must be cautious about subjecting their kids to the pressure of always having to measure up to their parents' expectations. Sometimes children of very conscientious parents grow up to feel that they are never appreciated with or for all their human frailties. They may be fearful of making mistakes and have an inner sense that they are not and never will be good enough. The conscientious parent may, in fact, be very proud of his or her offspring, but may be unable to express the approval or just plain affection that the child craves. If there is a non-conscientious parent in the family, however, he or she may be able to provide enough sentiment, reassurance, and hugs to make up for the other parent's distance and stiffness.

Tips on Dealing With the Conscientious Person in Your Life

1. Be humorously tolerant. Let the conscientious person have his or her habits. Instead of shrieking, "For God's sake, come to bed. It's three a.m. You can work out the computer glitch in the morning." Smile and say to yourself, "That's my Ernie. He can't relax until he figures it out."

2. Stay flexible. Just because Ernie stays up all night tinkering with the computer doesn't mean you have to lose sleep. Go to bed and during all those waking hours in which your conscientious mate is working, develop your own interests and activities.

3. Don't wait for the conscientious person to change. Bring your strengths to the relationship and use them. For example, your conscientious mate may be reluctant to experiment with just about anything. Therefore, you might want to bring some spontaneity into the relationship. Whereas he or she would never be able to.

4. Don't expect compliments or easy expressions of affection. These are not a barometer of how a conscientious person feels about you. Your conscientious husband may fail to say a word about your appearance after you've spent half a day dressing for the dinner party. Rest assured that he sees how fabulous you look and is beaming inwardly.

5. Avoid arguments and power struggles. Conscientious people must win. It's a part of their nature. Conscientious men and women are consummate arguers and may nit pick and split hairs until you walk out or give up. You can often prevent an escalation of hostility simply by listening to what the person has to say, no matter how provocative, and responding, "I understand what you're saying," or a similarly neutral comment.

6. Appreciate and enjoy the security and stability that the conscientious person brings to the relationship. Be reassured that he or she takes care of the details of your life so well. Tell the person how much you appreciate and depend on him or her. Conscientious people like to be needed. While you're at it, tell your conscientious husband, wife, father, or mother how much you care for him or her. Everyone needs to hear that even if the conscientious are not good at saying it.

Making the Most of Your Conscientious Style

Great organizers and list makers, conscientious individuals can harness these skills to overcome some of the pitfalls of their personality style. The potential stress-related health risks of their style make an urgent priority of broadening one's personal life and learning to relax.

Exercise 1: Make a list of ten relaxing non-work activities that will enhance your leisure time. Consider possibilities such as noncompetitive sports, family picnics, going to a movie or concert, taking a walk in the park or along the beach, and so forth. Consult your family or partner for suggestions. Next, choose one of these activities to pursue this coming weekend. If you can't make the decision, read on.

Exercise 2: Consult your list of possible leisure time activities. Number them from one to ten in priority order. You must use all ten numbers and no two items can receive the same number. Now plan only the first priority activity for this coming weekend. If you begin to worry whether your choice was the best one, ignore your doubts. Just smile and say to yourself, "There I go again—worrying and doubting my decisions. I mustn't take myself so serious all the time." Make a list and establish priorities each time you have trouble choosing among various options in any area of life.

Exercise 3: When you have difficulty making a decision, always keep in mind that it often makes no difference which decision you make as long as you do something. If you have to choose between two apparently equal alternatives, consider simply flipping a coin. You can always try the other alternative later. This exercise will also help tackle the common tendency of conscientious people to do nothing, i.e., procrastinate until the "perfect" solution presents itself.

Exercise 4: Is your boss or your spouse on your back because you spend too much time on your tasks? To manage your time more efficiently, aim for results that are good enough, not perfect. If your boss asks you to prepare a quick report, find out precisely what he or she wishes included in it and cover those points only and let it go. In all your efforts, determine what the job requires and do only that. Resist your tendency to include additional material or to do extra work. Instead of concentrating on the minor flaws, pay attention to how pleased other people are with you for getting the job done. Tell yourself, "Good enough is just right." Sometimes, of course, good enough will require 100 percent effort. If you practice this exercise consistently, you will find that you have the necessary energy and enthusiasm to do thorough and brilliant work and to get it done on time.

Exercise 5: Every time you catch yourself making mistakes, say to yourself, "Ah ha, I'm human." Odd as this may sound, you need to appreciate that nobody's perfect (including you) and that you berate yourself too much for human errors. Try a variation of this exercise when you catch people you're hard on having an occasional lapse, "Ah ha, she/he is human."

Obsessive-Compulsive Personality Disorder

The difference between conscientious style and obsessive-compulsive personality disorder, indeed between any of the styles and its accompanying disorder is one of degree and consequence. Individuals suffering from this disorder are so exceedingly conscientious that they can no longer adapt to the demands of reality or meet their personal and professional goals. And to others, they may seem exasperating or even impossible to deal with. Obsessive-compulsive personality disorder can be described as follows: A pervasive pattern of preoccupation with orderliness, perfectionism, and mental and interpersonal control at the expense of flexibility, openness and efficiency beginning by early adulthood and present in a variety of contexts as indicated by four or more of the following:

1. Preoccupied with details, rules, lists, order, organization, or schedules to the extent that the major point of the activity is lost.

2. Perfectionism that interferes with task completion and/or inability to complete a project because their own overly strict standards are not met.

3. Excessively devoted to work and productivity that excludes leisure activities and friendships not necessary for obvious economic necessity.

4. Overly conscientious, scrupulous, and inflexible about matters of reality, ethics, or values not accounted for by culture or religious identification.

5. Unable to discard worn out or worthless objects even when they have no sentimental value.

6. Reluctant to delegate tasks or to work with others unless they submit exactly to his or her way of doing things.

7. Adopts a miserly spending style toward both self and others. Money is viewed as something to be hoarded for future catastrophes.

8. Shows rigidity and stubbornness.

How to Survive an Obsessive-Compulsive or Very Conscientious Boss

Obsessive-compulsive/very conscientious bosses can be overly critical, demanding, and even tyrannical when you make just a small mistake. What they will demand—more attention to neatness, small details, perfection in general, and procedures—is much greater than will be demanded by people with personalities dominated by other disorders or styles. They equate overtime with devotion to your job. Often they think that if you go home on time, you're going home early. Never let this type of boss know that you think the workday ordinarily ought to end at 5:00 p.m. Put in a little overtime every once in a while and always make sure the boss knows about it. But don't come in late the next day or take an extra long lunch to compensate for that extra time. These bosses are very mindful of rules and regulations, especially those concerning timeliness.

But keep in mind when the going gets rough, your obsessive-compulsive or very conscientious boss achieved his or her position through sheer ability. Your boss may be rigid and lack some in personal skills, but he or she is, or used to be, extremely competent. Under this person's tutelage, you can learn a great deal. If you treat such bosses the same way they treat those in authority over them—with loyalty, deference, and respect—in time, they will begin to trust you and delegate more substantial work. In general, however, don't be discouraged if your obsessive-compulsive/very conscientious boss does not encourage you to find creative or innovative approaches to your work. Learn to do the job in the boss's extremely thorough way, and later you'll have a solid ground from which to experiment when you move on later.

Know too, that the obsessive-compulsive/very conscientious boss deeply appreciate a job well done, even if he or she can't comfortably show it. Once you prove yourself, the boss will be loyal to you too, which can be very reassuring. He or she will prove a staunch ally and will go to bat for you if necessary with the powers that be. But if you get on his or her bad side, you may stay there long past your due. For once an idea gets into this person's mind, it's hard to get rid of. Obsessive-compulsive/very conscientious individuals can and often do hold grudges. So help them have it "their" way, but try not to get in their way!

3

The Self-Confident Style

S elf-confident individuals stand out. They're the leaders, the shining lights, the attention getters in their public or private spheres. Theirs is a star quality born of self-regard, self-respect, self-certainty, all those self words that denote a faith in one's self and a commitment to one's self-styled purpose. Combined with the ambition that marks this style, that magical self-regard can transform idle dreams into real accomplishment.

The self-confident personality style is one of the two most goal directed of all the fourteen. Self-confident men and women know what they want and they get it. Many of them have the charisma to attract plenty of others to their goals. They are usually extroverted and intensely political. They know how to work the crowd, how to motivate it, and how to lead it. Hitch onto their band wagons and you'll be well rewarded.

The self-confident style adds go-getting power to other personality styles. For example, it counteracts the conscientious person's tendency to get side tracked by details and it fuels the adventurous person's great feats of daring. It propels any personality pattern into the realm of success. Indeed, the self-confident style confers an ability to be successful more than any other style except the aggressive personality style.

The Nine Characteristics

The following nine traits and behaviors are clues to the presence of the self-confident style. A person who reveals a strong self-confident tendency will intensely demonstrate many of these behaviors.

1. Self-regard. Self-confident individuals believe in themselves and in their abilities. They have no doubt that they are unique and special and there is a reason for their being on this planet.

2. The red carpet. They expect others to treat them well at all times.

3. Ambition. Self-confident people are unabashedly open about their aspirations and possibilities.

4. Politics. They are able to take advantage of the strengths and abilities of other people in order to achieve their goals, and they are shrewd in their dealings with others.

5. Competition. They are able competitors. They love getting to the top and they enjoy staying there.

6. Stature. They identify with people of rank and status.

7. Dreams. Self-confident individuals are able to visualize themselves as the hero, the star, the best in their world, or the most accomplished in their field.

8. Self-awareness. These individuals have a keen awareness of their thoughts and feelings and their overall inner state of being.

9. Poise. People with the self-confident personality style accept compliments, praise, and admiration gracefully and with self-possession.

The Six Domains of Self-Confident Functioning
Self—the Joy of Being Me

The self is the reigning domain of the self-confident style. It gives this style its special character and power and all the other domains fall under its sway. It provides purpose, structure, and meaning to the life of the self-confident individual for whom, in short, the world is "me."

It is impossible to describe this personality style without recourse to words that reflect back on the self—self-made, self-possessed, self-respect, self-propelled, self-reliant, self-fulfillment, self-enrichment, self-asserting, self-loved, self-esteem, self-starter, and so on. As this style becomes extreme, other self words increasingly come into play including self-aggrandizing, self-preoccupation, selfish, and even self-destructive. Here, as with all of the fourteen personality styles, the key domains can achieve too much control of the proud possessor's life. Looking out for number one, perhaps the catch phrase of this style, can reap a life harvest for self-confident individuals, their families and devotees. Whereas for narcissistic individuals, it may threaten to destroy them and those around them.

Charmed Lives

Self-confident people believe in themselves. They are prepared to work hard, to plan, and to endure hardship if necessary to get what they feel they deserve. Other perhaps equally qualified people may be assailed by self-doubt and thus led astray by setbacks. A strong self-confident personality style protects against these demons.

From the moment he got his first electric guitar, rock star Jay Cunningham believed he would be great in the rock and roll pantheon—a dream that was shared by untold numbers of other young people. Jay Cunningham was more than thirty years old before he cut a hit record and even then, he was just part of a larger band. Nevertheless, he knew he'd make it. He'd formed band after band, made demos, courted producers, cut singles that went nowhere, played obscure clubs, but after a decade in the business, he still refused to give up. He believed in himself so much that others ended up believing in him too. He found backers for the demo tapes and promoters who would donate their time. When they saw the way he occupied the center of the stage in a concert, and heard the sureness in his voice, they knew he was made for this part. He is exactly where he belongs.

This is also true with Caitlyn in her own way. From Caitlyn's childhood on, she saw her future as a wife and mother with all the trappings of the good life. To her, this meant fine houses, servants, cars, jewels, and "name" schools for her children. Caitlyn has never been embarrassed by or defensive about her ambitions.

Caitlyn, whose personality shows a strong streak also of the conscientious style, did not come from a family of means. She put herself through school and then worked hard and well as a secretary to support herself and her widowed mother while waiting for her expected prince to appear. He came in the form of Joey, her last boss. Joey, an outstanding design engineer and promoter type, showed a lot of ambition and promise. He gave her everything she wanted—a house in the suburbs, the cottage in the country, the housekeeper, the diamonds, and the free time to shop and to linger at the club. After their children were in school, he even bought her a small fashion boutique to run because she had always said she had better taste than any of the exclusive stores in their town. For Caitlyn's part, in addition to running her store, she took good care of her husband and their two children and she put up with Joey even when other people couldn't. As long as he treated her with respect and deference, Caitlyn dealt with his tantrums, his sometimes boorish and bullying behavior toward his associates, his employees, and some of their friends, and his cheating in business.

Caitlyn had no illusions about Joey. She often said to him and to others that she would leave him in a second if he treated her one tenth as badly as he treated other people. Then Joey began to suffer reverses in his business. He blamed his losses on his associates and his employees. Night after night he came home angry, looking to Caitlyn for solace from abuses he felt he suffered at the hands of others. But the great strain on their finances made Caitlyn short tempered and less accepting of Joey. She found she could not tolerate his constant complaining. She began to let the saleswoman who worked for her have more responsibility so she could spend more time at the club in the company of a rich retired widower who had always shown her much consideration. The wealthy widower and Caitlyn were not sleeping together, but Joey wouldn't believe it. He became possessed with jealous rage. During one of their now frequent fights, Joey lost control and struck Caitlyn. That night, she took the kids and moved to a hotel suite. She never went back to Joey. In the divorce settlement, she received both houses, the new Mercedes, and considerable child support. She sold the suburban house and the boutique when she decided to marry her widower friend. Now Caitlyn and her children can be found at one of the best addresses in her city where she lives the good life that she always felt that she deserves.

Status, Image, and Power

Self-confident individuals believe that they were "born under a lucky star," and their lives seem to bear it out. Usually what they want involves status and image and/or power. They want to be department heads at the very best universities, to belong to the best clubs, to live in the classiest neighborhoods, and to send their kids to the most renowned schools. If they are celebrity types, they'll have gorgeous bodies and wear fabulous clothes. If they are intellectuals, academics, or politicians, they'll sit on the most powerful and prestigious commit-tees, the ones that get the most TV time. Their image consciousness is genuine. They seek to be and succeed in becoming what they believe they are to begin with—important, deserving people.

Tender Spot

Self-confident men and women are at most times, cognizant of and comfortable with their strengths. They are not, as a rule, so keenly aware of or so comfortable with their short-comings. To those who have a lot of this personality style, even the most constructive criticism feels barbed.

Professor Henry Winston criticized Tanya's political science term paper. He told her that her research was weak and that she depended too much on her interesting, but unsupported opinions. She was a good student and he generously allowed her the opportunity to rewrite the paper before he graded it. Tanya had always held Professor Win-ston in high esteem, but she considered his criticism insulting and now began to think of his seminar as a waste of time. Nonetheless, she remained cooperative. She reworked the paper as the professor sug-gested, not because she fully understood his point, but because she wanted a good grade. Had Tanya been open to her teacher's construc-tive remarks, she might have saved herself embarrassment in later years.

Two years after graduate school, Tanya lost a job as a political speech writer for much the same reason—over confidence in her opinions without the backup or hard information that the candidate needed. Fortunately, when Tanya went into politics a few years later, she found someone else to research her own speeches. She had the self-confident ability to delegate important tasks that she really didn't want to do. Today, she makes an excellent political party chairperson for her state.

Work, Leadership, and Success

Men and women with a strong self-confident personality style are outgoing, highly energetic, competitive people who are able to absorb data easily, to see the big picture, to make decisions, to plan, to set priorities and goals, and to delegate. This is the person whom you, as chairman of the board, want to put your new corporation on the map.

At work as well as in every other aspect of their lives, self-confident individuals are instinctively political. They are naturals at understanding the power structure of any organization and at establishing effective political alliances. They can be jealous of those in power and, like their aggressive brethren, they are not squeamish about attempting to unseat them. They will "play politics" to get ahead. Whereas work-hard-to-go-places conscientious types will keep their noses so close to the grindstone that they will miss out on the power plays that could carry them to the top. Outgoing and political as they are, self-confident men and women often work very comfortably and effectively with others. For this personality style, people are a means to a successful end. To those in authority and/or from whom there is something to gain, they will be deferential and cooperative. To their own staffs in exchange for their loyalty, self-confident men and women will be very generous with money, perks, and support. People against whom they compete can also serve as a measure of their own importance.

The Self-Confident Leader

Self-confident style individuals are genuine, often gifted leaders. They are happy to delegate to members of their staff not only the dirty work, but responsible undertakings. Unlike highly conscientious types, they often allow their direct reports autonomy and leeway as long as the job gets done. They are quite skilled at building an effective highly motivated team of which they must be the absolute centers. As long as everybody acknowledges who is boss, self-confident leaders do not insist on the strict hierarchial structure that the aggressive manager needs to function effectively. But the team must work to achieve the goals of the self-confident leader, not those of the individual team members. Start to compete with or criticize the goals of the self-confident leader or boss or insist on sharing the credit and/or glory and you'll be off that team or at the bottom of the heap before you realize what you did to deserve it. Innately competitive, self-confident individuals are like race horses. They run all the faster when anyone edges up on them. They thrive on the competition and they love staying one step ahead at all times. They respect the same inclination in others as long as they are not in direct competition and can make excellent mentors provided you stay on their good side.

Tips on Working for Self-Confident People

1. Be absolutely loyal. Don't criticize or compete with them. Don't expect to share the limelight or to take credit. Be content to aspire to the number two position.

2. Don't expect your self-confident boss to provide direction. Likely, he or she will expect you to know what to do, so be sure you are clear about the objectives before you undertake any task. Don't hesitate to ask.

3. You may be an important member of the boss's team, but don't expect your self-confident boss to be attentive to you as an individual. Don't take it personally.

4. Self-confident bosses expect you to be interested in them, however. They may be susceptible to flattery, so if you're working on a raise or a promotion or trying to sell your point of view, a bit of "buttering up" may smooth the way.

Careers for the Self-Confident

If this is your dominate style, follow ambitions that lead toward leadership and the limelight. Many performers, broadcasters, and politicians have a predominance of this personality style. In all cases, choose careers in which you work with or influence others. Self-confident folks need other people around them.

Relationships—Good at Being Loved

Self-confident men and women are popular and attractive. Their sense of themselves and their certainty in their projects draw others to them and they are very good at being loved. They are not in any way shy or embarrassed by the attention they receive from a person who loves them. Self-confident people need to be needed and they will work hard to gain and maintain the person's loving admiration. They know what to do to get your attention and how to win you over.

David Woos Susan

When self-confident David, a twice divorced fifty-year old salesman, fell head over heels for Susan, she was slow to warm up. A salesman in her own right, she had recently endured a painful divorce and was not eager to begin another involvement. But David began to spin his web of endearments. He cooked elaborate dinners for the beautiful Susan. He sent her flowers. He brought munchies for her miniature terrier. He found her a new housekeeper when her housekeeper quit. Very slowly, Susan's heart opened to this wonderfully attentive man. Increasingly, they were seen in each other's company in their various work and social circles. But 40-year old Susan still wished to keep her independence. At last after nearly a year, she invited David to live with her in her waterside mansion. David moved in that very day.

Some of David's oldest friends who had lived through his two previous marriages wondered cynically whether it would all fall apart now that Susan would have him. These friends had witnessed David when he was in love and charming a woman. They had also watched him turn his back on the women he had won over. Would he stop his impressive attentions to Susan or would they continue? That was the question they all waited to see the answer to.

The answer was "no" because Susan continued to impress and challenge David intellectually and in every other area of their relationship. He had enormous respect for this accomplished woman who was always just a little removed emotionally. David was never sure that he possessed her in any way whatsoever. This uncertainty kept him continually on his toes.

And Susan did not need from David the kind of love she had sought when she was married as a young person. She had grown up over these last 20 years and she knew it. Back then, her husband had understood Susan and treasured her for her outward beauty. Now she wanted David's respect and acceptance, but she no longer needed a man to truly "know her." For this, she relied on her old friends and long-time colleagues. She found David a stimulating and exciting companion and she enjoyed the merger of their two sales careers. She admired his self-certain style—it was a match among equals she felt. Susan understood David. She understood better than he did that he would never deeply love her.

People like David whose personality patterns are unmistakably dominated by the self-confident style are so strongly ruled by the self-domain that they do not gain sufficient distance from their own thoughts and feelings to provide unstinting, unselfish love. Often, they believe that the people close to them feel what they feel or think what they think. Although they thrive on the love that others provide and they appreciate what others do for them, they may find it difficult to comprehend that the people who are important to them may have separate individual needs. They get so wrapped up in their ambitions, they just don't notice. This is why they are often shocked to discover, for instance, that their spouses have been unhappy for many years. By contrast, a devoted person, exquisitely sensitive to a loved one's feelings, would have picked up the signs of discontent early, perhaps even before the unhappy spouse became fully aware of his or her own distress. A self-confident spouse assumes that his or her own happiness spells a contented relationship for both of them. This, of course, is not always true. But understanding this is often difficult for the self-confident husband or wife to get a handle on.

The Self-Confident Parent

Self-confident parents can confer a star quality on their children too. They teach them to aim high and to expect the best for themselves. They offer a model of self-esteem, ambition, drive, self-discipline, and social success. Strongly self-confident partners, however, may not recognize or credit their children's individual differences or needs. Because they tend to assume that the kids are all chips off the old block, it may not occur to them to step out of the spotlight long enough to let the children know what it feels like to be the center of the universe on their own merits. Some children of extremely self-confident parents grow up to be good at giving love, but to feel unworthy of receiving it.

The non-self-confident parent may be able to remind his or her moderately self-confident spouse to look at things from the child's point of view. Strength in some of the other personality styles such as conscientious, devoted, self-sacrificing, and dramatic may protect a moderately self-confident parent from this style's predisposition to be insensitive to others' emotional needs.

Emotional, Self-Control, and the Real World

Self-confident individuals have a temper and when they're crossed or slighted, they'll show it. In addition, they can be envious of others whom they perceive as more successful than themselves. But their strong sense of self, their success orientation, and their political savvy usually protect them from letting their less "admirable" feelings get the best of them, at least in public.

As we have seen, individuals with this personality style, depending on the degree to which they are dominated by it, will have some or much difficulty experiencing love. They can and do feel powerful attractions and emotional fulfillment. However, their moods are characteristically optimistic, energetic, even hyper at times. When the style crosses over to the narcissistic personality disorder, however, depression becomes a great risk.

In general, self-control is strong in self-confident types. Their strength in achieving their goals reflect their self-discipline and ability to keep conflicting impulses at bay. When they slip, it is more from grandiosity than from problems with impulse control. Individuals whose personalities are heavily dominated by this style may see the real world unrealistically as their own personal stage. As with the politician who makes no attempt to conceal his philandering and whose career is shattered when the truth is revealed, some overly self-confident individuals lose sight of their faults, their vulnerabilities, and their relative place in the scheme of things. We will explore this further when we discuss the narcissistic personality disorder in the following pages.

Tips on Dealing With the Self-Confident Person in Your Life

1. Self-confident individuals need to be number one. To love a self-confident person requires that you accept, admire, and respect this aspect of his or her character. Appreciate the considerable gifts and the strengths that this person brings to the relationship. Enjoy the fruits of your partner's success and the interesting life he or she may provide.

2. To hold this person's attention, pay a lot of attention. Your love and loyalty are very important to the self-confident person in your life. You bring to the relationship the ability to love and your mate counts on it. Accept that you may be more capable of selfless love than is your self-confident partner. Give your love without keeping track of who is giving more. If you need to be loved more intensely and equally, however, accept that this person is not for you.

3. Be careful not to tie your self-esteem to the amount of love and attention the self-confident person in your life shows you or by the extent to which he or she really understands you. Love yourself no matter what. This message is especially important for children of highly self-confident parents.

4. Many self-confident types will alternately move emotionally close and then apparently lose interest in you, especially after a relationship has become established. Be aware of this back and forth pattern. Try to wait it out while maintaining your own emotional balance and do not jump to the conclusion that your self-confident partner no longer has feelings for you. More likely, he or she has become preoccupied with other concerns. Remind the self-confident person that you exist and that you continue to care for him or her.

5. When you need to confront your self-confident partner, simply state how you feel or what you observe without judging him or her. Remember that for all their self-esteem, self-confident people have difficulty dealing with criticism. Be sure, at the same time, to express your admiration and praise. Keep in mind that although the self-confident individual may not admit that you have a point, he or she will try to deal with it. Self-confident individuals can step back from themselves and correct their behavior even if they are not so good in the "you're right–I'm wrong" department.

6. Continually make your feelings known even about apparently obvious matters. Don't count on a self-confident individual to sense or keep track of them—they are notoriously poor at reading between the lines. Keeping your partner informed about your feelings and attitudes

will enable him or her to understand you better and avoid conflict
later.

Making the Most of Your Self-Confident Style

Your ability to be successful and your nerve to go after it set you
apart from all other personality styles. You can call upon these singular
advantages in order to smooth out some of the problem areas that may
plague you. You are probably aware of your capabilities to strengthen
your personality and help it work at best advantage for you. You may
need to develop a more realistic sense of your own short-comings.

Exercise 1: Make a list in answer to this question. What's not
totally great about me? One item may be, "I'm not as responsive to
others/not as interested in them as I like them to be in me."

Exercise 2: Try to see yourself as others see you. Again, concentrate
on your weak areas. Ask yourself, "What would my mother, my father,
my husband or wife, my best friend, my teachers, my colleagues, etc.
say is not totally great about me?"

Exercise 3: Observe your reactions to criticism. Do not feel hurt or
humiliated or attack when people say negative things about you or
your work. Try to live with these feelings instead of lashing out at, distancing yourself from, or maybe disliking the people who offer criticism. The more you watch your reactions, the easier they will be to
bear.

Exercise 4: This exercise takes advantage of your ability to concentrate in order to improve your relationships. During any conversation
or interaction, especially with people whom you deal with frequently
ask yourself, "Who is this person?" Collect data. Concentrate on each
person's way of talking, facial expressions, characteristic body posture,
tones of voice, mannerisms and motions, clothing styles, jewelry, eye
color, teeth, and so on. In this way, you will paint an increasingly
detailed, interesting, rich portrait of the people with whom you come
in contact. This increasingly detailed portrait of the people around you

will enable you to understand them in ways you otherwise may find very difficult. Most of all, it will heighten your sensitivity to how they feel and what they think.

Exercise 5: Once a day ask each member of your household or your spouse or best friend a question about himself or herself. Ask perhaps, "What is it that you like about that book?" A question that elicits an opinion about you, such as, "What did you think about my speech today?," doesn't count. You might also try, at least once a week, to ask people who are closest to you in your personal life what you can do for them. This is always a good idea because the self-confident person tends to think about relationships in terms of what the other person can do for them.

The Narcissistic Personality Disorder

In Greek mythology, Narcissus was a young man who loved no one. He was tricked into falling in love with his own reflection in a pool of water. He could not embrace this watery image and he pined away. Eventually, he was transformed into a flower. In American psychiatry, narcissistic personality disorder defines a pathological condition char-acterized by self-centeredness and self-interest, grandiosity, lack of empathy, and manipulativeness. While individuals with this condition often achieve high positions, their lives are not satisfying. If they work in public life, they may create scandals that humiliate and undo them. Persons with this disorder cannot ultimately find happiness or fulfill-ment in their accomplishments or in their relationships. Yet as is true with persons who suffer any of the disorders, they may not realize that the way they think, feel, and behave distorts their lives. The narcissistic personality disorder can be present in a pervasive pattern of grandios-ity, a need for admiration, and a lack of empathy beginning by early childhood and present in a variety of contexts as indicated by at least five or more of the following:

1. Has a grandiose sense of self-importance. That is, exaggerates achievements and talents, expects to be recognized as superior without commiserate achievements.

2. Preoccupied with fantasies of unlimited success, power, brilliance, beauty, or ideal love.

3. Believes that he or she is special and unique, can be understood only by or should associate with other special or high status people.

4. Requires excessive admiration.

5. Has a sense of entitlement, unreasonable expectations of especially favorable treatment or automatic compliance with his or her expectations.

6. Is interpersonally exploitative. Takes advantage of others to achieve his or her own ends.

7. Lacks empathy. Is unwilling to recognize or identify with the feelings and needs of others.

8. Is often envious of others or believes that others are envious of him or her.

9. Shows arrogant, haughty behaviors or attitudes.

Self-Importance at Work and With Other People

With narcissistic personality disorder, one can be very successful, particularly in worlds of power, such as politics and corporations. Sufferers are often smooth and charming with manic energy, able to talk their way in the door and convince people of their special abilities. Those who can prove they have these abilities often are tolerated as talented, but difficult people. They exploit others to get ahead and they expect and demand special treatment.

Stan Ferguson, a lawyer who headed a department subdivision at a major law school, continually undermined his own effectiveness by battling arrogantly with the department chairman and becoming bitterly enraged when his way was rejected. Someone with self-confident style would be loath to commit such political errors. But Stan's personality disorder distorted his ability to size up a situation and to perceive the larger complexities. He believed that he alone could take on the chairman because, as he assumed everyone in the department recognized, he was better than all of them, including the boss. Fortunately, therapy saved him from quickly destroying a promising career.

Narcissistic individuals cannot bear criticism. Some react inwardly with devastating hurt and shame that far outweigh the actual remark. Others react with inappropriate rage, even tantrums and in the process, manipulate others to accede to their demands. Obsessive compulsive individuals may be crushed when they are criticized, but they will work hard to get back in the criticizer's good graces. Narcissistic individuals, on the other hand, attempt to destroy the attacker. We spoke about self-confident Caitlyn earlier in this chapter. Her ex-husband, Joey, who suffered from a mixed narcissistic, histrionic, and anti-social personality disorder with paranoid features, threw violent tantrums whenever he was crossed. In his business, he often hired young free lance commercial designers whom he frequently neglected to pay. He expected them to understand his "special" circumstances and agree to wait until his financial pressures eased. These young people were hardly in a financial position themselves to do without even a day's pay. But when they would press him, often growing heated and criticizing his ethics, Joey would fly into a rage, attack the quality of their work, insult them, and threaten to ruin them. Most of these talented men and women would have loved to walk away from Joey, but they were new in the business, they lacked confidence, and Joey had convinced them that they could go nowhere without him. So they continued to work for Joey who, when things were going right, would be very seductive, flattering, and encouraging.

All narcissistic individuals share the inability to empathize. They cannot recognize or experience how other people feel. These individuals may be oblivious to the hurt their remarks may inflict upon others. They are known to say things in front of former partners, such as, "my new partner has brought more to this firm than anyone ever brought in the past." They may even boast of having outstanding physical health in front of someone who is quite ill. Individuals with this disorder may be sexually very active, and they are the types who seduce and abandon. They form few genuine emotional commitments. Needless to say, relationships with persons suffering from this disorder are very hard on the partner whose worth in the relationship may depend only on how well he or she can bolster the narcissistic partner's self-esteem.

Narcissistic individuals must, at all times, be admired. They manipulate others to this end, they work to achieve admirable successes, yet they are consumed with feelings of envy and rage and disdain for others. They grow depressed and find little satisfaction or contentment from their work or from the people in their lives.

4

The Devoted Style

D evoted types care and this caring is what make their lives worth living. You won't find anyone more loving, more concerned for your needs or feelings or the needs and feelings of a group. At their best, individuals with this type are the loyal, considerate, ever-so-helpful players on the team whether it is the couple, the family, the assembly-line department, the religious or charitable organization, or the military unit. Their needs are those of the group or its leader and their happiness comes from the fulfillment of the others' directives and goals. Devoted people are the ones who tell you, "I'm happy if you're happy," and mean it when they say it.

The devoted style is common in our society and it occurs among both men and women. Traditionally this helping and giving personality style has been particularly encouraged and approved among women. The customary view of the good wife has been of a tender-hearted, devoted woman who lives through her husband and relies on him to make the worldly decisions for her while she dedicates herself to providing a fulfilling home life for the family. As views of women's roles have changed in this society, some women with this personality style may have mixed feelings about expressing it. Today's cultural pressures on women to step out of the shadows of other people, both in and out of the home, leave one feeling that wanting to make someone else happy is something to be ashamed of. While these women struggle to come to terms with all sides of their personality patterns, more men are feeling freer to enjoy their own nurturing tendencies. In any case, as we will see throughout our discussion, the devoted personality plays itself out in many ways in the personality profiles of males as well as females.

The Seven Characteristics

The following seven traits and behaviors are clues to the presence of the devoted style. A person who reveals a strong devoted tendency will demonstrate more of these behaviors more intensely than someone who has less of this style.

1. Commitment. Individuals with the devoted personality style are thoroughly dedicated to the relationships in their lives. They place the highest value on sustained relationships, they respect the institution of marriage as well as unofficial avowals of commitment, and they work hard to keep their relationships together.

2. Togetherness. They prefer the company of one or more people to being alone.

3. Teamwork. People with this personality style would rather follow than lead. They are cooperative and respectful of authority and institutions. They easily rely on others and take direction well.

4. Deference. When making decisions, they are happy to seek out others' opinions and to follow their advice.

5. Harmony. Devoted individuals are careful to promote good feelings between themselves and the important people in their lives. To promote harmony, they tend to be polite, agreeable, and tactful.

6. Consideration. They are thoughtful of others and good at pleasing them. Devoted people will endure personal discomfort to do a good turn for the key people in their lives.

7. Attachment. Relationships provide life's meaning for this personality style. Even after a painful loss of someone around whom their life was centered, they are able to form new meaningful bonds.

The Six Domains of Devoted Functioning Relationships—My World Is You

For devoted men and women, the domain of relationships is key. Other people are their reason for being, lending purpose to their lives and fulfillment to their dreams. Their attachments center them in the universe and make them feel complete.

People with the devoted style prominent in their personalities form relationships easily and they devote themselves to pleasing the principle people in their lives. They remember your birthday, they bring a hot meal when you're sick, they think about you, they listen to you, and they keep up with what's going on in your life. They are gifted hosts and hostesses, careful that their guests match up well, that the food is prepared to everyone's taste, and that conversation never lags. Because they pay so much attention to you, they always seem to anticipate your needs. The phone rings, it's your devoted friend or family member who somehow knows you need someone to talk to.

It feels good to have such considerate, undivided attention and if you feel good, so does the devoted person. An individual with this personality style will often endure discomfort or hardship to make sure that those close to them do not.

Keepers of the Flame

People with a predominance of this style will do more of the work and make more of the sacrifices involved with keeping a relationship going without keeping score or complaining about the apparent inequality of things. Consider the case of Maggie, who has been married to Kyle for fourteen years. She met Kyle when he was studying engineering at a Midwestern university. At that time, Maggie was just on the threshold of making a name for herself as a photographer of city scapes. They married when he finished his graduate studies and Kyle's career took off. He was recognized for a particular engineering design which was much in demand. Kyle was not content to work for others, however. He dreamed of owning his own engineering firm and of employing and directing others. But they were young and finances were tight. Nevertheless, Maggie encouraged Kyle to follow his dream. Soon, Kyle had put together all the necessary arrangements to start his own business and so off they went to pursue Kyle's dream.

When Maggie told a friend that she and Kyle would be moving to the State of Maine where the best opportunity for Kyle presented itself, the friend was appalled. Had Maggie abandoned her own love of photography? Had she given everything up for Kyle? So it seemed. And as a matter of fact, she was comfortable doing just that. Maggie understood that her friend was disappointed in her decision to walk away from a promising career, but to Maggie, it made perfect sense. She knew that the sacrifice was enormous and it would cost her a great deal in terms of her own dreams and aspirations. But she would go wherever Kyle needed to go. He was her husband. "Can't he at least stick it out here a few more years until you are more established?" asked the friend. Maggie shrugged, "I don't know," she said. "I don't think I'll ask him."

In the years that followed, Maggie would assume most of the responsibilities for maintaining a good marriage and for raising the two children. It seemed to Maggie a reasonable sacrifice to make for the person she loved. She never looked back, never regretted, and she never thought about what might have been. Instead, she devoted herself to her husband, to her children, and to her husband's career. Those who have known Maggie across the years would say that it is hard to know what she feels in her most private moments about the road not taken. She doesn't talk much about herself. Her letters to her old friends are filled with news of Kyle and the children. Unquestionably, Kyle is the center of her universe. He may never achieve all the acclaim as an engineer that he believes he is capable of, but Maggie believes in him. No matter what her old friends may think about his influence on her, organizing their married life around him is what she wants to do. It is the life she has chosen and it is the life that suits her very well.

The Balance of Power

Kyle is by no means an ogre. He loves his wife deeply and dedicates much if not all of his spare time to her and the children. Often, he stops to thank the heavens for gracing him with such a woman as Maggie. He consults Maggie in everything and if ever she said, "No, I can't go along with that," he would have second thoughts about proceeding and very likely would not. However, with devoted types, there is a risk that they will hook up with overbearing, control-hungry mates. This is because within their relationships, devoted types like Maggie automatically assume the less dominate, more passive caretaking role. They prefer to rely on the judgment of the central person in their lives to make the major life decisions. Thus, relationships that devoted individuals form are mercifully free of power struggles. Trust is paramount, the lines of family authority are clear, and so decision making often boils down to "whatever you say dear." That can work well as long as the devoted person does not sacrifice his or her best interests. This balance of power also works well with people who also have substantial self-sacrificing style in their pattern and the mate is responsible, has no major personality problems, and does not take advantage of the devoted style of their mate.

Set Up On The Pedestal

Devoted men and women rarely tire of their mates. They idolize them and place them, along with most other people in their lives, on pedestals. The devoted partners make sure that their spouses remain on their thrones. They need it this way for their own place in the world to become secure and comfortable. They like to involve the mate in all aspects of their lives and they ask their opinions about any old thing, "How do you like this dress? Do you think I ought to sell stocks and buy bonds? I have to pick out new wallpaper for this room. Can you come and tell me what you think?" Often this devoted idealization of the mate is more subtle in people who have more mixed personality patterns than Maggie. Either way, when the dominate personality style is the devoted style, the person is comfortable placing others at the center of their universe.

Stress

Trouble in relationships is a severe source of stress for the devoted person, second only to a breakup itself. Individuals with this personality style take criticism hard and feel personally responsible for things that go wrong in the relationship. They may spend more energy than other people worrying about the short or long-term fidelity of their spouses. And when they are worried about the relationship, they may need excessive affection and reassurance in order to forestall periods of anxiety or depression. They cope with these stresses by taking it upon themselves to make things better. They aim to please. Unfortunately, this coping style often compounds their problems. The mates of overly devoted individuals may already have been exasperated with their compliance and lack of initiative. What they may need to see now is a show of strength from their devoted mates. But when the devoted person is being threatened, he or she may become more deeply entrenched in their personality style. In response to a question such as, "Where would you like to eat?" all the stress-devoted partner can answer is, "Wherever you want is okay with me."

The end of a relationship through breakup or through death of a spouse may feel like the end of the world to a devoted person. Devoted types do not do well alone when depression becomes a real risk. The actual extent of the devoted style may not become apparent in an individual until such an occurrence. Often the spouses of devoted people are happy to be the responsible ones in the family. But when the spouse is no longer present, the over-protected, devoted partner may discover for the first time that he or she is prepared to make the decisions and show the initiative required for life on his or her own.

Devoted men and women cope with loss by filling the void as soon as possible. Some devoted people go from relationship to relationship rather than be alone with themselves even for a few months. The tendency to rebound immediately is a strong clue to the presence of the devoted style in a person's personality profile. Nonetheless, the fact that they are able to create new relationships is to their credit. Some people, such as those with vigilant or sensitive personality styles, unlike the devoted personalities, cope with the pain of loss by steering clear of opportunities to love again.

The Devoted Parent

Few others are more nurturing than devoted parents, especially when their children are babies. Devoted individuals are exquisitely sensitive to the needs and feelings of their infants and they take care of them without discomfort or complaint. Indeed, they are so good at understanding and fulfilling the dependency needs of their young ones that they must take care not to overprotect them and keep them dependent when they begin to take steps toward autonomy. Devoted parents should at all times be sure to work on helping their kids test and appreciate the rewards of independence. Single devoted parents may have some problems making important decisions for themselves and their children. By and large, however, moderately devoted parents will give easily and happily to their children and will be remembered with great love.

Emotions, Self-Control, and the Real World Attached Self

Since devoted people find contentment through attachments, their sense of themselves may be weak. They don't necessary appear unconfident or fragile. Many people with moderately devoted traits lead active, productive lives as long as they are within a successful caring, mutually respectful relationship. Individuals with a great deal of this style, often feel that they don't measure up to the idealized partner, and they may be hesitant to voice their opinions. As the style becomes extreme, they may change themselves to suit others, even going so far as to assume the opinions of their partners. When men and women with this style are not involved in a relationship, they may feel that there's something wrong with them.

Frequently, devoted people think of themselves and their mates as one. Thus, the devoted wife who says, "We don't think we're going to the toy manufacturer's convention," means that her husband, who always attends alone, has decided not to go to the convention this year. A veterinarian's devoted wife, who serves as his receptionist, confused a caller who asked for her husband when she responded, "We're in surgery now."

Emotionally, people with this personality style can be steady and open if they are attached. If they are not involved in a relationship or if they are having trouble as a couple, they may become depressed, anxious, and worried.

They can express and accept love, this is their gift. They may have difficulty showing strong, negative feelings, including anger if these feelings put them in conflict with the people they care for. When they are angry, they are more likely to brood and become resentful than to express it directly.

Self-control is not usually a problem for people with this personality style, at least when the relationships are proceeding well. When they are worried about their relationships, they may need an excessive amount of reassurance, and after a loss, they may seek symbolic substitutes such as food. As soon as they find a new number one, they snap out of it.

The real world for the devoted person is one in which other people loom rather large. Or, in other words, it is a world in which the devoted person can, without fully realizing it, feel a bit small and needy like a child carrying less weight compared with idealized, apparently more substantial, others.

Work in the Service of Others

Devoted men and women can be good hard workers who do whatever is required to please the boss. They take orders well, cooperate with their co-workers, have little need to put their own imprint on the work, or to share the credit or glory. When their work life is functioning smoothly, they do need frequent expressions of appreciation. They work well with conscientious bosses who prefer to be in direct control of their employees' work. While self-confident bosses appreciate the loyal, noncompetitive nature of devoted people, they may expect their direct reports to show more initiative and independence than is characteristic of someone with this personality style.

People whose personalities are dominated by the devoted style are generally content to steer clear of the "fast lane." They tend not to be avid competitors or eager decision makers. However, because they are often so cooperative and competitive at doing what they are asked, they may be promoted into positions that require some non-devoted, creative decision making. Unfortunately, these management level jobs may prove their undoing.

The Devoted Leader

A person who is ruled by the devoted style generally avoids becoming a manager or any leadership position for that matter. Since this style is common in mixed personality patterns, however, many men and women in management positions possess their fair share of devoted traits. Such moderately devoted managers will prove to be sensitive, friendly, encouraging, and caring toward their staffs. Often, they will go out of their way to make the work situation pleasant and rewarding. They are quick to express their gratitude for a job well done. They may rely on key staff members to make or contribute to important decisions, but they may worry too much about what direct reports think of them and will thus have difficulty asserting their authority during conflict. Assertiveness training may be of great help to the leader with some degree of the devoted style.

Careers For the Devoted Style

Men and women with a devoted personality style thrive in jobs and careers in which they take direct orders and/or fulfill the needs of others from secretarial work to administrative assistants to a secure position in the family business to line work or middle management in a corporation. Service careers such as nursing, working with children, and social worker are naturals for this personality style. A streak of devoted style balanced among other personality styles can benefit psychotherapists. Devoted volunteers are God-sends for service agencies where there is no end of need for people who can give so much of themselves to others.

If this is the dominant style in your personality, steer clear of any work that does not involve other people and/or that requires you to spend most of your time making, implementing, and being responsible for decisions. It is just not the right fit for you.

Tips on Dealing with the Devoted Person in Your Life

1. The devoted person in your life likes to help and to please. Don't fight it and don't feel guilty for accepting it. Enjoy!

2. Don't take the attentions of this person for granted. The devoted person in your life may be so good at anticipating your desires and putting you first that you may not recognize that he or she has unfulfilled and unexpressed needs. Devoted types often seem more confident and assertive than they actually are. When they want something from you, they may not ask. Indeed, they may wait for you to anticipate their needs the way they anticipate yours. Foremost among their needs is reassurance. Devoted people are extremely sensitive to your feelings about them. Express your love and appreciation frequently and honestly. If the devoted person in your life is your employee, express your

appreciation for the good work and stop and consider whether you owe this person a raise. Devoted types may be reluctant to request a raise or to remind you that it is time for one. They may assume that if they deserved it, you'd provide it.

3. Keep in mind that criticizing or blowing your top with a devoted type will likely lead to self-doubt and self-blame—not particularly constructive reactions. When you need to resolve a conflict with a devoted person or deal with unpleasant personal business, contribute as much reassurance as you can. Resist the temptation to allow the devoted person to shoulder the blame for everything that goes wrong between the two of you, which he or she may be all too willing to do. At the same time, don't provide so much reassurance that you neglect to work out a solution to your conflict.

4. Take the stated opinions of this person with a grain of salt. The more devoted a person is, the more that person will express an opinion that he or she thinks you want to hear. Underneath it all, this devoted person may have an altogether different opinion. If you say, "What do you think about going on a camping vacation for a change?" Your mate, hearing the enthusiasm in your voice, may say, "Oh sure." In reality, he or she may prefer to go on a cruise. Unless you make sure that this person's opinion is a true one, you may be stuck in the woods with a less than cheerful partner.

Making the Most of Your Devoted Style

You know how to love and how to give. You are keenly aware of other people's needs and feelings. Now turn your attention to yourself and see what you can do on your own behalf and let other people know who you are and what they can do for you. You are diplomatic and you like to promote harmony. To this end, you may tend to agree with the people who are important to you, perhaps stifling your own opinions. By this, you run the risk of appearing less interesting to the people whose opinions you care about most.

Exercise 1: Whenever someone asks you for your opinions, say what you honestly think. For example: if your mate asks you what you would like to do tonight, don't answer, "I don't care, whatever you want is fine with me." Instead, think of an answer. If you can't come up with one, say, "I don't know right now, but I'll think about it." Your devoted personality style may make it difficult for you to express your anger, in addition to your opinions, for fear that you'll rock the relationship boat. However, trying to suppress your feelings such as anger may lead you to express your anger sideways such as by pouting, by getting a headache, or by becoming uncooperative. These expressions of anger tend to be destructive to a relationship.

Exercise 2: Get it off your chest. Express your anger directly. Tell people what you are angry about and why instead of allowing it to distort your behavior. If you can't get yourself to do that, start by making lists of all the things you are angry about. Then, when you are alone, pretend the person you are angry at is in the room and that you are telling him or her what you are angry about. Devoted people like you prefer to rely on other people and to let them make their decisions for them. It is important to keep in mind that just going along with the wishes of others for the sake of going along may lead to dissatisfaction with the results of those decisions now or years from now. Also, decision making is an essential survival skill necessary to avoid becoming helpless and dependent should you lose the person or people you rely upon most.

Exercise 3: Practice decision making. Each time you are about to seek someone else's opinion or advice in making a decision, stop and think whether you can make up your own mind or come up with the answer yourself. If you have a big problem with decisions, concentrate on minor decisions first such as what to wear today, which movie to see, or where to go to dinner. When you get better at these, start practicing on the more important ones such as whether to look for another job or what kind, where, and when to buy a house.

Exercise 4: Your total devotion to your family or your mate is admirable. Make sure you do not give up all your other interests though. Develop or rekindle your own activities—go bowling once a week, join a charitable organization or the volunteer fire department, volunteer at your local hospital, sign up for a class, whatever you think you would like to do. In order to remain balanced and to avoid over dependence on your spouse, you need other connections to the world. Remember that most people no longer have the extended family network to fall back on when they grow old or face aloneness. In this day and age, the better you learn how to take care of yourself, the more independent dignity you will have in later life.

Exercise 5: Develop the life skills you lack. For example: learn to do the banking and pay bills, shop for food and cook a meal, find out how to buy a car, how to claim insurance benefits, how to make travel reservations, and how to plan social activities in the event that your spouse takes care of these tasks for you. These responsibilities may all fall to you sooner or later should your mate die or fall ill. Life will go on more easily if you learn what to do.

The Dependent Personality Disorder

People suffering from dependent personality disorder, the pathological extreme of the devoted style, have the misfortune to experience themselves as helpless, weak, empty and inferior. By attaching themselves to another person, they gain the strength and self-esteem to survive. Yet, they live in fear of losing the person that is so necessary to them. They can't bear the very thought of being alone. The dependent personality disorder can be described as follows: A pervasive and excessive need to be taken care of that leads to submissive and clinging behavior and fears of separation beginning by early adulthood and present in a variety of contexts as indicated by five or more of the following:

1. Has difficulty making everyday decisions without an excessive amount of advice and reassurance from others.

2. Leaves others to assume responsibility for most major areas of his or her life.

3. Has difficulty expressing disagreement with others because of fear of loss of support or approval. Note: Does not include realistic fears of retribution.

4. Has difficulty initiating projects or doing things on his or her own because of a lack of self-confidence or abilities rather than a lack of motivation or energy.

5. Goes to excessive lengths to obtain nurturance and support from others to the point of volunteering to do things that are unpleasant.

6. Feels uncomfortable or helpless when alone because of exaggerated fears of being unable to care for him or herself.

7. Urgently seeks another relationship as a source of care and support when a close relationship ends.

8. Is unrealistically preoccupied with fears of being left to take care of himself or herself.

The Overwhelming Need For Another

Dependent people sometimes referred to popularly as, "co-dependent," lead their lives determined not to disturb or offend the people who become the entire focus of their lives. They yield up their individuality and autonomy at the doorstep, becoming placating, submissive, self-deprecating, undemanding, and apologetic without self-assurance or ambition. They attach themselves uncritically and may run the risk of being victimized by partners who take advantage of their passivity. If the relationship becomes unsteady, dependent individuals will appear helpless and clinging. But if they form a solid relationship with a partner who will provide the reassurance, strength, and protection they need, these dependent individuals seem content and comfortable. To others, they appear kind, gentle, generous, and humble.

Their tendency to depreciate themselves before others, "You are so smart, you'll understand that book so much better than I did," can seem a genteel and thoughtful manner of complimenting you for your intelligence. It is not, however. Despite all apparent evidence to the contrary, they honestly believe that they are inadequate in everything from books to abilities to mental capacity. Underneath the smiling face of a dependent person, lurks someone who has little or no confidence coupled with a huge need for reassurance. This man or woman reaches out to gain self-esteem from other people. If you say, "Nonsense, you're extremely smart." Your dependent friend may be able to believe it, but only for a moment. Primarily dependent people acquire the self-esteem they lack through their attachments to other people. Dependent individuals tend to reveal a cheerful demeanor to the world. This sunny expression may mask their internal suffering. People with dependent personality disorder may be very reluctant to confide their darker feelings to anyone lest these truths burden or upset others or otherwise undermine their relationships. Even a mate of many years may be unaware of the dependent partner's inner life. Indeed, dependent individuals are very often unaware themselves of the extent of their depression and rejection as well as their need to be dependent. Instead, many of them prefer to pretend that the world is a story book place with happy endings everywhere.

Others may mask their psychological helplessness by feeling frail and, therefore, requiring other people, including medical personnel, to take charge and to pay attention.

5

The Dramatic Style

D ramatic types are all heart. They have been granted the gift of feeling with which they color the lives of everyone around them. When paired with great talent, dramatic men and women can transform human emotion into the highest art form. Even in their daily lives, their wit, their laughter, their sense of beauty, their flamboyance, and their sensuality can lift the spirits of a room full of strangers. All the world's a stage for individuals with this very common personality style. Life is never dull or boring for them and certainly not for those who share it with them. Dramatic people fill their world with excitement—things "happen" in their lives.

The Seven Characteristics

The following seven traits and behaviors are clues to the presence of the dramatic style. A person who reveals a strong dramatic tendency will demonstrate more of these behaviors more intensely than someone who has less of this style.

1. Feelings. Dramatic men and women live in an emotional world. They are sensation oriented, emotionally demonstrative, and physically affectionate. They react emotionally to events and can shift quickly from mood to mood.

2. Color. They experience life vividly and expansively. They have rich imaginations, they tell entertaining stories, and they are drawn to romance and melodrama.

3. Attention. Dramatic people like to be seen and noticed. They are often the center of attention and they rise to the occasion when all eyes are on them.

4. Appearance. They pay a lot of attention to grooming and they enjoy clothes, style, and fashion.

5. Sexual attraction. In appearance and behavior, dramatic individuals enjoy their sexuality. They are seductive, engaging and charming, tempters and temptresses.

6. Engagement. Easily putting their trust in others, they are able to become quickly involved in relationships.

7. The spirit is willing. People with dramatic personality style eagerly respond to new ideas and suggestions from others.

The Six Domains of Dramatic Functioning

The rich, complex lives of dramatic men and women are governed simultaneously by two key domains—emotions and relationships.

Emotions—the Heart Speaks

The men and women who possess this personality style know the world through their emotions. How they feel about someone or something gives them all the information they need. The conscientious person, the voice of reason, sees a movie and offers a factual critique of the performances, the direction, the cinematography, the sound track, the costumes, and the script. The dramatic person may sum it up in one word—"Wow." It's the impact of life that counts and what they seek.

They dwell in a world of flamboyant color and they extract passion from every experience. Their lives often seem so much more eventful than other peoples, they are full of exciting tales, they transform the ordinary happenings of life into real theater.

Listen to how Valerie explains to her friend why she was late meeting her for lunch at a restaurant. Note how one of the tedious daily frustrations of life in a large city, finding a parking space, turns into a lively afternoon adventure.

"I was halfway to the subway when I realized I hadn't moved my car. The spot I was in was only good for another half hour. God! I raced back into my building to get the key, but the elevator was stuck, so I ran up a million stairs, found my key, flew down again, ran out to my car. Would you believe a parking space materialized before my very eyes. My fairy godmother was with me today. So I'm backing into the space and suddenly I hear this vroom, vroom, this total leather guy on a motorcycle has pulled in behind me. I get out of my car, he gets off his bike and I tell you, I've never seen a human being so big. He just glowers down at me and I think the guy must be a hell's angel. If I open my mouth, he'll kill me. But this teeny, weeny little voice comes out of me and squeaks, 'Excuse me, large leather person, but I was here first.' There's this long pause in which I'm convinced I'm in my last moments on earth and then the leather hulk says, 'okay lady.' He grins—what a set of teeth—then he swings his leg back over his Harley and vrooms away. Would you believe it? I taught a hell's angel how to be a good American!" Valerie lapsed into delighted laughter. Her friend, who had sat waiting nearly half an hour, forgot her annoyance, charmed by the colorful tale and Valerie's talent for turning a potentially stressful experience into an enjoyable one.

Expression and Impression

Dramatic men and women generally display their emotions freely and openly. They possess no competing emotionally reticent styles, their emotions are there for everyone to see. No stiff upper lips for them. They are good-natured, sentimental, and effusive. They enjoy melodrama, intrigue, and gossip, and they are easily moved. They react powerfully and often immediately to events.

Because they are so reactive, their feelings can change very quickly—from joy to fury to misery to despair, depending on the day's experiences. Predominately dramatic people tend to express their moods with whatever degree of passion they feel. If a very dramatic person is mad at you, watch out. But they don't hold grudges and they expect other people not to hold grudges as well.

They seek emotional experiences in life and they may have little appreciation for life's drier side. The dramatic style tends to bring with it impatience and/or anxiety with details, routines, organizing, planning, and finances. Highly dramatic individuals will often steer clear of weighty conversation, preferring gossip and intrigue. When they read a newspaper, they may skim the headlines, skim the politics and finance, and concentrate on the murders, the human interest and life style stories, entertainment and/or the sports sections. The conscientious person prefers to read the whole paper straight through, word for word. A person with a mixed dramatic/conscientious style, a very common pattern, may read the "good stuff" first, then turn to the beginning of the paper and dutifully read what he or she "should."

When you listen to a dramatic person tell a tale, note their absence of factual description. Like impressionist painters, they create a picture without relying on realistic details. "He's so big!" Valerie says of the man on the motorcycle. How big? As big as the impression of the man on the motorcycle that forms in the mind of the listener. She says, "I ran up a million stairs." Instead of mentioning the number of stories. In this way, dramatic people may distort factual reality, but they do convey the emotional impact of their experiences.

Overall, they live their lives intensely. To plumb the emotional heights and depths of any experience, all aspects of their lives, their work, their relationships, their imaginations, their leisure time activities are infused with stimulating, extroverted energy. With little tolerance for boredom, dramatic men and women usually do not wait for life to happen to them. They don a dashing costume, they go out on the town, they laugh until everyone else laughs with them, they actively provoke experience by stirring the passions of other people.

Relationships—Stirring the Passions

Dramatic men and women are highly social. Like fish in water, they are in their element when surrounded by others. The central focus of their lives is to win friends and to influence people. Dramatic men and women rouse others, energize them, charm them until they drop their reserve and open their hearts. Dramatic individuals are the life of the party—happiest when the atmosphere is highly charged and all eyes are on them.

Dramatic men and women genuinely like other people and are very attentive to what pleases them and makes them comfortable. Many are gifted with profound intuition about other peoples' feelings and are extremely skilled at reading people by their gestures, their tones of voice, their body language. These social gifts ensure their places on everybody's party list.

Sally always invites her friend, Lucy, to dinner when her husband, Don, brings home some of his straight-laced, out-of-town clients. Lucy gets them all talking and relaxed before the soup is on. All woman, she dresses with an eye-catching flare, she smells wonderful, her eyes are wide with enraptured interest as she listens to these business men and women answer her questions about what they do and where they come from. She draws out what makes these out-of-towners feel important and good about themselves. She wants to know about them and she intrigues everyone at the table. "It's like living a kind of romance when Lucy is around," Sally says, "There's a feeling of excitement and possibility. Everything is so striking, so interesting, so vivid. She weaves a spell. Don's clients have a wonderful time—we all do."

The Seduction

Dramatic individuals are particularly effective in the early stages of a relationship. They know how to draw people to them, using their own natural sensuality and flirtatiousness to stir others' passions to make the person they are focusing on feel like the center of the universe. They are open with compliments, flattery, and appreciation. Like devoted people, they seem to have an uncanny sense of a person's desires and needs. They watch and listen with attention to what you like, want, and need, and they'll go to great lengths to provide it for you.

When the object of the dramatic individual's attention responds with admiration and desire, the relationship ignites and passions are set aflame. In an emotional connection with someone, the dramatic person experiences profound infatuation. She or he is fully open to the new love, trusting, and accepting. While in the best of situations, solid relationships can spring from such emotional heat, the dramatic person's feelings can create a vulnerability to impassioned wistful thinking. This individual wants so much for the ardor to continue that he or she may well misread important cues.

Tom, an up-and-coming actor and singer with Hollywood good looks and Broadway talent, had little difficulty meeting attractive, intelligent women. The women he would really fall for were usually very glamorous and even more successful than he was. In his infatuation, he would suddenly begin to see their every gesture, word, glance as a confirmation of their equally profound feelings for him. But he wouldn't necessarily be taking in all the relevant information and acting appropriately. Kimberly, the last woman to break his heart, was a cosmetic industry executive whose career was on the front burner of her life when Tom began taking her out. She was much taken with Tom, which was obvious to all. What was equally obvious to everyone except Tom was that Kimberly's attention was not about to be diverted from the fast track her career was on right at the time. Tom was sure that he was dead center of her universe. When she told him she didn't have room in her life now for the encompassing commitment he wanted from her, he felt like he had been hit with a bolt of lightning on a sunny day. Where could it have come from? But Kimberly had never been trying to lead him down a garden path. What Tom had done, in his dramatic way, was read only the "good" signs that she loved and cared for him. But he selectively ignored information that would round out the story—that her soul was in her work right now and that if he wanted a deep relationship to develop, he'd have to give her space and time. Vigilant and sensitive people also misread other people frequently, but in an opposite way from dramatic types. Vigilant and sensitive types look to others for signs of questionable motives or criticism. Dramatic people over interpret the "come-hither" side. Faced with someone's ambivalence, vigilant and sensitive will see only the negative section while the dramatic person will react to only the good vibes. In such ways, all three types end up charting an inaccurate course with people based on incomplete information. Vigilant and sensitive people hold back from others or even push them away when these people might be well-disposed to them if they only let down their guard. Dramatic individuals assume an involvement that may not have had time to develop, so they sometimes scare away the people who count most.

Related to the dramatic openness to people is an easy willingness to respond to others' ideas, suggestions, and activities—a very likable trait. Highly dramatic people will sometimes need to question their responses. Do they really want to go along with an activity or are they so bedazzled by the attention of people they like or so taken with a fad that they are sometimes too easily swayed?

Keeping the Fire Lit

A dramatic individual requires a high degree of excitement. So when the ardor tempers, as usually happens after the infatuation phase, this person may become bored. People whose personalities are powerfully dominated by this style may have difficulty sustaining relationships over the longer, duller run. Some, like the operatic temptress, Carmen, may lose interest after the successful seduction. Others may seek affairs outside their primary relationship in order to keep the level of exciting attention sufficiently high. Some may flirt, tease, and collect admirers while remaining sexually faithful to their partners.

Their low tolerance for boredom in relationships may inspire some dramatic types to an inventiveness that would benefit any relationship. They may plan vacations, parties, or other entertainments to keep life at a high pitch. They keep making friends and populating their lives with stimulating people. If all works well, life with a dramatic partner can be passionate and interesting. It will never be dull or quiet.

Stress

Life with dramatic people can also be stormy. Considering their strong and immediate reactions, trouble in a relationship will be a major blow to the self-esteem of the dramatic individual. Trouble can ensue when the partner cannot deal with the very dramatic spouse's passionate outbursts and/or seductive behavior. It can arise when the dramatic individual does not receive sufficient admiration, attention, or expression of feeling from his or her mate. It can result also when the couple cannot establish a routine that compensates for the extremely dramatic partner's inability or reluctance to handle life's mundane chores, like balancing the checkbook, keeping track of important papers, saving tax receipts, or staying within the credit card limits.

To cope with stress and anxiety, dramatic types like to look on the bright side. They prefer to repress the unpleasant in order to sustain an optimistic outlook. They keep telling themselves that everything will work out. Action helps them forget.

Jason, a civil engineer, flew into a rage when his dramatic wife, Gloria, neglected to record a two thousand dollar check. "I've bounced the mortgage payment and the car payment. How could you screw up the credit rating I've taken years to build?" He yelled on the verge of tears. Money had always been a big problem in their marriage. Gloria believed that Jason, who she felt was a little uptight, worried far too much about it. "You can straighten it out with them. I know they trust you and will realize it was an honest mistake." Gloria tried to reassure her husband, "I tell you what," she said as her face brightened, "Let's take our minds off this little misunderstanding and go dancing." At that, fire started coming out of Jason's nostrils, or so Gloria insisted when relating this scene to her mother.

Being alone is another source of stress for dramatic individuals. Without a partner or lover in whose eyes to shine, many dramatic people feel unhappy with themselves. For the dramatic person who has never had to take care of him or herself, having to deal with money and other responsibilities after the loss of a long-time partner may provoke extreme anxiety. The state of being alone may not last long though. Usually, a person with this personality style will attend parties and social gatherings as soon as possible, putting on a happy face and casting a delightful spell over new admirers.

The Dramatic Parent

Dramatic men and women can be emotionally understanding and accessible parents and they encourage creativity and aesthetic appreciation in their children. But they may become disorganized and let important details slip such as forgetting teacher conferences, field trip permissions, little league games, even tuition payments. This can be embarrassing and confusing for a child who may conclude that the parent doesn't care. The non-dramatic parent should be aware of responsibilities that the dramatic parent has toward the child and make sure that they are met.

Overall, dramatic parents are fun, active, and energetic, offering their kids a wide range of experiences out in the world. They may need help in teaching their children restraint and frustration tolerance and, as the style becomes extreme, some dramatic parents may be overly needy of loving feedback from their kids and will have a hard time letting them go their own independent way. Ideally, the non-dramatic parent will be able to reassure the dramatic one that he or she is being a good, loving parent and help the dramatic parent know when to back off.

Self—the Importance of Image

Outward and other directed as they are, these intensely social beings tend to define themselves from the outside in. They see themselves as others see them. Ask a strongly dramatic person to describe him or herself and you might hear, "People say I'm very friendly," or "My family is always telling me how funny I am," or "My teachers say I'm very talented." The self-confident person would say, "I'm friendly," or "I'm funny," or "I'm talented."

Similarly because their self-definition comes from outside themselves, how they look to others, the image they present is extremely important to them. They are what they wear. Dramatic people often are great dressers. Theirs is a talent for costume and style, for creating a visual image. Their eyes always trained outward to the reactions of others. They tend to outfit themselves in the fads and fashions of the social groups with which they identify themselves. They dress to go out with great care, never just throwing something on any old thing. Some will dress, redress, and dress yet again before they are satisfied that they look right. People who are clearly dominated by this personality style may have difficulty appreciating the maxim that beauty comes from the inside.

One of the consequences of being intensely other directed and emotionally reactive is that the dramatic individuals will, with varying degrees, lack a calm, consistent, centered sense of self. For this reason, people with this personality style usually require reassurance and feedback—call it applause—from others in order to maintain their self-confidence. They need to hear that the meal they just cooked tastes good, that they are attractive, that their artistic performances are moving, their athletic feats astonishing, and especially that they are loved.

Self-Control, Resisting the Urge

This passionate, pleasure loving personality style comes with a low frustration tolerance. Unless they have some of a more reflective or thoughtful style to balance them, emotionally ruled individuals will be spontaneous, impulsive, impetuous, and impatient. They want what they want now. "Please let me open my present now, I can't bear waiting until my birthday," a dramatic person pleads.

Toby, a rather dramatic sportscaster, couldn't find his gold-plated fountain pen when he went to write in his journal one morning. He didn't use the pen that much since he'd started using a lap top, but that pen was an important symbol to him and he searched high and low for it to no avail. He couldn't wait, even until the next day, to see if it turned up around his apartment, although common sense told him it would. That afternoon, he spent almost two hundred dollars on a new pen which he could ill afford. Ten days later when Toby cleaned his apartment, he found the old pen which had fallen behind his bed. The department store would not take back the new pen because Toby had already used it. Toby says that if it happens again, he'll do exactly the same thing rather than be without his lucky gold pen for ten days.

Temptation to act on impulse grows harder to resist as the degree of dramatic style becomes greater. Self-control in everything from eating, to spending, to keeping secrets, or controlling a hot temper will prove relatively difficult for a dramatic person. This is because dramatic individuals live best in the heart-felt moment which makes it difficult to resist immediate gratification. Also, dramatic types like to take their minds off their worries as soon as possible. A bit of self-indulgence can lift their spirits intensely. Another reason why this style confers a vulnerability to self-control problems is that dramatic individuals are not natural planners. For many people, restraint in spending comes from planning and keeping to a budget. Success in losing weight comes from determining in advance what and how much you are going to eat over how long a period. Success in keeping the lid on your anger results from anticipating the damage it may cause. Fortunately for many dramatic types, a healthy streak of a counter-balancing restraining personality style, such as conscientious, self-confident, vigilant, serious, solitary, or aggressive in one's overall pattern can make it easier to resist the urge. Otherwise, they find they are continually dieting or watching their spending. Extremely dramatic people will probably find they have a difficult time with emotional control. As the dramatic style becomes histrionic personality disorder, temper tantrums become increasingly common.

Real World, Wistful Thinking

For dramatic men and women, the real world is a storybook land where romance lives. They have rich fantasy lives like Valerie who made a hell's angel out of a man on a motorcycle. They spot heros and villains wherever they turn. Other people become larger than life characters in a cosmic melodrama. Talented, balanced, and dramatic individuals may transform their story-book world into art and entertainment that gains and holds public attention in the real world. Some of them have a great talent for creating inspiring and/or romantic stories with broadly drawn good guys and bad guys in which the bad guys get what's coming to them and the good guys share a happy ending.

In the world of romance, dreams come true. Dramatic men and women, although they have their despairing moods, want to believe in happy endings. Their optimism about the present and future can be inspiring; "everything will work out," is their motto. Given their tendency to cope with stress by ignoring unpleasant reality, dramatic individuals must take care not to substitute a wish for an uncomfortable truth that they'd rather not deal with.

Work: Creative Flair

Dramatic people love an exciting work situation in which they can make an impact. They are idea people, often brilliant in their hunches and they can persuade others to back their projects. What they may fail to do, however, is follow through with the details. But if they can find people to do it for them, they can make their dreams a reality.

Years ago, Max, a successful trial attorney with an ability to move juries to decide cases in his favor, came up with an idea whose time had come. One night Max, who was twice divorced, was fantasizing about how to find the woman of his dreams. Wouldn't it be great, he mused, if all the available women in the world could appear to you one after another on a movie screen. You could watch them, listen to them, and pick the ones you wanted.

Although the concept of video tape dating services is old news now, no one had thought of such a thing when Max had his brilliant idea. He took a leave of absence from the law firm and traveled to major cities around the country gathering backers. Max had a deep, sonorous voice and an ability to spin a moving story. He intrigued many people from coast to coast with his project and they dug deep into their pockets to help finance it. Within the year, Max had opened 30 on-screen dating offices. He put ads in papers and ran TV commercials featuring himself. People responded by the thousands. The only problem was that Max hadn't begun to organize the production side. He hadn't even hired a production staff. As happens so frequently to individuals with the dramatic personality style, Max had come up with and promoted a great idea, but he had failed to execute it.

He was beginning to see his great idea collapse into a bunch of bad debts when finally he put an ad in the paper for an executive manager. Louise was the eighth person he interviewed. He knew as soon as she walked in that she was the person for the job. Louise was astonished to be offered the job after a five-minute interview. Max's hunch was right, and Louise put together a plan and was in production in key locations within six weeks. Max has long since sold his dating services for a huge profit. Louise, in all her conscientious competence, has gone on to become head of production for a cable TV station.

Their tendency to operate on hunches and insights instead of reasoning things through may make life difficult for dramatic types if the institutions they work for insist that they proceed with outlines, plans, budgets, and detailed follow through. However, dramatic individuals can contribute greatly in the entertainment world—broadcast, advertising, and associated industries, which welcome dramatic individuals on their creative staffs and demand less regimentation from them than from other employees. Usually the creative personnel are encouraged to dress as they please. For example: whereas suits are the expected dress for the business staff, one creative hotshot at a New York advertising agency was given a piano for his office. Not because he was responsible for the music, but because playing the piano helped him relax and generate ideas. A suggestion for management: pamper your dramatic employees, tell them how much you appreciate them, let them work the way they please and they'll reward you with excellent work.

Many successful entrepreneurs, like Max and his dating service enterprise, have a strong streak of dramatic style. These people can charm, sell, wheel and deal, promote. If they can manage to put together a strong organization to back them up and take care of the administrative details, they can often create quite a successful enterprise.

The Dramatic Leader

Dramatic men and women can be strong leaders, skilled and inspiring their direct reports to work hard. They need to have a capable and strong conscientious secretary or assistant whom they trust to keep the work moving and to make sure that routine responsibilities are met. They often appreciate a job well done and are generous to those who work hard on their behalf. Similarly, they do not hide their anger. They may lambast a report who displeases them, even threatening to fire the unfortunate offender. Often they do not follow through on their threats. They may be emotionally changeable individuals, gruff and uncommunicative on one day, cheerful and enthusiastic on another. If you work for such a person, do not take your boss's emotional reactions personally. Avoid a confrontation, lay low, maintain your own emotional balance, and wait for the boss to show a more expansive mood before you ask for your raise.

Careers for the Dramatic

The creative and performing arts, or the creative sides of business and industry, are natural choices for talented dramatic people. Overall, seek careers that make use of your style's extraordinary ability to influence other people. Anything from public relations, to teaching, to sales, and sales promotion. This style's sensitivity to emotions can be an asset in the helping professions.

Avoid routine, repetitive, and technical work of any kind and seek a non-regimented work environment. Working for yourself may appeal to you, but it could be your downfall unless you have an agent and/or can afford to hire someone to assist with the paperwork, help you handle the finances, and prod you to be disciplined and productive when you feel strongly tempted to goof off.

Dramatic on the Inside

For many people who have a heavy streak of the dramatic style, it marks the character of their inner lives rather than their outward behavior. Other strong styles in the personality pattern will influence how "out front" a dramatic person is. For example: if the conscientious style shares top billing with the dramatic, as it often does, it will add social and emotional reserve and self-control. The sensitive and the solitary styles will temper the dramatic's gregarious and emotional expression. The vigilant style will contribute independence and caution and the devoted style will moderate the individual's drive to get out there and move the world. But inwardly, regardless of the outward appearance, a dramatic individual's emotions and love of attention remain rich and strong.

Tips on Dealing With the Dramatic Person in Your Life

1. You are attracted to the dramatic person's spontaneity, passion, sensuality, and the ability to have a good time. Now don't clip this bird's wings. Let the dramatic person in your life dress you up and drag you out to social gatherings. Don't fight it when he or she insists you take vacations, go out dancing, or give parties. Allow the dramatic person in your life his or her emotional freedom, and enjoy the range of experience that will result for you.

2. Appreciate, praise, flatter, and give feedback. The dramatic person in your life needs you to react openly and verbally, especially about your positive feelings at all times. React to his or her appearance, cooking, business, and personal successes, romantic gestures, giving, and so on.

Most important, say how much you love this person. Don't hold back. There's no such thing as too much of a good thing with this personality style. But be sure to be honest. If you don't mean the good things you are saying, the intuitive dramatic person will know it.

3. Be romantic. Bring flowers, candy, gifts, and send valentines and mushy cards for every occasion. Even if the dramatic person in your life is a friend, relative, or parent, these sentimental attentions will delight and thrill him or her. Similarly, neglecting these expressions of affection may make dramatic types feel that you don't care.

4. Be realistic about this person's relative inability or reluctance to handle certain responsibilities, including money. Handle the finances or the financial planning yourself if need be. Better, supervise or double check essential details. For example, if your dramatic partner writes checks, periodically ask if he or she has recorded them all. Individuals with this style frequently forget. Encourage this person to do better, but never expect him or her to do as well as you do in this aspect of life. Similarly, remind this person to keep track of responsibilities such as meetings and phone calls, especially those that relate to children.

5. Don't hold grudges. Dramatic people don't hold things in and the dramatic person in your life may be emotionally tempestuous. You and this person may have a loud fight and he or she may express a ferocious anger. A few hours later, the dramatic individual will have forgotten all about it. He or she will not understand why you are still stewing. Try to let go of your own anger and annoyance. Don't take this dramatic person's emotional reactions personally and don't be frightened by the drama.

6. Avoid jealousy. Dramatic individuals like to charm other people. If you're the jealous type, stop and think whether there's anything to be jealous about. If everything is going well between the two of you at home, it is quite possible this person is merely enjoying the reactions of others and will not carry things further.

Making the Most of Your Dramatic Style

Your sources of self-esteem come from outside yourself which may make your inner life unsteady. Finding sources inside yourself will help ensure some inner calm.

Exercise 1: Think about or make a list of what you like about yourself. Be sure to look at yourself through your own eyes. For example: Do not say, "I'm glad that other people like me." Instead, try to rephrase your own point of view such as, "I like that I am friendly."

Exercise 2: Pat yourself on the back every time you find yourself needing somebody's reaction, reassure yourself. After cooking a meal, tell yourself how good it tastes. When you dress to go out, look in the mirror and appreciate how nice you look. When you are worried that someone doesn't love you, tell yourself that you are worthy of love whether or not that person cares. Don't let your value of yourself be determined purely on the basis of how others respond to you.

Exercise 3: To balance your natural spontaneity, work on restraint and planning. Stop and count to ten. The next time you are about to act on impulse of any kind—to spend, to leave work, to eat, to drink, and especially to vent your feelings, stop for a moment. Count slowly to ten. Think whether or not you want to proceed with what you are about to do. If you don't want to proceed, but can't resist the urge, see how long you can hold out. Practice this exercise at every opportunity. Get used to stopping yourself between urge and action.

Exercise 4: Plan. Every time you have a task to accomplish at home or at work, write down all the steps necessary to complete it. Resist the urge to throw down your pen or pencil halfway through.

Exercise 5: You are very intuitive about other people, but you lead with your feelings and when you are powerfully attracted to someone, your judgment may fly out the window. So stand back and observe. Collect details and information about this person. Leave your feelings aside. What color are this person's hair and eyes? How big are his or her feet? What style shoes is this person wearing? What color are his or her clothes? Ask questions. Where does this person work? Is he or she married? Where does he or she live? Make this exercise a game. The more details you fill in, the higher your "score."

Exercise 6: Face it. You like to take your mind off unpleasant truths. However, some truths grow more unpleasant if you ignore them. Try keeping all aspects of real life in the front of your mind and see how that feels. It's okay to feel anxious if you take action to deal directly with the difficulty, the anxiety will often go away. It is all within your power to face reality, not just on a regular basis, but on a daily basis.

Histrionic Personality Disorder

Men and women who have histrionic personality disorder live in an exaggerated emotional world in which they do anything they can to get attention because without it, they are nothing or so they feel. The histrionic personality disorder is demonstrated by a pervasive pattern of excessive emotionality and attention seeking beginning by early adulthood and present in a variety of contexts as indicated by five or more of the following:

1. The person is uncomfortable in situations in which he or she is not the center of attention.

2. Their interaction with others is often characterized by inappropriate sexually seductive or provocative behavior.

3. The person displays rapidly shifting and shallow expression of emotions.

4. The person consistently uses physical appearance to draw attention to self.

5. This person has a style of speech that is excessively expressionistic and lacking in detail.

6. This person shows self-dramatization, theatricality and exaggerated expression of emotion.

7. This person is suggestible, i.e., easily influenced by others or circumstances.

8. This person considers relationships to be more intimate than they actually are.

Emotions Out of Control

The men and women who suffer from this personality disorder are often unaware of, or uninformed about the world around them. This is because they are so involved in their own emotional dramas. Everything is a production. A minor setback becomes a major disaster. A small pleasure becomes the greatest joy of their lives.

Yet for all their intensity, the histrionic individual seems unconvincing. As he negotiated deals throughout the day, a middle-aged entrepreneur named Dave would go from "This is the happiest day of my life," to "I can't stand it anymore, I'm getting out of this business," depending on the way the deal went. Everyday, it was the same litany. "Yes, Dave," his colleagues would respond unsympathetically, no longer taking him seriously.

Like children, people with this disorder react instantly and their emotions often seem infantile. Their feelings change frequently. They can't stand frustration or disappointment, and they cannot delay gratification of their needs. They act self-centered and when they can't get what they want, they become greatly upset. Like some youngsters, they are prone to throwing tantrums. The sexuality of some histrionic individuals may be equally childlike. Men and women with this disorder often dress and act very seductively. Yet, for many, it's just a tease. Take them up on it and they run or get offended, although some are sexually promiscuous. Many persons with this disorder are sexually naive and often inhibited.

Coping With Histrionic People

An essential rule is not to over react to their over reactions. This isn't easy since they are manipulative and know how to "press your buttons." Don't engage them and don't sulk or pout. Later, when things are quieter, be friendly, but firm about what you require from the relationship. Be sure at the same time to reassure this histrionic individual of your loving feelings and of your good will for him or her. If you no longer have these feelings, then you should ask yourself if you are prepared to end the relationship. Ending relationships with histrionic people, whether it be a personal or professional relationship can be very difficult. They find it nearly impossible to let go and may make life difficult, even hazardous for themselves and the other person.

6

The Vigilant Style

Nothing escapes the notice of the men and women who have vigilant personality style. These individuals possess an exceptional awareness of their environment. Call them survivors. Their sensory antennae continuously scanning the people and situations around them, alert them immediately to what is awry, out-of-place, dissonant, or dangerous, especially in their dealings with other people. Vigilant types have a special kind of hearing. They are immediately aware of the mixed messages, the hidden motivations, the evasions, and the subtlest distortions of the truth that allude or delude less gifted observers. With such a focus, vigilant individuals naturally assume the roles of social critic, watch dog, and crusader in their private or our public domain. They are ready to spring upon the improprieties, especially the abuses of power that poison human affairs.

The Six Characteristics

The following six traits and behaviors are clues to the presence of the vigilant style. A person who reveals a strong vigilant tendency will demonstrate more of these behaviors more intensely than someone with less of this style in his or her personality.

1. Autonomy. Vigilant style individuals possess a resilient independence. They keep their own counsel, they require no outside reassurance or advice, they make decisions easily and they can take care of themselves.

2. Caution. They are careful in their dealings with others, preferring to size up a person before entering into a relationship.

3. Perceptiveness. They are good listeners with an ear for subtly, tone, and multiple levels of communication.

4. Self-defense. Individuals with vigilant style are feisty and do not hesitate to stand up for themselves, especially when they are under attack.

5. Alertness to criticism. They take criticism very seriously without becoming intimidated.

6. Fidelity. They place a high premium on fidelity and loyalty. They work hard to earn it and they never take it for granted.

The Six Domains of Vigilant Functioning
Relations—Who's in Charge Here?
Part I

Individuals with vigilant personality style are acutely aware of power and authority in their relationships. Throughout all aspects of their lives, they seek to maintain their freedom and independence from domination. Vigilant individuals cannot be subordinated. This is their organizing principle. Thus for this style, the domain of relationships, characterized by their insistent autonomy, is key. In relation to other people, in no uncertain terms, vigilant types are always in charge of their own destiny.

Caution and reserve mark all their dealings with people. But they are not necessarily cold and unfriendly, nor do they prefer to do without relationships. Although they may be uneasy among strangers and slow to warm up, vigilant individuals can be gregarious and comfortable among people once they get to know them, but they are slow to commit. Unlike the devoted type who is comfortable with dependence and will jump in with both feet, the vigilant individual will enter one slow step at a time. Even within their established relationships, loyal though they may be, most vigilant types hold back part of themselves until they are certain that a person who shows interest in them can be trusted not to hurt or disappoint them. Vigilant types prefer to watch and evaluate.

Vigilant men and women are gifted people watchers. Pam, who is fifty-one years old, has been dating Ted, age fifty-five, for four years. Ted, whose personality is characterized by strong vigilant, conscientious, and sensitive styles, is a bioengineering consultant. They met when he undertook a project at the company where Pam was working at the time. They worked together daily on the project for more than three months.

"I was attracted to him from the first day," confides Pam. "I didn't know much about him for a long time since he isn't very open about himself, and I was reluctant to ask. I didn't know if he was married or single, where he lived, how he liked to spend his time, but I had a lot of respect for the way he worked. I appreciated his sharp intellect and his fabulous concentration. And he was so polite to me and so handsome. I liked his Clint Eastwood reserve. I started having romantic fantasies about him."

Pam, whose chief personality styles are conscientious, dramatic, and devoted, is not shy. She does not hesitate to initiate relationships with others. She has learned not to mix business with pleasure, so she did not act on her attraction to Ted until the project ended. By that time, she had learned from a colleague that Ted had never been married although he had had a series of long, involvements over the years. Since Ted had not shown any personal interest in her while he had been consulting at her agency, she decided on an indirect approach to test the waters. She called him and told him she was thinking of going out on her own as a consultant. Would he have lunch with her and offer some advice?

Ted said he'd be glad to. "At our lunch," Pam said, "he was friendly and full of good advice, but he didn't let down his professional guard. I was beginning to think this was a lost cause when he made a comment about my relationship with my boss, Marty. He said he'd noticed that Marty and I were locked in a battle for control. I wasn't sure what he was referring to and he reminded me of a day two months earlier when I had a run-in with Marty over a minor matter. When I couldn't remember the incident, Ted reminded me that I had worn a red suit to work that day and that I had to leave early to go my son's engagement party."

"'I was dumbfounded.' Ted had noticed what I had worn, where I was going, what my boss and I had said to each other, and what was the underlying tenor of our relationship. Ted asked me whether I wanted to leave the agency because I felt politically squashed by my boss. That was it exactly, but I had only just figured it out myself. I certainly never discussed this or anything else about office politics with him when he was working with us. I was flabbergasted by how perceptive he was, and flattered by how much he'd noticed about me. It turns out he knew so much about me and how my mind worked that it was almost as if he's been tape recording my thoughts and staring at me the whole time he was working there."

However, although Pam and Ted met for several more lunches, emotionally he moved no closer to her. He asked a number of questions about her life, her two grown children, her late husband. They discussed her work and he shared his insights about her. He didn't ask her out for an evening and he was closed mouth about himself. He would talk about his work, or about his interest in sports, if Pam asked, but he never seemed comfortable sharing his feelings. Pam assumed that he was involved with someone else or that he simply wasn't interested in her. If she hadn't been invited to a business-related dance at which she felt obliged to show up with an escort, she would have given up on Ted for lack of any sign that he was interested in her.

The fourth time they met for lunch, Pam asked if Ted would join her at the fancy dress ball. She said, "I was prepared for him to look embarrassed and say no. So when he said he would be glad to go, I was so surprised, I blushed like a school girl."

That was the first of four years worth of dates. They had had a great time, they discovered that they both loved dancing and they kissed goodnight. But Ted didn't call afterward, which disappointed Pam tremendously. After a few days of no word from Ted, she called him. He sounded glad to hear from her. She told him that she had concert tickets and asked if he'd like to go. Sure, he accepted her invitation and they continued to see each other, usually at Pam's suggestion.

Vigilant style individuals like Ted often will not actively pursue a relationship and they are usually misunderstood as noncommittal because their reserve continues even when they have been involved with someone for a long time. But Pam was determined and she worked hard to forge a relationship with Ted. She had confidence that in time he would relax with her, although a few of her close friends advised her that he was just stringing her along. He wasn't ever going to marry her, they pointed out. After all, he'd never really committed himself to anyone and look how old he was.

Ted never wanted to talk about the relationship. He didn't want to share his feelings about her and he never offered to take Pam home to meet his parents. The first time she suggested that she accompany him to Nebraska for Christmas, his eyes opened wide with alarm. The next time two years later he said, maybe next year. The third time, Ted decided instead of going home to see his folks, that he would join Pam and her children for the holidays.

Currently, Ted and Pam are not exactly engaged, but they are together virtually every night. Pam believes that he is only now becoming able to trust her and let down emotionally a little more. She would like to get married, but she knows him well enough not to bring that up. And she has the good sense that an ultimatum, "marry me or else," would never work with Ted. Vigilant types will never succumb to a power play. She is hoping that they will just slide into marriage the way they have slid into everything else.

For all his reserve and his lifetime attachment to his bachelorhood, Ted is dedicated to Pam. He is quietly possessive of her and acknowledges to himself that he is deeply involved with her. He believes in loyalty and has no interest in seeking out other women. True to his vigilant style though, he operates best at an emotional distance where he is fully in possession of himself. But Pam has a lot going for her in his mind. She lets him be who he is and all the other women in his life, of which there had been many, had always given him the shape up or ship out speech. So, of course, he shipped out. Marriage makes him very nervous. He doesn't like the idea of being tied to anybody by a legal contract. Why can't he have his cake and eat it too?

Underlying Motives

Vigilant individuals are almost always aware of other people's motives. A lot of Ted's reticence to become involved with Pam, and the women who proceeded her in his affections, was due to his concerns that the woman of the moment was trying to corner him into a relationship. Or, that she was just using him. She really had no intention of remaining true to him.

More than other styles, the vigilant carries with it an alertness to what people want from you. Varying with the degree of vigilance in their personality pattern, people with this style will watch for signs of disrespect and abuses of power in almost every relationship. Because they are on guard against it, they are not easily hoodwinked by others. They are capable of understanding the many levels of communication, spoken and otherwise. They can hear a false note, know a forked tongue, sense ambivalence. This ability serves them well in their dealings with people. When the vigilant style finds themselves being thanked profusely for staying late at work, they usually hear a double message, "Thanks for staying late," plus, "I'm angry at you for always leaving at 5:00." So, they will often start staying late every once in a while to demonstrate their loyalty. Vigilant types are anything but naive. If they can respond appropriately to the information they glean, they often prosper. With increasing amounts of this style, however, they run the risk of misinterpreting the signs that they perceive. Too, not everyone harbors a hidden intention, and just because a woman wants to spend more time with a man doesn't mean, as Ted so often felt, that she is out to entrap him. And so what if she is? Vigilant individuals often invest others with a power that they do not have. No one can force Ted into a relationship he doesn't want. As the vigilant personality style grows extreme, suspicion plagues these individuals and begins to undermine their relationships. They begin to overreact to the human flaws of others and assume that others are looking at them as closely as they are observing other people, which is far from true.

Age Factor

Pam is not trying to force Ted into marriage. She knows not to play games with him. True, Ted chokes on the, "I love you's," but she knows he's a good, upstanding person. And Ted knows, since he's continually on the lookout, that Pam harbors no ulterior motives. She loves him, that's all. Ted would like to get married before he dies, but he's no spring chicken.

Both Pam and Ted have age on their minds. Personality style, even disorder, tends to mellow with age. In her younger years, Pam might have tried a dramatic style manipulation to move Ted toward the altar. Now she can accept herself, Ted, and life more on their own terms. As for Ted, he's inching closer to saying, "I do." Maybe next year.

Inalienable Rights

Society needs individuals who are on guard against abuses of authority and power, and who can detect ulterior motives. Even though their watchfulness and their sensitivity to flaws may hamper their personal relationships, vigilant types often serve an important role in the world. They can be champions of the underdogs, protectors of the downtrodden, fighters for freedom from oppression. Vigilant are many of those who champion causes such as the environment and civil rights. They may serve as watch dogs over government and blow the whistle on corruption. They are good debaters and their strong opinions, their certainty about the righteousness of their mission, and their intense concentration on their goals make some of them attractive, even charismatic leaders. Under attack, they become even stronger. They rise powerfully to their own defense and the defense of their cause. Their courage inspires those who follow them. Vigilant men and women want to believe in a better world, yet wherever they turn, they are confronted with the evidence of human flaws and wrongdoings. They take them hard. They are idealists. They expect more from the human race than it seems to deliver.

Extreme vigilance, however, may make some individuals vulnerable to imagined fears and suspicions about other individuals, races, religions, or political organizations. These people may end up as rabble rousers, stirring up hate and fear, and championing the very organizations and causes that seek to oppress people and deny them their right to survive.

The Family Protector

As parents, vigilant men and women are loyal and protective, perhaps over protective if the style is very strong. They may encourage the mistrust of others in their offspring. When the kids begin to rebel or assert their independence, a vigilant parent may feel threatened and attempt to over control the kids. Nonetheless, even though vigilant parents may be emotionally undemonstrative, underneath they are deeply caring. Responsible and thoroughly dedicated to the welfare of their families, they are determined to protect them from all outside harm.

Stress

Vigilant style men and women need to feel that they are firmly in control. This is why it takes so much time for them to become comfortable in relationships and commit themselves trustingly to other people. The loss of that control causes the most extreme stress for vigilant people. People with this personality style will find it hard to come to terms with disappointment in a relationship. When a relationship at work or at home begins to come apart or they feel they are losing control over their own destiny, vigilant types will take the loss or change as a personal betrayal. It is not their style automatically to conclude,

"Well, some things just don't work out," or "I guess we just weren't made for each other," or "We did the best we could. No one's to blame."

Self-defense is their principle coping style. Vigilant individuals tend to focus on the other person's errors. They don't like to hear about what they did wrong and can be very touchy about criticism. They can't take it. They don't lapse into tears or collapse into self-doubt, but they feel attacked and will react by defending themselves.

Vigilant individuals are not natural compromisers. Although they may react bitterly to the end of a relationship, their resilient autonomy serves them well. They prove that they are survivors. They can and do take care of themselves. Like conscientious people, they will often jump into hard work. They will, of course, be wary of new relationships, and will not enter new ones for the long time it takes for their wounds to heal.

Work—Who's In Charge Here?
Part II

As you will see under "Careers for the Vigilant," many types of work are open to vigilant style individuals. They are observant, careful, perceptive, sensitive to subtlety, tactical, alert, not easily fooled—qualities that serve them and their employers well in the work domain. They tend to be as serious and industrious about their work as they are about the rest of their lives, especially when they have conscientious or moderate serious personality traits as well. They work hard. They can be very ambitious and they can be very successful, depending on how well they handle their relationships with those who are in authority in their work domain. Vigilant individuals will be sensitive and alert to the power structure of any organization in which they operate. Coupled with their dislike of dependence and subordination, this sensitivity can make their place in the hierarchy unstable unless they have a self-confident streak to balance them. In which case, they will use their antenna to gather information, to maneuver quickly through the organizational maze.

Generally, the higher the degree of vigilance in one's personality pattern, the greater is the mistrust of authority and the greater the discomfort within the organization. Vigilant style individuals are inclined to feel that power will always be used against those who have less of it. This is sometimes true in the world, but not always. A strongly vigilant person will not be able to make this essential discrimination. Being perpetually on guard against possible abuses of authority at work or any other domain makes it harder for the vigilant person to make positive use of his or her power.

Phillip Versus The Corporation

A few years ago, vigilant-conscientious-dramatic style Phillip, a corporate trial lawyer, joined the legal staff of a major multinational corporation. He had been reluctant to leave his private legal practice, but the corporate officers wooed him for almost two years. They wanted him on their side because Phillip was often their all-too-worthy opponent. They kept upping the ante and finally made him an offer he couldn't refuse. He accepted after making sure that he would have substantial independence in his job.

Although he had no immediate supervisor, Phillip was beholden to the chief counsel and the other corporate officers, reasoning that the less he had to do with the "honchos," the better. Phillip steered clear of them. He attended only those meetings that were absolutely required, he avoided socializing with the higher ups, and he invited none of them to the elaborate party he planned when his personal staff celebrated a major court room victory.

While it suited Phillip's style to remain independent of the authority, he couldn't have made a worse political decision. The chief counsel, Phillip's mentor within the corporation, was deeply offended. Characteristic of many vigilant individuals in the work domain, Phillip had poor political instincts in the broad sense. While he could defend his own bailiwick against the greater power, he couldn't let down his guard. Instead of establishing himself within the power structure, because of his discomfort, he maintained a closed, defensive, mistrustful position. He made the organization the enemy and himself an outsider.

Then, a couple of months later, when the chief counsel questioned how he had decided to organize the defense in a major case against the corporation, Phillip became defensive. Instead of appreciating the input of this seasoned legal veteran, he took his questions as criticism, "You hired me to bring this substandard department up to par. If you don't like the way I do things, you should have hired some other guy." Phillip challenged rather than simply explaining his approach and convincing the chief counsel of its soundness. Phillip could win over a judge and jury, but when it came to people whom he thought were trying to interfere with his independence, he rushed to his defense rather than promoting his cause.

The corporation officers began to leave Phillip alone to do his work and to exclude him from political power. Phillip sensed this change in their attitude which only confirmed his feelings about them. After two and a half years, he abruptly left and returned to private practice where he feels free.

Recently, the corporation for which he had worked engaged him to represent them in a trial. Now Phillip and his erstwhile employers recognized that they have discovered the best relationship with one another.

Kid Gloves

Not all individuals with the vigilant style behave so truculently. On the surface, many are eager to please while inwardly, they feel apprehensive. Others are happy to create their own little niche where they do their jobs and escape the notice of the powerful people. They are willing to forgo the benefits of political ties. It takes enlightened management to deal well with vigilant style people. Like conscientious types, they often do their best work when they are given independent roles and are managed with a light hand.

Vigilant types rarely take advantage. Many people with this style will, however, be quick to spot and perhaps crusade against inequities in company policies and practices. They serve the watchdog role. It comes so very natural to many of them.

The Vigilant Leader

As leaders, vigilant style men and women need to be assured of the loyalty of their direct reports. To earn it, they will often be generous with favors, praise, and rewards. If they suspect disloyalty, they will be angry and unforgiving. An extremely vigilant leader may mistake ambition for disloyalty and make it difficult for the direct report to move on in the organization.

Generally, however, moderately vigilant style leaders take good care of their staff while perhaps promoting a view of upper management as something ominously powerful against which they will act as a protector. Indeed, if their direct reports run afoul of the organization or if policy seems to treat them unfairly, the vigilant leader will not hesitate to fight for their rights.

Since individuals with this personality style need to be or to feel in complete command, as leaders, they will not be comfortable delegating important, i.e., politically powerful responsibilities. Vigilant leaders make it their business to be fully informed about the working of their departments. If there is extra work to be done, they will often put in more than a leader's share of the time, not only to earn their staff's loyalty, but to keep an eye on what is going on. Like their conscientious brethren, many individuals with the vigilant personality style will choose a more independent track within an organization where they can perform their duties without having to worry about managing other people.

Careers for the Vigilant

Vigilant style individuals often work best in fields in which they can operate outside of direct, full-time authority. With their exceptional astuteness, their ability to focus their attention and their gift of argument, they can be excellent critics, diagnosticians, academicians, lawyers, investigative reporters, and researchers. Their perceptive savvy, including their ability to understand the multiple levels of communication, helps them in detective work as interviewers, in sales, and as long as the vigilant style is at a moderate level, as psychotherapists. And because many people with this style naturally identify or sympathize with the underdog or the oppressed, vigilant people can contribute to the effectiveness of social and political causes.

Strongly vigilant individuals may prefer working with machines rather than people. Like conscientious people, vigilant types are often very competent and comfortable with mechanical things. Their ability to concentrate serves them well in this area.

Real World—Standing Tall Amid the Dangers

Vigilant men and women have a definite sense of themselves. Most have an inner sense of rightness. They believe that they are the sane ones in an insane world. They have strong opinions. They don't often doubt themselves. But, as mentioned earlier, they have a hard time admitting their mistakes and accepting criticism. Their antennae are focused outward. It is easier for vigilant types to detect the faults of other people.

For the vigilant person, the real world is something of a mine field—it is populated with people who might take advantage. This alertness can be very useful in urban environments and unsafe neighborhoods. Vigilant individuals don't like surprises. In anticipating danger, they are prepared for any emergency. They react quickly like Penny, who suddenly turned and stepped away from a stranger before she fully realized that he was trying to grab her pocket book. Or like

David, vigilant to an extreme, who flashes his headlights the moment he sees a car coming toward him with its brights on. David does not realize that he has a faster reaction time than most people and that he doesn't give other drivers time to lower their beams. Instead, David repeatedly gets annoyed that so many people have the rudeness to shine their lights in his eyes. Whatever actual or exaggerated dangers vigilant style people perceive in the real world, they quickly show the world that they can stand up for themselves.

The Vigilant Idealist

Vigilant men and women want to believe in a better world. Yet, they are confronted wherever they turn with the evidence of our flaws and wrong doings. They take them hard. They are idealists. They expect more from the human race than it seems to deliver and their expectations sometimes, as in the following example, helps some of us humans to reach a little higher. Richard Harris was a writer for the New Yorker. Upon his death, the following eulogy appeared in that magazine and demonstrated the heights to which the vigilant, as well as the serious personality style can reach:

> Richard Harris was what one editor here used to call a hard case. His judgments often seemed harsh. He did not give the benefit of the doubt. He tended to find almost any situation worse than it had first appeared. When he came across a sunny scene, his eyes invariably fell on what was in the shadow—the unworthy motive, the cowardly evasion, the failure to measure up. He viewed the world with an unfiltered gaze. Applying that gaze as a reporter for this magazine, he was able to turn out penetrating and prodigious articles on the American legislative and judicial process. The work exhausted him, but it never mellowed him. When he died last month at the age of sixty-one, he was still a hard case. He cared a lot.
>   Like many deeply skeptical reporters, he was a closet idealist, accustomed to almost constant disappointment. He was, someone close to him once said, "a gloomy optimist." Unlike Diogenes, the

cynic, who walked around in broad daylight with a lantern "in search of an honest man," Harris actually hoped to find one. Occasionally, he did. In a couple of cases, the honest man turned out to be, of all things, a United States Senator. He set great store by old fashioned idealistic values. His idealism was reflected in some of the titles he used. Even though he would have pointed out somewhat testily that they were used ironically, "a sacred trust," and "honor bound," and most of all, "justice." An acquaintance could disappoint just as easily as a congressman could. He often found himself having to cross people off his list. He was a man of great charm. His comments were often witty, his manners bordered on the courtly, but he did not consider the spreading of good cheer to be among his responsibilities. He was often angry. The people who knew him well, people who hadn't been crossed off the list, people who had somehow found their way back on, even some people who believed they were probably off for good, thought of him as a splendid companion and a fiercely loyal friend. His friends were sometimes exhilarated by contemplating the possibility that they were actually living up to his expectations. "He made it difficult," the person closest to him at his death said last week, "But he was worth the trouble."

Emotions and Self-Control

Emotional reserve marks this style except when vigilant types feel threatened or challenged. Then they will show you through argument or outbursts of temper that they are not to be challenged.

Otherwise, vigilant individuals reign in their expressions of feelings and resist giving into impulse. This is a "head" not a "heart" style. Vigilant people do not like emotional risks. Without some dramatic, mercurial, or devoted styles in their pattern, vigilant individuals have a hard time abandoning themselves fully to their feelings. Tenderness may be difficult at least until the person is finally ready to trust and to commit. Vigilant individuals have a hard time with "I love you's" and prefer that their mates understand them and not require verbal reassurance. They are possessive and can be extremely jealous, although they probably don't talk about it.

Humor may be their only outlet. Some vigilant style men and women with their acute awareness of subtlety, ambiguity, and irony, have a well developed, though sometimes biting, sense of humor.

Tips On Dealing With the Vigilant Person In Your Life

1. The vigilant person in your life may appear very confident, independent, tough, and assertive. You may not realize how much this person needs your respect. Express, show, and otherwise prove it often.

2. If the vigilant person in your life is new on the scene and you would like to get to know him or her better, do not hesitate to pursue this person. Even though he or she may be painfully slow to reciprocate and to begin to trust you, persistence usually pays off. Go the whole distance. This advice is especially intended for women who may be hesitate to initiate a relationship and to be the one to keep it going.

3. Do not misinterpret the vigilant's reserve as indifference. Unless he or she has a streak of a more emotionally outgoing style, do not expect that you can break through this wall and force the vigilant person to show you his or her deeper feelings. Don't even try. Accept the emotional reserve and if the relationship is solid and stable, trust that this person cares deeply for you.

4. Avoid competition and power struggles. The vigilant person needs to feel in complete control of his or her destiny. Respect that. Otherwise, the vigilant person in your life will begin to distance himself or herself from you.

5. Expect defensiveness when you criticize or confront this person. It's a natural reaction for someone with this personality style to resist accepting blame. Let the reaction run its course and don't start defending yourself if he or she tries to shift the blame to you. The best way to confront a vigilant person is simply to express your feelings without criticizing or finding fault. Try saying that you care and are looking for

a way to better your relationship, not to blame anybody. It's easy to get into a boxing match with a vigilant style person, trading attack for attack, argument for argument until one of you crumbles. This is presumably not your style. You be the one to steer your attempts to resolve conflict toward a more constructive end.

6. Take the lead socially. The vigilant person in your life will appreciate your greater ease in getting to know people and making plans with them.

7. Don't tease. Vigilant persons often have a good sense of humor, but not about themselves.

8. If the vigilant person in your life is unjustifiably jealous or worried about your loyalty, don't be flippant or dismiss these concerns as silly. Don't underestimate the seriousness of such worries to a vigilant person. Reassure your mate or your friend of your devotion.

9. Accept that if you slight this person, unintentionally or otherwise, he or she will have a long memory. The vigilant person in your life is often unforgiving, so forgive yourself and be patient.

Making the Most of Your Vigilant Style

Your mind and your senses are always on monitoring the environment and other people. Being in such a state of ready alert can make you physically and emotionally tense. Therefore, the first order of business is the following:

Exercise 1. Relax. Include more activities in your life that you know will loosen you up. Concentrate especially on relatively mindless pursuits that temporarily shut down your "scanner," i.e., go for a run, take a swim, listen to music—don't just put it in the background, take up meditation, practice muscle relaxation exercises, get a massage, sit in a hot bath and let the tension slip out of your body and keep thoughts from tumbling through your head by concentrating on the heat of the water and how good you are beginning to feel. If anxiety starts to do battle with your on-coming relaxation, tell yourself it's just part of the process.

Exercise 2. Every time you find yourself wondering about some-one's ulterior motive, think about or make a list of two other motives that could explain the same action. For example, at a recent wedding reception, you handed the newly weds their gift. Almost two months have passed and still no thank-you note. You think, "They hate it and are so appalled at my bad taste that they can't figure out what to say to me." Now think of two other explanations. One, they are over-whelmed with other things. Two, they tend to procrastinate and have put off writing their thank-you notes. In other words, it has nothing to do with you, it has to do with them and how prompt they are in writ-ing such notes.

Exercise 3. If someone really is harboring a hidden motive, so what? Let's say a colleague from your office tells you he has a couple of tickets to a ball game and he asks you if you would like to join him. You've never been friendly with this person and you think, "He's asking me because he knows I'm in the boss's good graces. He wants me to put in a good word for him when he comes up for promotion." So what? He can't make you do anything you don't want to. Consider taking him up on it, motive or no motive. Enjoy the game.

Exercise 4. The next time someone criticizes you, catch yourself in the act of justifying your behavior. Stop and think whether the criti-cizer has a point. Realize that it's okay to be in the wrong or to make an error. Everybody does at one time or another. If you say, "I see your point," you get a thousand points. If you think the criticizer is a fool, you earn a thousand points by saying, "I'll think about what you have said," or something similar. This is no admission of guilt, but will usu-ally put an end to an unpleasant situation.

Exercise 5. After each fight with your friends, or mate or parent, in private make a list of what you did to contribute to it. Pat yourself on the back for being so honest. Keep the list in mind if you find yourself getting into the same argument again with the same person. The fact is, you cannot argue a person out of an emotion and that also means that no one can argue you out of an emotion. All you can do is listen and give each other a fair hearing. Another way of dealing with arguments is to remind yourself whenever you feel the inclination to blame others or assign fault that you should consider laughing at yourself, shrugging your shoulders, and confessing, "Sometimes things just go wrong and it's no one's fault."

Paranoid Personality Disorder

Paranoid people expect the worse of others. They're apprehensive, suspicious, uncompromising, and argumentative. They are convinced of their rightness beyond a shadow of a doubt. Individuals with paranoid personality disorder are on guard against a hostile universe where bad things happen or are always about to happen to them at the hands of other people. Note that paranoid personality disorder is different from paranoid or delusional disorder and paranoid schizophrenia. Paranoid personality disorder can be defined as follows: A pervasive distrust and suspicion of others such that their motives are interpreted as malevolent beginning by early adulthood and present in a variety of contexts as indicated by four or more of the following:

1. Suspects, without sufficient basis, that others are exploiting, harming, or deceiving him or her.

2. Is preoccupied with unjustified doubts about the loyalty or trustworthiness of friends or associates.

3. Is reluctant to confide in others because of unwarranted fear that the information will be used maliciously against him or her.

4. Reads hidden, demeaning, or threatening meanings into benign remarks or events.

5. Persistently bears grudges, i.e., is unforgiving of insults, injuries, or slights.

6. Perceives attacks on his or her character or reputation that are not apparent to others and is quick to react angrily or to counter attack.

7. Has recurrent suspicions without justification regarding fidelity of spouse or friends.

Enemies

The men and women who suffer from this personality disorder are consumed with mistrust. They are sure that other people mean them harm or humiliation or at least will let them down. They may be hostile, stubborn, uncooperative, hypersensitive to the tiniest slights, defensive, sarcastic, belligerent, cold, envious, rigid, secretive, argumentative. All these behaviors serve to keep them from getting too close to other people. Individuals with paranoid personality disorder must not let down their guard and give way to trust and intimacy less the other person take advantage of their weaknesses. It is obvious that their relationships are troubled, both at work and in their private lives. Although often superior in intelligence, alertness, forcefulness, and ambition, these types can be quite successful at work, but will have difficulty with bosses and co-workers. Their envy of people in authority betrays itself in their belligerence or sometimes in their attempts to ingratiate themselves. In either case, they are quite uncomfortable with people of higher rank or position. Individuals with paranoid personality disorder will be able to sustain relationships only with those whom they perceive as non-threatening.

While those who have severe personality disorders may never marry, others may find comfort with spouses who are compliant and dependent. Most people with this disorder do not betray their inner most thoughts to other people and they are careful about how they appear. As a result, the people in their lives may not suspect the extent of their suspicions and mistrust. They are perpetually searching the environment to find confirmation of their doubts about other people. And they always find what they are looking for—often because they provoke it themselves. If a paranoid person is sure that you will not remain loyal, he or she may voice so many suspicions that you throw up your hands and say, "I've got to go out with other people. I can't stand this anymore." "You see," declares the paranoid individual, "I knew I couldn't trust you." A paranoid person is never wrong. It's always the other person's fault or the fault of fate. When James lost a big sale, he came home and blamed his wife. If she hadn't been arguing with him so much, he wouldn't have been so tense during the negotiation, he told her. After she divorced him, he blamed fate for dealing him a bad hand. The bottom line: to live with a paranoid person is to live perpetually in the defendant's box—always being interrogated.

These men and women may magnify every slight and then sue you for it. Many paranoid individuals threaten law suits and often follow through.

Coping With Paranoid People

You have to love a paranoid person completely. Any criticism or annoyance you express will hurt this person intolerably and you find yourself on the long list of people who have wronged him or her. To cope with such a person, back off. Don't try to talk him or her out of any suspicions or you will soon be seen as a co-conspirator yourself. Avoid confrontations and try to stay clear of arguments. If this person is important to you, try to get him or her to seek help. Consider going for help as a couple or in support of this person. Whatever you do, don't be confrontational. It simply won't work.

7

The Sensitive Style

Sensitive people come into possession of their powers when their world is small and they know the people in it. For this commonly occurring personality style familiarity breeds comfort, contentment, and inspiration. These men and women, although they avoid a wide social network and shun celebrity, can achieve great recognition for their creativity. Nestled in an emotionally secure environment with a few family members or friends, the sensitive styles' imagination and spirit of exploration know no bounds. With their minds, feelings, and fantasies, sensitive people find freedom.

The Six Characteristics

The following six traits and behaviors are clues to the presence of the sensitive style. A person who reveals a strong, sensitive tendency will demonstrate more of these behaviors more intensely than someone with less of this style in his or her personality.

1. Familiarity. Individuals with a sensitive personality style prefer the known to the unknown. They are comfortable with, even inspired by, habit, repetition, and routine.

2. Concern. Sensitive individuals care deeply about what other people think of them.

3. Circumspection. They behave with deliberate discretion in their dealings with others. They do not make hasty judgments or jump in before they know what is appropriate.

4. Polite and reserved. Socially, they take care to maintain a courteous, self-restrained demeanor.

5. Role. They function best in scripted settings, vocationally and socially, when they know precisely what is expected of them, how they are supposed to relate to others, and what they are expected to say.

6. Privacy. Sensitive men and women are not quick to share their innermost thoughts and feelings with others, even those they know well.

The Six Domains of Sensitive Functioning

Two domains, emotions and relationships, in tandem shape the experience of the sensitive individual.

Emotions—Safe At Home

Each of the fourteen styles offer a way of ensuring emotional security. The devoted, for example, finds it through attachment to another person. The vigilant through independence and self-reliance. Individuals with the sensitive personality style gain emotional security by building a small world they can call their own. They are territorial and family centered, they form deep life-long personal attachments with their families and/or a few close friends. Their home is their castle which they make comfortable, personal, and attractive. They are always glad to be home. Inside the bounds of their own territory, they are emotionally free. They can be warm, giving, open, spontaneous, creative. But outside their security spheres, like fish out of water, sensitive types feel vulnerable. They move into new situations uneasily, becoming cautious and holding themselves in emotional reserve. Among strangers, they are rarely in top form. They may even feel vaguely threatened, out of their element, guarded, anxious, worried. But they mask their discomfort beneath a polite, if cool, facade. Few of the strangers they encounter at a large gathering would guess how uneasy they feel.

The Sensitive "Snow Queen"

Joel, an internist and medical school faculty member tells about his initial impressions of his wife, Emily, a surgeon. "We met at a hospital function. Emily was a new resident. My chairman was talking to her and when I came up, he introduced us. We shook hands, but in a moment, Emily politely excused herself and stepped away. I kept talking to my chairman, but I followed Emily out of the corner of my eye. She went to the bar and got a drink and then stood off to the side, looking rather cool and arrogant. Surgeons, you know, have a reputation for being "holier than thou" and I assumed she had stepped on her pedestal to escape us common folk. My chairman caught me watching Emily and he said, 'She's a nice person. You should get to know her.' I said, 'Somehow I don't think "nice" is the word for her,' and my chairman laughed.

I kept running into Emily around the hospital and she was always pleasant, but distant, but really attractive. I liked that dark, deep, mysterious look. And she had a very good reputation as a surgeon, although nobody seemed to know her very well.

When Christmas came around I went to visit my old college roommate, Eddie, and his new wife, Trish, at their country place. We were invited for Christmas Eve for a gathering at the weekend home of some family friends of Trish's. I had never met these people. We got to their house and who do you think was standing in the kitchen ladling eggnog—Emily! It turns out it was her family's home and she and Trish had known each other since they were children. I expected the usual cool hello, but when she looked over and saw me, her eyes lit up. She immediately came over and extended her hand. "Joel, how wonderful to see you here. So you're Eddie's old buddy. Small world."

I couldn't believe it. The Snow Queen greeting me like some long lost friend. We were together all evening. I swear she was the warmest, sweetest and yes, nicest woman I have ever met. We made plans to see each other back in the city. Later when I told Trish about Emily's behavior toward me all those months, she told me that Emily was actually quite shy. She said she was a homebody, not interested in a whole lot of people, but very close to her family and a few old friends."

By entering into Emily's familiar world, Joel could see the relaxed, easy, warm side of Emily. And once he became part of that world, Emily could relax and be comfortable with him no matter where they were.

They began to date in the city. Emily invited him to her apartment. Joel was impressed by how comfortable and homey she had it. His place was nondescript, just a place to spend the night, but hers was a nest, a home. The centerpiece, an ebony grand piano, where Emily told him she spent some of her happiest hours. Joel asked if she would play something for him. She said no. The piano was a private experience for her, not for entertaining other people. Joel, a highly dramatic person, was smitten. He was ready to run out and get married by their fourth date. Emily didn't exactly jump into his arms though.

Sensitive types take their time getting to know people and they're very slow to open up. Several times she had to tell Joel that she wasn't ready to be as serious as he wished. Joel tried not to pressure her and slowly she grew attached to him. They spent a lot of time with Eddie and Trish and with Emily's family. Eventually she grew comfortable enough to play the piano in his presence. More than two years went by before she agreed to become his wife. They had a small wedding, just the immediate families and a few close friends. Eddie and Trish were the best man and the matron of honor. Joel and Emily live a quiet life, keeping much to themselves. Emily's career keeps her very busy outside their home, but she returns home with pleasure and obvious relief. She tries to avoid socializing with colleagues, but she'll go if Joel will go with her. She prefers not to go to Joel's obligatory functions, but she will if it's important to him. He likes for her to accompany him, but occasionally they agree that she'll stay home if he feels she'll cramp his political style. Joel likes to travel and Emily always puts up a fuss about going, claiming she's too busy or she has to plant the garden in the country or some such excuse. But she always has a good time once she overcomes her reluctance. She'd never been to Europe and Joel finally convinced her to go with him to Paris a couple of years ago. She loved it there, although she didn't like going off to sightsee or to shop by herself. They went to Paris again this year where Joel had a conference. Having been there before, Emily was clearly more relaxed and willing to go out on her own. Joel suggested they go to Italy next year, but Emily says she would like to return to Paris a third time and really get to know the place.

Sensitive Explorer

Emily is not a reticent person. In the operating room, she quite competently welds her scalpel. The human body, inside and out, is familiar territory to her and like other sensitive people, she likes to know every detail about everything in her environment. Sensitive types are not dilatants. The more they know about something, the more they are inspired to know. Emily studies, experiments, learns in her work and in her music and in her gardening and in her cooking.

Sensitive types prefer to explore the known rather than the unknown. That's why Emily would be happy to return to Paris the third time. Some sensitive people travel easily within their own regions or within the country, but are reluctant to go abroad. Many moderately sensitive individuals enjoy travel as long as they can go with someone they're used to being with. Others will travel anywhere as long as they know someone who lives there.

The Counterphobic Sensitive Explorers

In other words, it is usual for the sensitive style to be content with the known or search for the familiar within the unfamiliar in order to move farther out into the world. But some sensitive types reveal an opposite tendency. They leap right into the unknown despite or rather because of their inner anxiety. These sensitive individuals demonstrate what is known as a "counterphobic" coping style. For example: Carson, a sensitive travel photographer had never liked going off to strange places by himself. He got into that type of photography when an editor friend, thinking he was doing Carson a favor, offered him an opportunity to cover an African safari. Only Carson's psychiatrist knew the anxiety the offer caused him. Carson was scared to death of going off to a country he'd never been to, a continent he'd never set foot on, and having to perform at his best. He was sure he would fail, fall apart, or reveal himself to be incompetent.

Even so, Carson didn't want to turn down the opportunity. He said he'd be terribly disappointed in himself if he let his fears control him. Several times before the departure he was tempted to cancel the whole thing, but he managed to go on the safari and to do the piece. The resulting work was so good that Carson received more travel assignments.

This result is not atypical for counterphobic, sensitive people. In their efforts to demystify the strange and unfamiliar and tame the terror, sensitive types become sharply aware of their environment and what they have to do within it. Carson's anxious attention to the details all around him translated into remarkable photographs. Carson has been traveling around the world for years now and he is not as nervous about it as he used to be. Yet, still he worries and grows fearful, especially before he sets out. He can't completely explain what he's alarmed about. "I think it's that my feeling of inner safety and security is upset each time I go even though nothing bad has ever happened and even though I'm always glad to have gone. I always feel this dread, this sense of foreboding. I have a very interesting life." Carson adds "And I guess this is the price I pay. It's ironic, that I'm a travel photographer, but I never really feel comfortable unless I'm home."

Be Prepared

Sensitive men and women are worriers. What if there's a hurricane while we're in the Caribbean? What if I lose my camera? What if the heat goes off while we're away and the pipes burst? What if the baby sitter loses our number and can't call to tell us that the baby is sick?

How do sensitive people deal with the "what ifs?" If their sensitivity is extreme, they stay home. If they're like most reasonably sensitive people, however, they invoke the Boy Scout motto, "Be Prepared."

In one way or another because they can't bear the possibility of surprise, sensitive people are prepared for any contingency. They generally gather information on everything they're about to undertake. They pack everything they could possibly need on a trip, they call home frequently, they carry an umbrella when there's a chance of rain, they carry numerous guidebooks, phone books, extra pairs of glasses. Sensitive people do not like to be surprised. Therefore, they do all they can to be prepared for whatever they might face.

Inner Journeys

Just because they become uneasy when they're tackling the unfamiliar doesn't mean sensitive types are not curious or adventurous in their own way. They are avid readers, for example: Surgeon Emily delights in every word and photograph in <u>National Geographic</u> to which she has subscribed for years. She's a great lover of literature and somehow manages to read at least a novel a month on top of everything else she has to do.

Although they may impose some limits on their physical world or cross boundaries with discomfort, sensitive types can often invest in an explorer's energy and fantasy, imagination, and creation, their minds and feelings free and easy in the unknowns of "inner space." Emily's piano jazz improvisations transport her, and anyone who happens to be fortunate enough to be nearby, to untold distances.

Relationships—a Few Familiar Faces

The sensitive personality style is other directed. These people need the approval of others in order to feel best about themselves and comfortable in the world. Individuals with this style genuinely like other people and want them in their lives, but only to a degree. In a warm, solid relationship with one person or with a small group of friends or family members, their self-confidence peaks. Put sensitive individuals in a large gathering and they will begin thinking of ways to excuse themselves and head for home.

The sensitive's self-confidence exists in an inverse ratio to the number of people, especially strangers, whom they must endure at one time. Unlike vigilant types who tend to doubt strangers until their intentions are known, sensitive individuals doubt themselves in the presence of people they don't know. They want to feel that they have made a good impression, but as the crowd increases, the number of people to impress becomes overwhelming. They begin to feel self-conscious, to worry that their discomfort will cause them to say something stupid or silly.

As the sensitive style approaches avoidant personality disorder, the anguish these individuals experience over other people's reaction to them becomes so great that they must refuse all social functions, no matter how much they would like to go. With more moderate amounts of the style, these people will be most comfortable socializing on the arm of someone else or, if they came alone, to hunt out someone they know or failing that, to count the minutes until they can go home. When they know the people around them and are sure of their affection and respect, sensitive types are relieved of their social anxieties and their personalities shine forth. Thus, they usually build their lives around a few people around whom they are happy. "You're always welcome here, you're family," they will say to their close friends, but they will be slow to establish new ties. Until they begin to trust a new person's feelings for them, they'll seal off their emotions and confidences around a polite, well-mannered, emotionally distant facade.

The Facade Problem

Because they are so reticent with new people, extremely sensitive people can have great difficulty establishing the truly intimate relationship with anyone. They may begin relationships only to see them dissipate and fade away. The problem comes from the sensitive tendency to hold themselves in reserve and their reticence to be themselves. All sensitive people are private with their innermost thoughts and feelings. To some extent, they all believe that to impress somebody new, they have to put on a facade. Very sensitive types are sure that if they reveal their so-called true selves, they won't measure up to what the other person wants. So they end up masking what, in fact, makes them interesting and attractive—their likes and dislikes, their quirks and idiosyncracies, their very individuality.

Sensitive Parents

They are good parents, attentive to their offspring and watchful of their safety. The moderately sensitive parent will anticipate and protect the kids from the dangers "out there." "Wear your boots because it's supposed to snow. Don't talk to strangers because you never know. If someone bothers you, here's what to do. Carry your name and address in your pocket in case you get lost," and so on. These parents will worry that something might happen when their kids go off to camp or to college or out on a date. Similarly, they usually give their children a strong sense of home and family. The kids know they always have a place to turn. The children feel secure and later will look back and appreciate that they were so well cared for and that they learned so well how to take care of themselves. The extremely sensitive or avoidant parent, however, must take care not to impose his or her anxieties on the children and make them fearful of taking chances.

Stress

Stress for this personality style comes from having to brave the unfamiliar. It also comes from criticism. Sensitive men and women care so greatly about how people react to them that disapproval and criticism hurt a lot, although sometimes you'd never know it from their reserved demeanor. They react either by staying clear of the criticizer if he or she is outside their central sphere or by trying to improve their behavior or performance in order to win back the favor of someone who is important to them. To deal with the stress of the unknown, sensitive types cope in one of three ways: (1) they find someone else to brave it with, (2) They back off from the challenge, or, (3) in some cases, they jump right in.

This last is a counterphobic coping style mentioned earlier. Like Carson, the travel photographer does what is feared the most in order to master the terror, or at least to avoid being mastered by it. The sensitive types, however, are quite happy to structure their lives around comfort and predictability, and feel little need to wrestle with their inner demons.

Since sensitive individuals count on having one close person in their lives to rely on, breakups are highly anxiety provoking. To cope, they'll seek familiar faces. They will be reluctant to get out and meet new people and they often attempt to return to former relationships. If they have no old loves to take up with, their social reserve may make it hard for them to meet new people and get a relationship going, which they will find very depressing.

Self, Self-Control, and Real World: Facing the Unknown

In the safety of their known worlds, sensitive individuals have a good sense of who they are and what they can do. Outside these boundaries, however, in the wide world of strangers (people with whom they are not yet comfortable) they temporarily lose perspective. Other people become huge, powerful, and potentially threatening, whereas they themselves shrink and weaken or go into hiding. In this "Alice in Wonderland" transformation, sensitive men and women lose their certainty about themselves though, they have good self-discipline and self-control. They use it to shape their behavior and keep their feelings and discomforts to themselves. The last thing they want to do is make waves and call attention to themselves. Their only risk of self-control problems is if they begin to medicate their social unease with alcohol, recreational drugs, or tranquilizers and come to depend upon these substances for "chemical courage." However, if appropriately pre-scribed, and with supervised use, tranquilizers can be a very useful part of treatment for people with debilitating anxiety.

To the sensitive person, the real world is full of threats. Beyond the limits of their territory, there are beasts in the forest so they stick close to the hearth, or return relieved after venturing away.

Work: Home Away From Home

Individuals with the sensitive style bring many good qualities to the workplace if they can build a comfortable work "nest" and find a struc-tured role from which to operate. Then they are reliable, steady, and effective. Highly sensitive people work best with a few co-workers with whom, in time, they become familiar. The workplace, office, or depart-ment becomes their little family—their safe haven to which they return day after day. They like to stay put in their jobs, having little need to seek variety for its own sake.

Sensitive types tend to be thorough and they concentrate well on their work. Because they care what other people think of them, they try hard to do good work. They are uneasy dealing with management unless their workplace is small and has a family type environment. In general, they don't like to deal with unfamiliar people. Some very sen-sitive people are reluctant to telephone strangers even in the course of their routine work, such as calling a repairman.

Structure and Role

Contributing to their effectiveness at work is their comfort with routine. Every type of work, in or out of the home, has its daily repeti-tions. For some personality styles, the dramatic included, routine is tantamount to drudgery. It saps their strength and motivation. For the sensitive individual, however, routine provides a welcome structure to the day. For similar reasons, sensitive types like to find roles in which they know what is expected of them and don't have to readjust each day. Indeed, their vocational roles often provide a welcome identity that they can use in their interactions with others in unfamiliar settings.

As a division reporter, Rita knew how to conduct probing interviews with people for her work. Yet in a social situation, she would become tongue-tied when trying to talk to a new person. She figured out that if she thought of herself as a reporter even in her private life, she could approach people and ask questions. Celebrities with a strong streak of sensitive style inching up behind a more "out there" style, [and there are a surprising number of famous people who are certain that, as themselves, no one would find them appealing,] frequently cope with people in just such a way by carrying their professional personas wherever they go. In fact, sensitive people role play automatically.

The Sensitive Leader

Men and women of this style often are more ambitious on behalf of their work than on their own political behalf. They will do the best work they can and are happy to please higher ups. They may wish to be promoted into a leadership position in order to do more challenging work, but they are not eager to increase their exposure to upper management. Sensitive leaders do not like to deal with people outside their immediate unit and may appoint a direct report to act as their liaison. Although if they also have a counterbalancing, socially capable style, such as the dramatic, they'll be able to work the hierarchy and attend necessary work related social situations despite their inner queasiness about exposing their "real" selves. A sensitive person can benefit from a long-term relationship with a mentor upon whose sensitive opinion and guidance he or she can comfortably rely.

Sensitive leaders promote a family environment among their own staffs. They will appear aloof and cold to newcomers until they are sure of them and their performance. They work best with staffs in which there is little turnover.

Careers For the Sensitive

If this is your predominate style, seek a career in which you have a defined role—an accountant, computer analyst, or a doctor for example in which your exposure to the public is limited or your interactions are structured. Sensitive individuals may do well with clients because they can take refuge in professionalism which allows them to be involved with their clients' interest, yet not be emotionally involved. But sensitive types are uneasy with strangers whom they must consult or influence. So steer clear of such fields as contracting, public relations, or sales, for example. Also avoid jobs or careers that will require public speaking. They will create an enormous amount of anxiety which you may or may not be able to overcome. Due to the sensitive style's ease with routine, repetition, and habit, as well as their ability to concentrate, they do very well in the technological fields.

Tips on Dealing With the Sensitive Person in Your Life

1. Count your blessings. Treasure the closeness and loyalty that your sensitive person offers you. Recognize that you are among a favored few in this person's life. Appreciate the home life this person makes possible and his or her dedication to friendship and family values.

2. Accept the sensitive person complete with shortcomings. If your sensitive mate becomes stiff or withdrawn among strangers, or is otherwise not him or herself in company, so what? It's no reflection on you.

3. Avoid emotional torture. Don't insist that a sensitive person do things he or she shuns just to please you. Sensitive individuals want you to be happy with them, but there are some things they just can't stand doing. The reluctance has nothing to do with you, so don't hold it against your sensitive friend or partner. If you like to socialize or to ski, for example, and the sensitive person in your life prefers to stay home, consider going by yourself occasionally. Sensitive people often

are happy to spend time alone as long as there is someone in their lives whom they will soon be with again.

4. Compromise. If you want to fly away on a vacation, and your not so adventurous companion wants to stay closer to home, consider a third alternative. Perhaps going to a nearby retreat where he or she can understand what is going on would be the better choice. Sensitive people want to please the important people in their lives so your willingness to compromise may encourage them to take a few steps farther than they would ordinarily go.

5. Help. Act as a guide to the unfamiliar. Go to social events with this person and accompany him or her on jaunts into unfamiliar territory. But don't overdo it. You want to help this person overcome certain limitations, not to make him or her dependent on you. Reassure, encourage, and praise every step forward. Remember that if you can help this person over a few barriers, you'll both have a good time and your sensitive partner, family member, or friend will remember the experience with pleasure.

6. Recognize the signs. You're both due to leave for a dinner with your new boss and his wife. Your sensitive companion suddenly feels ill, gets cranky, or is late getting ready. Avoid a fight. Say, "I'll bet you're nervous about tonight." Reassure the sensitive person that everyone is going to like him or her.

7. Talk about it. If the sensitive person's anxieties are cramping your style, don't keep it to yourself. Don't attack your loved one for having these difficulties. Rather, express the problems openly and directly. Say you're interested in finding a solution that accommodates both of you.

Making the Most of Your Sensitive Style

Your love for the familiar allows you to build a comfortable, personable environment that could get you into a rut. So practice a little preventive medicine.

Exercise 1: Do something different. Every once in a while, change one or more of your routines just for the sake of change. Try a new restaurant, take a different route to work, rearrange the furniture in your living room, take a different kind of vacation, anything.

Exercise 2: Do it anyway. The less you expose yourself to uncomfortable situations, the harder it will be to overcome the anxiety in the future. Conversely, the more you expose yourself, the easier it is to dissolve the discomfort. So do what it is you would prefer to avoid. Every time you find yourself tempted to avoid a challenge or to refuse an opportunity because of your anxiety, do the opposite. If somebody invites you to a party and you are inclined to say no, say yes, and then go! If you want to leave the party, stay. Take small steps, don't expect to conquer everything in one week. Give yourself credit for even the tiniest progress.

Exercise 3: Be who you are. Your imperfections give you character and make you interesting and appealing. It's your efforts to hide your human imperfections that make you stiff, uncomfortable, and possibly unapproachable. If you accept your flaws, others may find it easier to accept you with them.

Exercise 4: Stay inside yourself. Many sensitive people look at themselves as if through other people's eyes. When playing the piano, you think the neighbors think you are playing terribly. When you give a speech, you think the audience thinks you are stupid and uninteresting. When you're at a social gathering, you think that the stranger you're talking to thinks you're boring. You try to change your behavior or performance in order to please someone that you think is criticizing you. You are guaranteed to lose your concentration on the task at hand each time you start focusing on other people's thoughts about you. You end up hitting the wrong note, losing your place in your speech, finding yourself at a loss for words. Every time you find yourself thinking about what another person is thinking, immediately stop those thoughts and continue with what you are doing. Like most of these exercises, this one gets easier with practice.

Exercise 5: In talking to somebody, periodically look him or her in the eye. Reluctance or inability to establish eye contact can indicate that you feel in some way threatened by that person. But if you can establish moments of eye contact despite your discomfort, you'll find it easier to gain acceptance and confidence. If you can't do it, at least hold your head higher so that it is not comfortable to look down at the floor. This posture also signals confidence to others and perhaps you'll even begin to feel a little more confident after a while.

Avoidant Personality Disorder

The unhappy individuals with avoidant personality disorder are always on the outside looking in. They yearn to be involved with other people, but they can't endure the feeling when they get around others that they are unacceptable and unlovable. They feel incapable of changing, so they withdraw in order to survive.

Avoidant personality disorder can best be defined as a pervasive pattern of social inhibition, feelings of inadequacy, and hypersensitivity to negative evaluation beginning by early adulthood, and present in a variety of contexts as indicated by four or more of the following:

1. Avoids occupational activities that involve significant interpersonal contact because of fears of criticism, disapproval, or rejection.

2. Is unwilling to get involved with people unless certain of being liked.

3. Shows restraint within intimate relationships because of the fear of being shamed or ridiculed.

4. Is preoccupied with being criticized or rejected in social situations.

5. Is inhibited in new interpersonal situations because of feelings of inadequacy.

6. Views self as socially inept, personally unappealing, or inferior to others.

7. Is unusually reluctant to take personal risk or to engage in any new activities because they may prove embarrassing.

Damned If You Do—Damned If You Don't

Avoidant men and women are trapped in a distressing universe. They are so afraid of being rejected by other people, and so convinced they will be that they retreat from others to spare themselves the agony they anticipate. When they can't avoid others, they stand aloof, looking down or away rather than making contact. As a result, they live socially impoverished lives. The painful irony for people with this personality disorder is that although the avoidance of close relationships relieve them of the anxiety of waiting for the rejecting ax to fall, it removes them from what they deeply desire—the acceptance, approval, and love of other people. Unlike people with schizoid personality disorder who don't want anything to do with others, avoidant individuals are lonely loners. They are aching to be a part of things if only they knew how.

No wonder they withdraw. Their experiences with other people are like recurring nightmares. On one hand, they are sure that others are going to treat them badly. On the other hand, their awkward self-consciousness is indeed off-putting. What avoidant people fear seems always to happen. People don't accept them. In truth, others don't know what to make of avoidant people. Because of their detachment, others often conclude that avoidant people are cold and don't want to be included.

So, avoidant individuals feel isolated, unwanted, painfully different, and incompetent no matter what they do. Emotionally they rarely feel comfortable. If they're not anxious, they're depressed. Often they are both. But at least when they are away from others, they don't have to experience that terrible anticipation of humiliation and rejection.

Coping With Avoidant People

Because avoidant people withdraw from others unless you are part of their family, few people will find themselves deeply involved with an avoidant person. The way to cope is to recognize the reality of avoidant anxiety and sensitivity to criticism and how it impairs these people. To deal with a mildly avoidant person, one must be genuinely sensitive and understanding. Likewise, be very kind and reassuring and completely accepting. But don't start doing for them what they are afraid to do for themselves. And look around, see how many people you encounter in your life at work, for example, who fit the avoidant description—aloof, ill at ease, awkward, tense. Instead of dismissing these people as cold or unfriendly, take a second look. Maybe they really would like you to befriend them. Try reaching out. It just might work out.

8

The Leisurely Style

F ree to be me. No one can take away this right from a person who has a leisurely personality style. These men and women play by the rules and fulfill their responsibilities. But once they have put in their time, they will let no person, institution, or culture deprive them of their personal pursuit of happiness. To the leisurely personality style, the pursuit of happiness is what life is all about.

Some leisurely individuals find their happiness through creative pursuits, some by relaxing with a good book. What's important to them is not how they choose to enjoy themselves, but that they are guaranteed the opportunity. If threatened, these normally easy-going individuals will vigorously defend their fundamental right to do their "own thing."

The Seven Characteristics

The following seven traits and behaviors are clues to the presence of the leisurely style. A person who reveals a strong leisurely tendency will demonstrate more of these behaviors more intensely than someone with less of this style in his or her personality.

1. Inalienable rights. Leisurely men and women believe in their right to enjoy themselves on their own terms in their own time. They value and protect their comfort, their free time, and their individual pursuit of happiness.

2. Enough is enough. They agree to play by the rules, they deliver what is expected of them, and no more. They expect others to recognize and respect their limits.

3. The right to resist. Leisurely individuals cannot be exploited. They can comfortably resist acceding to demands that they deem unreasonable or above and beyond the call of duty.

4. Time is not a problem. Leisurely men and women are relaxed about time. Unlike Type A individuals, they are not obsessed by time urgency or the demands of the clock. To these individuals, haste makes waste and unnecessary anxiety. They are easy going and optimistic that whatever needs to get done will get done, eventually.

5. I'm okay. They are not over awed by authority. They accept themselves and their approach to life.

6. Wheel of fortune. Leisurely people believe that they are just as good as everyone else and as entitled to the best things in life. They maintain that blind luck often accounts for who fairs well and who fairs poorly.

7. Mixed feelings. Although they feel compelled to proceed in their own direction, when their choices put them in conflict with the people they care for, leisurely people are often of two minds about how to proceed. They do not like to risk important relationships, yet they need to feel free.

The Six Domains of Leisurely Functioning

Leisurely is another "double domain" style. For individuals of this common style, their domains of self and of relationships together are key to their personal destinies.

Self—the Right to Be Me

The inviable independence of the self is the first priority for leisurely individuals. They have the God-given right to be who they are, to feel good, to pursue their own pleasures and comforts in their own way. No person or institution can take these rights away from them as far as they are concerned. If the conscientious style is associated with the high-powered East Coast, and the inevitable question, "What do you do?," then the leisurely style is a more relaxed, West Coast personality stereotype associated with the question, "What are you in to?"

But no matter where they are found, leisurely men and women believe in themselves and in their inalienable right to use their personal time however they choose. They can operate well within systems—the family, the workplace, the community. Indeed, they need these complexes of other people in other to fulfill their basic human needs, but they do not identify with any outer authority.

Unlike the conscientious person who has a strong super ego and works extra hard to be an upstanding member of the workforce, the family, and the community, the leisurely person carries no such weighty self-critical burdens. After meeting his or her obligations, including those to the family, the leisurely person turns to what is most important—the pursuit of his or her private pleasure in life, be it sports, art, contemplating nature, or drinking a beer while watching TV.

Unlike self-confident types who feel that they are inherently special, better than others, closer to the center of the universe than most people, leisurely people perceive that along with everybody else, they are small cogs in the cosmic wheel. That's okay with them. Leisurely folks are comfortable with themselves. But even small cogs are entitled to lucky breaks which is how leisurely people perceive the differences between the haves and have nots. They dream of winning the lottery and they send in their ten million dollar sweepstake entries. Why not? It could happen. Most of all, they feel entitled to be happy and leisurely individuals claim this right vigorously. Leisurely individuals will not enslave themselves to anyone or anything or substitute anyone else's values for their own. They have a role to play, a job to do, certain services to perform, but they are independent and subject to their own dictates. Leisurely individuals do their part, but beyond that, they are free to feel good privately.

Relationships—You Don't Own Me

People who have a predominance of this personality style are deeply entwined with other people. They are family oriented and comfortable in groups. They like or even need to be taken care of and they enter into relationships easily. At the same time, like vigilant types, they are vaguely suspicious of others, especially of people in authority. Leisurely types expect others to ask too much of them. But while vigilant people stand emotionally clear of people until they are certain their autonomy is assured, leisurely men and women have a greater immediate need of companionship as well as a fool-proof defense against being ill used; if anyone asks them to sacrifice their self-determination, they simply refuse.

Leisurely individuals are very skilled at saying no. They will use the word as often as they must to ensure that they hold on to their own identities and the right to lead their lives their own way. Some men with this style might come off as "macho" or male chauvinistic, like Archie Bunker on the old "All in the Family" TV series. Archie went to work, provided for his family, and saw himself as a responsible, upstanding citizen, but he led his life the way he wanted when his workday was finished. After dinner, he did his own thing—sat in his chair to watch his TV, then out to a bar with his buddies. Edith, a strong, self-sacrificing type, rarely interfered with anything that gave her husband pleasure, and life functioned smoothly for them as long as she played by these rules. Archie was created as a caricature of a disagreeable, if comic, old-fashioned leisurely guy. Leisurely types, both male and female, in real life need not be intimidating, rigid, or unpleasant. But within their relationships, they will always be protective of their individual freedoms. And unlike Archie Bunker, they are likely to experience emotional pain when their desires and those of their loved ones conflict. Usually, they'll go their own way in the end, but not without a lot of soul searching and even guilt.

Phyllis Wants to Change the Rules

Anthony is a rather well-known artist. He is glad to be selling his paintings finally, but he understands that recognition for an artist is often short lived. He has never catered to the whims of any authority, the art market included, and he never will. He is forth-seven and his art is his joy and meaning in life. He'll get by—whether he sells or he doesn't sell. All he needs is the time to paint.

Susannah, his wife, has her own catering business which has seen them through the rough times. Her business pays for their son's private school. Anthony wouldn't mind if the child went to public school, but Susannah wants smaller classes and a more personal environment for her son so she pays for it.

Susannah is Anthony's second wife. They've been married for twelve years. They met shortly after Anthony's first wife, Phyllis, had left him. Phyllis had gotten fed up with Anthony. As she saw it, she was the one who had to go out and work, who had to cook and clean up when "all Anthony ever did was hang out in his studio and paint that stuff." Phyllis believed that if Anthony would only paint the kinds of pictures people were buying at the time, he could earn a good living and treat her better. Anthony agreed that if he prostituted himself to the market, they would be much better off financially. If others were making it now, it was just a matter of luck, not talent he told her contemptuously. But he was an artist dedicated not to money, but to creation. In that, he would never change, he told his young disillusioned wife, and he pointed out that he had never promised her any other life. Since the day they met back when she was nineteen and he was twenty-eight, had he ever said he would do anything besides paint his own way? "Well, no," Phyllis had conceded, "but I thought you'd be discovered and get famous and it would all be okay."

How romantic it had been for Phyllis, just out of high school, to meet this tall, big boned, long haired, intellectual artist and to live a kind of Bohemian life style. She loved taking care of him, cooking inexpensive stews, ironing his shirts, sleeping next to him on a mattress on the floor of his loft. Five days a week she went to work as a secretary at a plumbing supply company. Seven nights a week, she dined by candlelight with her young genius. They lived together before they were married, which her parents had tolerated, but when Phyllis told them she and Anthony had decided to get married, they objected. "What will you live on?," they wanted to know. "What kind of future can this man offer you?" Phyllis was twenty. These questions meant little to her. Her needs at that age were few—to be with and take care of the most exciting man she had ever known. "I know Anthony will be a great artist," she told her parents proudly. "And anyway, he can always go out and get a job." Four years later, Phyllis was tired of all the hard, dreary work so Anthony could have his art. Big deal. Nobody was buying. "A job?" He looked at her as if she was crazy. "Why should I get a job?" "Because I'm sick of doing everything," Phyllis cried. "What kind of a life do you think this is for me? I don't even have any decent clothes. We can't afford to go to a movie or eat out." That's when Anthony pointed out that nothing at all had changed—it's not as if things had taken a turn for the worse, that he had started withholding anything from her, or that he had stopped caring for her. He loved her and their life together as much as he ever had. He regretted that what they had had was collapsing

Over the next few weeks Anthony wavered between guilt and contrition [Maybe he did owe it to her to make a better living, maybe her unhappiness was his fault. No! I won't get a job. I can't give up my art!] Finally after one last confrontation, Anthony told Phyllis that if she wanted to be with him, this was the deal. He wanted her to stay, he said, but he'd never be anybody except who he was.

Phyllis decided she wanted something different out of life. Anthony was very unhappy with her, but despite his renewed agony, he didn't try to get her back. What was the point? She would never be happy sharing his life and he wouldn't be happy living any other way.

Susannah, on the other hand, wanted nothing more than to share Anthony's life. She was much older than Phyllis, the same age as

Anthony, in fact. She had built a satisfying career for herself, but had not found a man she loved enough to marry until she met Anthony. She was mature enough to recognize that Anthony was always going to be himself. He was not going to change. She admired his dedication to his art and his belief in himself no matter how well or how badly things were going for him success wise. Unlike Phyllis, Susannah loved Anthony's work. She understood it, was moved by it, and felt that what he painted and his ideas about art strengthened the bonds between them. Anthony and Susannah often engaged in passionate discussions about art that took them through the wee hours of the morning. It was, as far as she was concerned, a great relationship. It mattered little to Susannah that Anthony had not achieved success and perhaps never would. She could take care of the two of them if need be. And she knew that he loved her. One look at the tender, loving portraits of Susannah he began painting was enough to tell the world how he felt about her. Once his art was understood and accepted, Anthony could be a generous, appreciative, grateful, kind, fun-loving man. He was very physical and loved to hold Susannah tightly in his arms.

Susannah determined that no matter what, she would never try to change Anthony or to mold him to a different standard. But it wasn't always easy to avoid frustration. Anthony, typical of the leisurely style, could "dig in with his heels." Because he was finishing an important painting, he wouldn't come home from the studio to let the exterminator in when they had a terrible invasion of cockroaches and Susannah had to cater a large luncheon. He left most child care responsibilities to her, especially when their son was an infant, and he would never cook or clean up. He procrastinated so much over the income taxes that Susannah finally took charge of them. He'd always feel contrite, but not enough to change his ways. "All right, so I make more compromises than he does." Susannah says, "Perhaps I do more work to keep the relationship going and the family functioning. So what? I can handle these things. My husband gives me so much love and such great art. He's so grateful that I allow him the time to devote to his work; I feel so lucky in my life. I don't believe you can measure a marriage in terms of who does how much. "I do what I can do; Anthony does what he can do." We are both happy and productive. What more could I want?"

Leisurely Parents

They are responsible bread winners who are concerned about their children's basic needs. Their family life is a significant source of pleasure and is important to them. Leisurely parents have a gift for enjoying themselves and can share in their children's lives more memorably when they are all having simple family fun.

Leisurely parents tend to believe that what is best for them is best for the children, so they do not generally go out of their way to adapt to their children's needs or wants if these are different from their own. But they are not inflexible and will bend if someone can get through to them that they must.

As the leisurely style becomes passive aggressive personality disorder, though, dad or mom will be less likely to comprehend that the child could possibly have different needs. The parent will be remembered as a stubborn and selfish person, more interested in his or her own comfort than in the children's's welfare. With luck, this child will have one non-leisurely parent who will be more attentive.

Work—It's Just a Job

Predominately leisurely types often run into the same clash of values at work as in their personal relationships. They tend not to be get-ahead types since they work not for the sake of fame or success, but for security, for a pension, to finance their pursuit of pleasure, or just to have fun. Leisurely individuals are cooperative, good workers, but they don't take work home. They don't worry about it after hours. They don't do work that they do not believe is their responsibility and they don't do more than what is asked of them to please the boss or to feel better about themselves. They feel just fine about themselves. However, they don't necessarily see that their lack of apparent ambition and unwillingness to prove their dedication to their work might be the reason they receive less approval, encouragement, or rewards than their colleagues or co-workers who do go that extra distance. And, they may resent another person's success as unjustified. Still, they fulfill the requirements and can take pride in what they do. They generally don't find their meaning in life in the workplace and they will not allow themselves to be exploited by someone who does.

When a mixed personality pattern consisting of conscientious and/ or self-confident, trends along with the leisurely, however, many people do manage to find pleasure somewhere in the workplace. Some, like Anthony, will be able to merge business and pleasure. This is easiest to accomplish in creative work which can be highly and immediately pleasurable. Others will find pleasure in some aspects of their work [while putting off the rest of it]. For example: Alexander, the accountant suffering a mid-life crisis, loves the client relations part of his work. He spends hours talking to his clients when he should be preparing their tax returns. As a result, he has to sprint toward the tax filing deadline in a last minute frenzy. Still other leisurely types with mixed patterns will be fortunate enough to discover rewarding activities that are incidental to what they were hired to do. Alexander finds happiness on the company's baseball team. His colleagues and supervisors think he is an adequate accountant, but a truly inspired pitcher. Alexander lives for the baseball season.

"It's Not My Job"

This is the oft heard refrain of a leisurely employee when a boss demands work that is above and beyond the call of the leisurely person's job description. This attitude often annoys employers or supervisors because people in authority usually expect their employees to share their dedication and values even though they receive a smaller share of the rewards. But the leisurely person may well point out that he or she is not paid to empty waste baskets, photocopy bills, work past 5:00 and so on.

Betty, a leisurely child care worker was hired primarily to watch the Smith's three children after school until Mrs. Smith returned home from her job. The children and the friends who often came to play with them generally made a mess of the house. Betty didn't clean up after them. Every evening, Mrs. Smith came home to dirty dishes in the sink and a house in disarray. Finally, she spoke to Betty about it. Betty said she was paid to watch the kids, "You don't pay me to clean up after them." From Mrs. Smith's point of view, anyone who had Betty's job would want to pick up after them. But Betty was not about to be exploited as she saw it. She was dedicated to the kids though and they liked her, so Mrs. Smith offered to pay Betty more to clean up as well. But to her surprise, Betty refused. She didn't want to be a house-keeper, she said. She just wanted to look after kids. Mrs. Smith acknowledged intellectually that Betty had the right to draw the line, but when she walked into the messy house every afternoon, she couldn't help feeling that Betty had a "bad attitude." Mrs. Smith finally decided that she valued her children's happiness and Betty's skills as a care giver, so she kept Betty until the kids no longer needed child care.

Leisurely people are not Type A's. They work slowly and comfort-ably. They don't rush to beat the clock or meet what they believe is an unreasonable deadline. They are not driven to please the boss or to cre-ate perfection. They can do very good work and they can often stand a lot of tedium. But their job is rarely going to be the central focus of their lives. For leisurely individuals including some civil servants, union members, and career military people, work means putting in twenty or thirty years so that they can get a pension. Then they can do what they really want to do.

Workers' Rights

Leisurely types are at least mildly suspicious of authority in the workplace. They expect that the boss will want more than they are willing to give, which is often true. Especially when the job has no precise prescription or when the boss is conscientious, self-confident, aggressive, or serious. Leisurely individuals attempt to fulfill their obligations and they feel ill used if their supervisors or colleagues do not accept this as sufficient. If the boss asks them to do more or to work faster, they are likely to feel that they are being treated unfairly. Should the boss insist that they do more than their fair share, a leisurely person will threaten to file a grievance. Leisurely individuals are always aware of their rights. Fair is fair, anything else is exploitation. They take advantage of all their rights such as taking all the days off they are allowed and because of this, they may be unreasonably judged by their bosses as lazy or unmotivated. They are not necessarily tempted to work overtime by the promise of extra pay, but they may be interested if they are promised compensatory time off. Quitting time brings smiles to their faces.

Self-employed leisurely men and women have much the same attitude toward authority. They don't let their clients make excessive demands on them. Arthur is a free-lance graphic designer with a good streak of leisurely style in his personality pattern. He never takes rush jobs [fortunately he doesn't have to because his wife brings in a good income] and regardless of what he has to get done that day, he will not work from 2:00 to 3:00 so that he can eat his lunch and watch the afternoon talk show that he has been watching for years.

Leisurely Housework

Leisurely homemakers need to have time to themselves too. Their house will be neat enough, the meals good, if not elaborate [unless they get their kicks out of gourmet cooking] but nothing will be perfectly well kept or prepared. Taking care of the house and the family is one of the most demanding jobs, and leisurely individuals know where to set their limits. But they will run into trouble with spouses who don't think of housework as "real" work and will see their need to entertain themselves as self-indulgement. In addition, leisurely types who work outside the home may not recognize that their at-home mates have had much to do all day. When they come home from a long, hard day at work at their "real jobs," they may not be inclined to pitch in. They treasure their non-work hours too much to sacrifice them easily to chores, especially if they feel that someone else in the family can and should take care of those responsibilities.

Success Isn't Everything

Leisurely style individuals can be found in virtually all jobs and careers, but rarely at the top of any, which is fine with them. Since their overall comfort in life comes from how they enjoy themselves away from work, they'll rarely devote the time or push that hard for advancement. A pitfall of the leisurely style may be that some very leisurely people drift off course or lose direction in their lives. But this needn't happen. Leisurely individuals can do well and make good lives for themselves regardless of others who may try to impose higher aspirations on the leisurely type.

Cindy is a good example. She is a very bright, biochemist who left a job at a prestigious university in a major city to take a position at a relatively unknown college in a small town with less adequate research facilities. Her choice struck her ambitious colleagues as peculiar. But with the move, Cindy became a full professor, received immediate tenure, a lot more money and could afford to buy a house with several acres. She would no longer have to struggle, compete, and prove herself. Most important, she would have the space and the time to breed and raise Alaskan Huskies. Her work is interesting and provides good security. So what if she hasn't "made the most of her career," as her father, the president of a major corporation sees it. She has no desire to win a Nobel prize, to be recognized, or to even publish anything. She likes to teach and to raise dogs. Cindy is happy!

The Leisurely Leader

You won't find many predominate leisurely types above middle management because they're not ambitious in their careers. They don't want to devote themselves to getting ahead, don't care too much about working hard enough to make a lot of money, and are extremely reluctant to make the necessary sacrifices of personal time that the fast track demands.

Since leisurely individuals often work with the same company, government agency, or military branch their entire careers, they may rise to middle management levels. As leaders, they expect of their direct reports what they expect of themselves—a day's work for a day's pay. They don't push anybody too hard, but they do expect their staffs to follow the rules and not make life difficult. They are not particularly creative leaders and they are not great motivators. But in the bureaucracies in which they may find themselves, they don't rock the boat. They enable the wheels to keep turning and they fit right in.

Careers for the Leisurely

If this is your leading style, consider being born rich. Too late? Then seek a 9:00 to 5:00 job in which you know exactly what is expected of you. You may wish to seek a job with plenty of routine since people with your personality style often prefer their challenges outside the workplace. Whatever you choose to do, just be sure that you will not be expected to demonstrate devotion that is above and beyond the call of duty. That can happen, for example, in legal careers. Seek secure jobs, such as in the civil service, in union shops, and in the military or a tenured teaching position where the rewards for just doing your job can be great, especially in terms of pensions and benefits. But be aware that people who are more dedicated to their work will still receive the greater share of the approval, encouragement, and advancement. Self-employment may be a way to ensure that you have hours to yourself when you want them. But think first about whether you have sufficient self-discipline. Can you shift from play to work without someone else setting the rules? If your personality self-portrait reveals a conscientious trend in addition, working free lance or consulting may be a way of resolving conflicting trends within your personality.

Perhaps you can focus on your conscientiousness now by working hard for a fixed number of years and socking the money away. Then you can retire young and let your leisurely side take over. You might also try to combine business and pleasure by seeking work in an area that interests you on your own time. For example, if you spend a lot of time listening to music, perhaps you would enjoy working in a music store, for a music publisher, or a radio station. You may also satisfy your strong need for pleasure by doing creative work, or perhaps you can learn to schedule time for your leisurely yearnings in an otherwise hard-driving day

Emotions and Self-Control
Relax, Enjoy, Avoid Stress

People with a predominance of the leisurely style are like lizards warming in the sun—placid, patient, slow moving, steady, not likely to get upset. Mellow fellows, in other words. They are not all tied up in knots, they don't worry, they're not running to get their blood pressure checked every other day or sending their secretaries to the drug store for antacids. They make their daily lives as comfortable as they can and may well postpone the more onerous tasks such as work deadlines, income taxes, bill paying, Christmas shopping, cleaning the house, mowing the lawn until the last possible minute. Generally, they are emotionally balanced except when they are pushed to do more than they think is fair or when someone pressures them to change their priorities. These are primary sources of stress to leisurely individuals. In response, they feel drawn to do things the other person's way, but then they react by resisting in a more demonstrative way. Even so, when they are angry, leisurely types tend to be indirect about it. They will become grouchy and sullen, they will dawdle and procrastinate, they will assign blame elsewhere, but they will avoid a head-on confrontation.

Maybe a leisurely man will come home late the night that his wife has insisted he cook dinner. Or maybe he'll cook an awful dinner so that she'll never insist again. If a man asks his leisurely wife to sew his torn shirt, maybe she'll "forget" to do it. But if the problems don't go away, if she still wants him to share in the responsibilities of the house, or he insists that she do more for him, or if the boss insists that the leisurely employee take on more work or come in on Saturday, the leisurely person will indignantly justify his or her behavior and will even try to rally others to his or her side. ["Kids, you tell daddy that mommy doesn't have to sew his shirts just because she's a woman. Mommies have their rights too.] But if their relationships are consistently stressed by mates or supervisors who keep trying to make them do "their fair share," the sullenness may well become a way of life. If left alone to do their thing, leisurely people are blessed with the ability to find emotional comfort. They don't need much except a little leisure time in order to enjoy themselves. The leisurely style is, after all, a slow, easy, pleasure seeking one. Happiness can come from just sitting in front of the TV with a bag of chips and a beer. Generally, these individuals have good self-control, they're not driven to excesses.

But any pleasure seeking style can backfire. Beware of growing fat, flabby, alcoholic or drug dependent, or intellectually lazy, simply out of sheer bad habits. These are the kinds of things that the leisurely style must guard against.

Real Work—Keeping a Low Profile

To people with a predominance of this personality style, the real world is a fairly straight-forward place. It's populated with a lot of folks who claim authority over others and would have you working all the time at unimportant tasks. Leisurely individuals have a built in immunity to these claims for they perceive that work is only part of the real world. They protect their identities by keeping a low profile, fulfilling only those obligations to the system that they must, wishing for a stroke of good fortune to which they feel as entitled to as the next guy, and then, concentrating on what they want to do with their own time. Now that's living.

Tips on Dealing With the Leisurely Person In Your Life

1. Accept the leisurely person in your life as he or she is. Don't approach a relationship with such a person with the expectation of changing him or her to suit your needs. Rather, ask yourself what it is in this person that you like and find attractive. Appreciate all your leisurely friends, parents, children, or spouses for the qualities they possess rather than those they lack.

2. If you are having difficulty with a leisurely person, ask yourself if problems arise because you have different value systems. Perhaps you come from a push hard, get ahead, make a success of yourself tradition, while the leisurely person in your life sees more value in doing his or her own thing. Instead of judging one system as better than the other, ask yourself whether your two value systems can co-exist or merge to some degree. Perhaps you can take responsibility for the ambition and the leisurely individual can take the lead in the comfort and self-fulfillment side of things and together, you can share the benefits. In any case, try to understand this person's philosophy of life and point of view.

3. Be realistic. Life with a leisurely person may demand more sacrifices from you than from him or her. Can you make these without bitterness or resentment?

4. Make life easier for yourself. People with a leisurely personality style don't automatically tune in to what's important to you. Instead of waiting for this person to figure it out, let him or her know your basic essential expectations. If need be, let him or her know how to fulfill

these expectations. For example: if you want your leisurely spouse to come to a meeting at your child's school, say that it's important to you that you both attend. Mention the time, the place, and if necessary, what to wear. If your leisurely partner objects, ask him or her to do it for you. But save that special request for occasions that are deeply important to you.

5. Leisurely types can be stubborn about protecting their rights to do or to be as they please. Offer to assist in projects that need doing and/or make a deal. "Tell me what part I have to buy in order to fix the stereo. I'll go out and get it and all you have to do is put it in and we'll be able to listen to music again, okay?" But if he or she simply doesn't get around to it, don't nag or complain and don't take it personally. Be practical. Try to find another way to accomplish what you want the leisurely person to do. Take the stereo in for repairs.

6. When the leisurely person in your life starts stalling, refusing, or forgetting, ask "Are you angry about something?" People with this personality style have a hard time expressing their anger directly.

7. Try to share in the leisurely person's pleasures. Observe his or her habits and routines and join in. If he or she likes to go for a walk before or after dinner, go along. Pull up a chair and watch TV with your leisurely partner or play a hand of gin together. Learn to bowl or play tennis if necessary. Leisurely people don't need to be alone when they are doing their own thing. You will enrich your relationship and endear yourself to this person if you can rearrange your schedule or preferences to be with the leisurely person at the moments that are most comfortable and enjoyable in his or her day. And it is possible that he or she may become more willing to accommodate you.

8. Take good care of him or her. Leisurely people are suckers for pampering and loving attention.

Making the Most of Your Leisurely Style

Your self-driven style leads you to look inward more than outward. Broaden your prospective with Exercise 4 for the self-confident style,

"Who is this person?" Look back and see how this exercise teaches you to gather information about people. In your case, focus additionally on the ways the people in your life achieve pleasure. What's important to them? What makes them happy?

Exercise 1: Ask yourself whether there's anything you can do to help other people better enjoy their sources of happiness. For example, If your spouse achieves real pleasure from having an orderly yard, can you contribute? Maybe your spouse would appreciate some private time. What a gift it would be if you could take over the child care or some other task even for an hour. Don't think of it as work, but as a source of real pleasure to your spouse and to you. For the more pleasure you can help another person achieve, the greater your shared pleasures will be.

Exercise 2: Procrastination is the leisurely way to maximize the pleasurable moments in life as well as to resist the demands of authority as long as possible. But procrastinating can get you in trouble with other people and make you and those around you crazy at deadline time. So try thinking about deadlines in another way. It is a major pleasure in life to get things done on or before deadline. Former procrastinators will testify to this. Think about this also. If you do it today, you'll have more free time tomorrow without anybody being angry at you.

Exercise 3: Make it fun. For every chore or assignment you are supposed to complete, find a way to enjoy yourself now or later. For example: Wear a Walkman while raking leaves or washing the floor. Watch a movie on TV or DVD while getting your tax receipts together. If you have to do something at the office, reward yourself later. As soon as you complete the task, go out to a special restaurant or go to the theater that night or see a travel agent to start planning your next vacation. Reward yourself with whatever prize you would value.

Exercise 4: Do some of it. It's easy to tackle major tasks if you realize that you don't have to do the whole job at once. If you do it little by little, you don't have to give up all the fun in your life. For example: if you have a paper or report to prepare, instead of doing it all in one long effort over many hours, days, weeks, or months, just sit down and sketch out a rough outline right now. Or, tell yourself you can get up as soon as you've written the first two pages. Then put it aside and go play. Later or tomorrow, take on the next small piece. Small pieces add up quickly if you do them consistently.

Exercise 5: Do it now. As soon as you find yourself thinking about something you have to do that you are inclined to put off, do some of it right now. Then feel virtuous for having done it.

Exercise 6: Double the fun. Leisurely people are so good at finding ways to entertain themselves, that they may unwittingly become oblivious to others. If you are used to sitting down with a good book or the newspaper or taking long solitary bike rides, ask the people in your household to join you. You can discuss the news, read aloud to one another, or pedal together.

Exercise 7: When you find yourself waffling between doing what you want and acceding to someone's demands so that they won't be angry with you, to resolve your struggle, try to accomplish both aims. For example: Agree to cooperate in a requested task for a specific time period, then schedule an activity for yourself. Also, ask yourself whether you really don't want to do it or whether it's your habit to refuse to do things you are asked. If you find you're an automatic refuser, evaluate the task to see whether it's really objectionable. It may not be so bad. In any case, resist being resentful of the people whom you are trying to please. Look at the bright side. Now you're both happy.

Passive Aggressive Personality Disorder

Individuals with this disorder raise contrariness to an art form. They stall, they complain, they oppose, they dawdle, they "forget," they scorn those who try to help, and then they feel cheated that life hasn't offered them a better deal. Their inner and outer experience of life is bitter and unpleasurable, yet they cannot see that they themselves routinely close off all avenues of reward.

The passive aggressive personality disorder can best be described as a pattern of negativistic attitudes and passive resistance to demands for adequate performance beginning by early adulthood and present in a variety of contexts as indicated by four or more of the following:

1. Passively resist fulfilling routine social and occupational tasks.

2. Complaints of being misunderstood and unappreciated by others.

3. Is sullen and argumentative.

4. Unreasonably criticizes and scorns authority.

5. Expresses envy and resentment toward those apparently more fortunate.

6. Voices exaggerated and persistent complaints of personal misfortune.

7. Alternates between hostile defiance and contrition.

The Passive Aggressive Trap

Passive aggressive people do not recognize that they have done anything to make you angry or to cause them to fail. If things go wrong, it's your fault or the employer's fault. They are never openly defiant. Their actions are so indirect, so passive, that they evade responsibility. "You know how busy I am. I can't remember everything. So I forgot you don't like anchovies. You should have reminded me."

To the individuals who suffer from this disorder, compliance feels like submission and submission to their tender, fragile selves, is tantamount to humiliation. These are individuals who are both very angry and very needy. They often are angry over deep, forgotten hurts inflicted on them early in their childhoods by their parents or care givers on whom they depended completely for love, attention, and protection.

As adults, they remain very dependent on the important people in their lives, including parents, spouses, and employers. But their neediness scares them and revives the same old wounds. They can't get close without feeling angry and resentful, but they can't live without these people either.

What do they do with all their inner rage and hostility? They are afraid of acting aggressively toward those on whom they are so dependent. Instead, they resort to oppositional behavior which expresses their aggressive feelings in a covert, passive way hence the name, passive aggressive personality disorder.

Trapped between love and hate, passivity and assertion, these troubled human beings find small comfort, happiness, or pleasure. Like paranoid people, they externalize their suffering rather than look inward toward their pain. What happens to them, is certainly everybody else's fault, not their own. Then, when they passively drive spouses or employers to fury and punishment, they experience the feelings of injustice that they have carried with them all their lives. They subvert their love lives and their work lives. In one long-term study of a group of men, of all the personality disorders, the passive aggressive proved to be the one most associated with downward job mobility.

Coping With Passive Aggressive People

It is very hard to get through to these people about what they are doing to you and to themselves. Keep in mind that deep down, most passive aggressive people are very needy and they may not risk losing you should it come to that. A passive aggressive person who begins to suffer extreme anxiety or depression [perhaps as a result of a relationship coming apart] may agree to seek help. In any case, get help for your relationship. Dealing with the passive aggressive can be extraordinarily frustrating.

9

The Adventurous Style

Throw caution to the wind. Here come the adventurers who have taken those long leaps for human kind—crossing the oceans, breaking the sound barrier, and taking a walk on the moon. The men and women with this personality style venture where most mortals fear to tread. They are not bound by the same terrors that limit most of us. They live on the edge—challenging boundaries and restrictions, pitting themselves for better or for worse, in the thrilling game against their own mortality. "No risk, no reward" they say. Instead, for people with the adventurous personality style, the risk is the reward.

The Eight Characteristics

The following eight traits and behaviors are clues to the presence of the adventurous style. A person who reveals a strong adventurous tendency will demonstrate more of these behaviors more intensely than someone with less of this style in his or her personality.

1. Nonconformity. Men and women who have the adventurous personality style live by their own internal code of values. They are not strongly influenced by other people or by the norms of society.

2. Challenge. To live is to dare. Adventurers love the thrill of risk and routinely engage in high risk activities.

3. Mutual independence. They do not worry too much about others for they expect each human being to be responsible for himself or herself.

4. Persuasiveness. They are silver tongued, gifted in the gentle art of winning friends and influencing people.

5. Wanderlust. They love to keep moving. They settle down only to have the urge to pick up and go, explore, move out, move on. They do not worry about finding work and live well by their talents, skills, ingenuity, and wits.

6. Wild oats. In their childhood and adolescence, people with the adventurous personality style are usually high spirited, hell raisers and mischief makers.

7. True grit. They are courageous, physically bold and tough. They will stand up to anyone who dares to take advantage of them.

8. No regrets. Adventurers live in the present. They do not feel guilty about the past or anxious about the future. Life is meant to be experienced now.

The Six Domains of Adventurous Functioning

Self-control and the self-domains dominate the adventurous life.

Self and Self-Control—It's a Thrill to be Alive

Adventurous men and women are action-oriented extroverts hungry for the peak experience that lets them know just how powerfully alive they are. They need thrilling challenge the way most of us need food and shelter whether in sports, in their careers, in the stock market, or on the gambling tables. Fulfilling their thrill quotient is the reason for all levels of adventurers. How they do it is key. Will they risk other people's lives along with their own? Will they flaunt social order to get what they want? Will they calculate their own or other's risk. A little of the adventurous personality style goes a long way. With some of it, a person can often build a meaningful, certainly interesting life for him or herself. Too much is a real problem, especially for other people which we'll discuss in antisocial personality disorder.

In It For Me

As with all the styles for which the self domain is key, adventurous types are fundamentally out for themselves. They seek intense, visceral experience for their own sakes. If they have strength in the self-confident personality style as well, they'll be ambitious to break records and make a name for themselves in the process. Otherwise, the rush of adrenalin that results from triumph and danger may suffice.

Adventurous types do not need others to fuel their self-esteem or provide a purpose for their lives, and they don't make sacrifices for other people or at least not easily. This does not mean they cannot or do not relate to others as we will see when we discuss their relationship domain or that [like some warriors, for example] they cannot also advance a cause while in the service of their own experience. Other people often figure into adventurers' exciting plans as in leading a team of Antarctic explorers, but the meaning of the experience is not the fusing of souls or the love of a person, country, or cause. Rather what counts most is the aliveness that they experience in the moment. Neither do adventurous types require anyone's approval for what they seek out of life. As with self-confident types, belief in themselves is among their strong points. They have a definite inner sense of what's right and wrong for them. And if something is important to them, they'll do it no matter what anyone else thinks.

When Jenny cries, "Hank, how can you even consider racing your motorcycle? We have a baby now. What if you hurt yourself? What would we do?" Hank can only reply, "Hold on. This is what I do." Hank supports his family, he does his chores, but motorcycle racing is his soul. If Jenny wants to be with him, she's going to have to accept that. It truly is just the way Hank is.

The Here and Now

The adventurous personality style confers a freedom unknown to other personality styles. Depending on the degree of this style and their overall patterns, these men and women are relatively free of concern about consequences. They experience life as it unfolds in the present. They don't think ahead and they don't look back. They are alive to the impulse of the moment and can act on it more easily than someone who worries about the future or feels guilty about the past.

Living in the moment as they do, adventurous individuals experience fear more as thrilling than as chilling. Danger is a challenge, not a fear of what might happen. Thus, they may seem reckless—sailing into a storm, driving fast around mountain curves, or speculating in an uncertain economy. They count on their wits, ingenuity, physical prowess, and sheer guts to carry them through. Fear heightens their excitement, focuses their concentration, and sharpens their senses.

Living for the present experience without much thought for tomorrow, those who are dominated by this personality style are not planners. They do not plot courses toward future goals. They don't tolerate frustration and they resist discipline, especially that imposed by others and by society [but they may be exceedingly disciplined in their risk taking pursuits]. They don't anticipate. They are happy to deal with what happens when it happens.

Andy has bought thousands of dollars worth of stock on margin. He had few liquid assets, but that didn't worry him. The last time the stock market crashed, he couldn't come up with the cash. He still didn't worry about it. He turned to his father who said, sorry, he couldn't help him. Then he turned to his father-in-law telling him calmly that if he couldn't help him cover his losses, he and his wife and kids would be wiped out. Terrified of the consequences for his daughter and grandchildren, Andy's father-in-law came through for him. But Andy knew that even if his father-in-law refused him, he'd get by one way or another. Such is the typical adventurous view of the future. Adventurous types like Andy can make a million, lose two, and make another five. Within a year after the crash, Andy had repaid his father-in-law with interest.

Because they don't worry about going under, adventurous people are remarkably easy with money. Investing, gambling, spending, even giving it away is stimulating. It makes them feel powerful. It's living with a good "gut sense," but they can sometimes make a bundle. Or, they can lose everything which, as with Andy, is no big deal. They'll get back in the game again. They'll pay off their credit cards some day—no sense in getting upset about it. Of course other people are hardly so complacent when the money lost is their own. When the gamble pays off, they are glad to take profits in. When the bottom falls out of risky investments that the adventurer has made on their behalf, they express outrage that this person would have put them in such peril.

As the Spirits Move

Nobody is more fun, more appreciative of the possibilities than these eternal optimists. Back in the '60's when they were newlyweds, Beth and Richard met adventurous Shawn and his wife, Jena. The two couples quickly became friends, Beth and Richard, who were more conventional, were delighted with Shawn and Jena's spontaneity. Shawn could call Richard at the ad agency where he worked and say, "Hey, you don't really want to work late tonight. Jena and I are going to pick up Beth, then you and we're all going dancing." They'd get home at 3:00 or 4:00 a.m. and Richard would then have to stay up to complete his work. At Shawn and Jena's urging, they all experimented with drugs. They took LSD and expanded their minds as well as their rock and roll repertoire. They even considered group sex, but Beth and Richard decided against it. It was just a little too much for them.

Richard and Beth had never lived this way and were glad to cast off their conventionality for a while at a time when everyone else seemed to be doing it. But after a year or so of their fun-loving, spur-of-the-moment lifestyle, consequences started to pile up. Too tired and "spaced out," Richard blew an important presentation and the agency didn't get the client they were pitching. He was very close to being

fired. He and Beth talked. They realized that the future was too important to them to take chances with it. They guiltily told Shawn and Jena
that they couldn't keep up the pace with them. Shawn and Jena
thought Richard should abandon his soul-restricting career and move
to the country and live off the land as they had decided to do. Now,
many years later, Richard and Beth run a small literary publishing
company. Their lives are centered around their work and their two
kids, who are now in graduate school. They remember the 60's and
Shawn and Jena and are glad to have known them and to have done
the things that they did. But they are not strongly adventurous so to be
fulfilled, they needed to follow a path that was truer to their own personalities.

Shawn and Jena moved to the country and lived in a commune for a
while. Jena gave birth to a boy. She discovered that Shawn was
involved in menage a trois with two women in the commune. They
declared theirs an open marriage, an arrangement that was quite popular at the time. But Jena became overwhelmed with jealousy and
moved back to the city with the baby. She went back to school, remar-
ried, and now is a special education teacher and has three grown children.

Shawn, true to his adventurous personality style, was happy to keep
doing his thing. He farmed for a while, then turned to woodworking,
and sold his little boxes from time to time at craft fairs and flea markets. He's had a couple of brushes with the law over his possession of
small amounts of narcotics, but he's never had to serve time. Now he
and Judy, the woman he's lived with for a few years, sell used clothing
at flea markets. They're happy as can be, moving around the West as
the spirit moves.

Shawn is over fifty, but he says he feels nineteen. He's not admitting
the truth. For the first time in his life, he's begun to recognize that he
doesn't and never again will feel like a teenager. While the women he's
been with often end up worrying about security in their old age, the
thought never crossed Shawn's mind until recently. But he shrugs it

off, insisting he's always been able to figure out how to survive. This is the life he knows how to live and it's always worked for him.

You Can't Win Them All

Living in the now, reacting immediately to impulse, enjoying an unrestrained, nonconformance existence, and taking numerous risks can lead to a very exciting life. It can also exact a huge toll. Living according to whim without self-control or thought of consequences leads the extremely adventurous, more than any other personality style except the mercurial, quickly down the path toward problems—economic disasters, drug abuse, sexually transmitted diseases, difficulties with the law, and accidental injury.

The individual with the mixed personality pattern that includes the adventurous style may be protected by strengths from other styles. Conscientious, self-confident, and vigilant styles, for example, offer the foresight necessary to calculate the risk. The devoted style will bring a sensitivity to what loved ones feel and think. Even when the bets are hedged, when training and preparation are thorough, death, injury, or substantial loss can be the unfortunate results of dangerous sports, career brinkmanship, or high rolling.

Brooke and Her Clients Lose Big

Strength and a more responsible and restrained personality style may only conceal the person's adventurous streak from the outside world, possibly even from oneself. Brooke made a name for herself in investments on behalf of non-profit organizations. She seemed the essence of conscientiousness—a person of extraordinary habits [as just one example, she ate lunch at the same restaurant at exactly the same time everyday] and conservative demeanor. [She wore only navy or gray suits.] She devoted all her energies to her work. Also typical of a conscientious person, she was very thrifty with her own money and indeed kept her own funds in low-risk investments, like certificates of deposits at a time when interest rates were quite low and riskier investments schemes were paying off. She knew well about these rewards because her client organizations were seeing returns on the much less than A rated investments she had been making for them.

Although conscientiously adverse to taking chances with her own money, (she recognized her fearfulness and laughed at herself for it) Brooke was comfortable indulging her adventurous love of risk in her professional work which was why she'd been in the investment business and done so well in her career. Up to now, she'd always mixed just enough caution with an ability to move fast and take chances when conditions were right. When, in rather difficult economic times, she spotted an opportunity for her clients to profit handsomely, she acted all too adventurously and converted conservative holdings into speculations that paid off spectacularly until the market condition abruptly changed and her paper empire crumbled. Most of the risks she'd been taking in her professional life had worked out over the years, this one did not and when her adventurous bets fell, they fell big.

Because of Brooke, some very worthy organizations ceased to exist. The community was shocked to discover the "two sides" of this prominent person. Predominately adventurous people don't necessarily suffer from their falls as much as some others, but Brooke was more conscientious than adventurous and experienced emotional as well as professional collapse. Perhaps Brooke [and her clients] would have been better off if she had been able to be a bit more adventurous in her personal life and more conscientious on behalf of her clients.

Many people have such contradictions in their personality. The challenge is to recognize all the trends, understand their effects on all the domains of functioning and to direct their influence into life expansions rather than self-defeating conflict.

Emotions—What, Me Worry?

Predominately adventurous types don't hide their feelings. You know immediately when they're feeling sexual, enthusiastic, or angry.

Restraint does not mark this style, so if a very adventurous person has a bone to pick with you, stand back.

Most of the time, adventurous people are careful and eager to enjoy life. Whatever negative feelings or disappointments they experience are immediately routed into action or some daring adventure. They don't feel much stress except when they are frustrated and confined and can't act. Then, they become restless, angry, and disgruntled like a caged animal. They are good at righting themselves quickly and returning to their optimistic state. But age has a way of creeping up on very adventurous people. They are adolescents at heart. Unfortunately as they age, the gap with the genuinely youthful grows larger. They become less attractive to others. Infirmaries and other age-related limitations can be exceedingly difficult for them to accept, whereas in their 30's or 40's, most people have been dealing with the reality of their mortality and the narrowing of their omnipotence. For adventurers, the facts of limited life hit late and hard. Suddenly, depressing thoughts about the future intrude. Maybe life isn't the never-ending, exciting game they always thought it was. Despite a lifetime of challenging the odds, it has never occurred to them before now that death always wins.

However, most adventurous people cope well. They almost always land on their feet. They'll figure out some way to survive, maybe now at least, they'll begin to lead a calmer life, maybe get married late in life, or become serious about commitment for the first time. Or, perhaps they will maneuver their old bones into a wheelchair and go out and enter a marathon. "Hell, you only live once" is forever their motto!

An Adventurous Phase

Personality style, as we have mentioned before, tends to mellow with age. This is especially true of the adventurous style which is much more common, appropriate, and culturally acceptable in younger people. Many adults with the adventurous personality style were rowdy, rebellious kids. They may have been a handful for their parents, but they weren't criminals, just high-energy, high-spirited youngsters.

Maybe you were Dennis or Denise the menace when you were ten.
Maybe you stole a Hershey bar from a candy store. Perhaps you experimented with drugs or alcohol or you drag raced with your buddies
when you first got your driver's license or trashed your neighbor's mail-
box. Or perhaps you rebelled in college or graduate school and started
cutting classes and not studying until the dean told you to shape up or
ship out. Maybe you bummed around South America for two years
with no money, just picking up odd jobs and staying with new-found
friends who would feed you for a while. Maybe you were into sexual
conquests picking up people in bars and parties, never the same person
twice. We expect young people to sow their wild oats, "Don't worry
dear, Junior is just going through his adventurous phase." But we
count on that part of their personality to smooth out and lose intensity, or expect other styles to grow stronger so that these individuals
can go on to productive, safer, socially acceptable, secure lives. Usually
this is the case. The wisdom that comes with age tempers adventurers,
although it leaves them with residues of mischievousness and a strong
appreciation of challenge.

Real World—Playing the Game

Adventurers know what's what in the real world and they don't care.
Life is a game of getting around the rules and the conventional obligations and going beyond the established limits. Adventurers are determined to prove that they are the world's greatest players and gamblers.

Work—A Rolling Stone Gathers No Moss

To highly adventurous people, life is one big opportunity to do
what they please. They are slaves of no system. Their primary rule of
life and of work is that they must be faced with a challenge. They can
work well with discipline, concentration, and responsibility if their
work [and here we include their risk-taking sports and hobbies] provides this necessary challenge. Thus, people with this style can be
skilled fighter pilots, stunt persons, tight-rope walkers, sky diving

instructors, combat soldiers, and so on—careers in which one false move can be their last one.

If their personality combines a "head style," such as the conscientious with the "gut style" adventurous, they might rise to considerable accomplishment in their careers as heart surgeons perhaps or criminal lawyers, just the kind of challenges an adventurer can appreciate. Furthermore, adventurous types can be good talkers. They can talk anybody into anything, judges and juries included. [But as described in the discussion of Brooke earlier, personality style combinations such as this can also backfire when the individual fails to calculate the risks.]

With or without moderating influences, adventurous types are good workers when they want to be, as long as the work provides constant challenge, new projects, and renewed excitement. Although they may be entrepreneurs, they're not typically what one would call management material. Adventurers operate on instinct and ingenuity rather than on intellect. They tend to resist authority, they are poor planners, they deplore tedious follow through. They do not accept responsibility for their people and they don't handle money or budgets well.

Adventurers are easily bored. When they are not stimulated by their work, no matter how successful they are, they will peter out or move on. Financial reward usually is not sufficient motivation for adventurers to keep going when they have lost interest.

Tom commands a high fee as a systems consultant for manufacturers of high tech products, but to his wife's chagrin, he accepts only one or two jobs a year. They have just enough money to live on, whereas they could be quite comfortable if Tom took even half the jobs that are offered to him. But Tom is bored by most of the proposed projects. He'll work only if the assignment stimulates him. He'd rather travel. He just came back from a four month trek in the Himalayas. Sandra, his wife who stayed home with their two-year old, thinks they should build a nest egg, and buy a house instead of renting. She wants the conventional secure rewards of life, but Tom doesn't think there's anything they "should" do except enjoy their lives to the fullest.

Innovative and resourceful as they usually are, adventurous types can often find some way to outwit the conventional obligations that most people feel they can't escape. They create their own opportunities. They frequently manage to live happily without a permanent job, moving around from place to place working as life guards, ski instructors, sales people, entrepreneurs, stock brokers, waiters and waitresses, bouncers and truck drivers, or by marketing whatever skill they may have when they need money. They may outwit the system entirely. Adventurers live by an inner sense of right and wrong.

Like aggressive types, they may bend or break rules for expediency, or if they think the rules don't make sense. They can become extremely successful, especially if they have some aggressive style in their personalities as well. Some build their own commercial empires by wheeling and dealing and bending the rules wherever they find a flexible spot. Some tread in deeper waters. For example, to use historical examples: trading arms for hostages or striking it rich with insider stock tips. Whatever the case, they love the adventure of the moment and it is the adventure and the current moment that matters the most.

Careers for the Adventurous

If the adventurous is your leading style, you don't need us to tell you what to do. But if it's one of your styles, you might be more satisfied with your life if you recognize and accept your adventurous need for action, excitement, and change.

Avoid routine and drudgery. Look for work that involves frequent, time-limited, new projects such as in magazine and newspaper publishing. Stay clear of middle management or any other position in which you must be subordinate to others. In other words, be on a solo track. Look for work in high glamour, high excitement fields such as investment banking, advertising, or entertainment. Sales may appeal to you; you are a good persuader and may enjoy the challenge of working on commission. Consider marketing your skills on a free lance or consulting basis. Explore the possibility of turning a hobby into an income producer or hang in there when you're going through a boring phase in your work. Remember, as soon as you're finished for the day, you can go take your flying lesson. But remember to hedge your bets. Predominately, adventurous people can pick themselves up and go on after a big fall, but can you?

The Adventurous Leader

It is rare to find a predominately adventurous style in a regular nine to five job, let alone, in a senior leadership position and certainly not in a corporate setting. But sometimes, in a nontraditional creative enterprise, a highly adventurous person will have a brilliant idea and enough magnetism to attract others to join in the excitement and carry the idea through. Adventurous people certainly have style, but they are not leaders in any traditional sense. They have charisma though, and if the rewards keep coming in, "real" leaders may stick around and make sure bets are adequately hedged and the enterprise keeps functioning. But the adventurous leader may well lose interest once everything is up and running, become inattentive to what others are doing, and put at risk everything that he or she has inspired.

Adventurous Parents

They're not the best in any long-term relationship including those with children. They are not reliably there as parents since their wanderlust draws them away from home so often. They may care a lot for their children and may feel some sadness that they can't come through for them more. But they have to go their own way. When they are there with the children, adventurers tend to assume that what is good for them is good for the children or that what they want for their children is in the children's best interest.

They may expose their children to unnecessary risks and may not teach them caution. Nor do they think of the consequences to the family or the risk they take on their own behalf. They are not naturally tuned in to other people's feelings. Yet, for all the non-goods, adventurous style parents are exciting, interesting, and non-critical and can open up a big world for their children. They may prove irresponsible, impatient, and hot tempered, but they are full of energy, curiosity, and good spirit. They are romantic, swashbuckling figures. What is essential for their kids is one full-time, on the scene non-adventurous parent who will be sensitive, supportive, reliable, and protective.

Tips on Dealing With the Adventurous Person in Your Life

1. Have fun, but make sure you know exactly what's going on. The adventurous person in your life can make an exciting companion, but don't confuse what you may want out of a relationship with what he or she is actually offering you. Adventurous types are charming and disarming. This person may flatter, persuade, cajole, or even manipulate you into an affair or an adventure, but just because you share this intimacy doesn't mean the adventurer loves you or feels any responsibility toward you. If you are the traditional love and marriage type, look at the adventurous behavior closely. Ask questions. Understand that this person may be sleeping with others besides you. Realize that romantic, sexy, and exciting as he or she may be, this person will not satisfy your more traditional needs.

2. No illusions. Once you are in a relationship with an adventurous person, don't think "Aha, now I can change him or her." Accept what this person gives you and recognize that he or she is not likely to start adapting to your needs. You be the flexible one. If that's not your style and the adventurer doesn't provide what you need, it's up to you to get out.

3. Don't crowd. The adventurous person in your life needs freedom to do as he or she pleases. Be satisfied with a nontraditional relationship that includes perhaps separate vacations. Don't try to prevent the adventurer from taking off. This person is more likely to come back to you if you let him or her go in the first place.

4. Be responsible. The adventurous person in your life may not make decisions about money, children, safety in general the same way you would. Don't wait for him or her to do the right thing. Take appropriate measures for birth control and disease prevention, for financial security, and for the protection of your kids. Don't be a passive partner.

5. Know your limits. The adventurous types have a great tolerance and capacity for drugs and alcohol, for fear, and for risk. The adventurous person in your life will probably assume that you like what he or she likes, unless you make your preferences clear. If you are terrified of white water rafting, don't go. Stop after one or two drinks if that's enough for you.

6. Expect a lot of yourself, not the adventurous person in your life. To maintain a relationship with an adventurous person requires that you have strong self-esteem and don't need him or her to support you emotionally. Adventurous people are not spontaneously sensitive to other people's feelings and needs. So you have to be able to find sources of self-esteem from within yourself and to be able to say, without anger or resentment, "This is who I am, what I feel, and what I need."

Making the Most of Your Adventurous Style

Your strong points include your spontaneity, your ability to act, your strength, your fearlessness, your ability to experience pleasure, and your tendency to live life to the fullest. The trouble you run into results from impulsiveness and lack of forethought In this way, you resemble people with dramatic and mercurial personality styles.

Exercise 1: Think from your head, not from your appetites. Urges, desires, and whims are compelling and have their own satisfying feeling-logic. Acting in direct response to impulse bypasses the cerebral cortex, the thinking part of your brain. While you are counting to ten, concentrate on the thinking part of your brain and try to experience the difference between that and the feeling and sensation satisfying part of your brain.

Exercise 2: Your style is remarkably free of anxiety, thus the consequences of your actions or lifestyles may not occur to you. So worry a little. Each time you are about to take a risk, to invest money, or to gamble, or to go in an airplane, or on a motorcycle, to drink or take drugs, or to climb a mountain, anything at all, use your cerebral cortex to consider what could possibly go wrong. Think of two or more unfortunate possibilities. For example: if you are about to climb up on a bucking bronco at a rodeo, you might consider: (1) I could get killed; (2) I could get maimed.

Exercise 3: Safeguard yourself. For each of the possibilities on your risk list, figure out at least one way to protect yourself in advance. For example: if you could get killed competing in the rodeo, you could protect yourself by staying sober and competing with your wits about you. To safeguard yourself from at least some of the consequences of life as a disabled person, you could take out health and disability insurance or you could make sure you had a job that offered these benefits. If you are unable to figure out a safeguard for any of the risks on your list, consider not indulging in those activities.

Exercise 4: Worry about other people. Observe your interactions with others and note all the possible ways in which your behavior or decisions put them at risk. For example: your baby is napping and you want to go across the street for a while. What could go wrong if you leave him alone for 15 minutes? (1) The house could catch fire and the baby wouldn't be able to get out of his crib. (2) The baby could vomit and choke and you wouldn't be there to save him.

Exercise 5: Safeguard other people from the risk of your behavior. Wait to go across the street until your spouse comes back or until you get someone in to look after the sleeping baby, or don't go at all. If you find it difficult to understand how you may put others at risk, you may need to see things from their point of view. "Who is this person?" Concentrate on what the people who are important to you like, dislike, think, and feel. Try to see things through their eyes instead of your own. Look especially for ways in which they differ from you.

Exercise 6: Think about this. What do you want out of your life five, ten, twenty years from now? Try to choose the long-term benefit over the short-term gain.

Anti-Social Personality Disorder

Individuals with anti-social personality disorder, also known as psychopaths or sociopaths, could care less about the feelings of others or the rules of society. Where others seek to build, they destroy.

Anti-social personality disorder can best be defined as a pervasive pattern and disregard for and violation of the rights of others occurring since age fifteen years as indicated by three or more of the following:

1. Failure to conform to social norms with respect to lawful behavior as indicated by repeatedly performing acts that are grounds for arrest.

2. Deceitfulness as indicated by repeated lying, use of aliases or coning others for profit or personal pleasure.

3. Impulsivity or failure to plan ahead.

4. Irritability and aggressiveness as indicated by repeated physical fights or assaults.

5. Reckless disregard for safety of self and others.

6. Consistent irresponsibility as indicated by repeated failure to sustain consistent work behavior or honor financial obligations.

7. Lack of remorse as indicated by being indifferent to rationalization of hurting, mistreating, or stealing.

Missing Conscience and Compassion

Most of us internalize into our personal conscience the basic rules of society and culture. We believe that it is wrong to hurt or exploit others. We believe we should obey the intent of the law. We feel it is right to support and protect our children and so on. When we fail to live up to our moral codes, we feel guilty. Some people, such as conscientious types, have a stronger conscience and a resulting sense of guilt than do others. But those with anti-social personality disorder have little or none of either. They disdain the rules of society. They want what they want and they will take it, be it property, sex, or even life. They know the difference between right and wrong in the legal sense; they just don't care about it. They have little compassion or empathy for others and can often justify every cruel, destructive, malicious, or manipulative act. You will find many of the people with this disorder in jail, now or eventually. Anti-social personality disorder is among the two most common diagnoses among convicted felons occurring in as much as 75 percent of the prison population. [Alcohol abuse is the other diagnosis that vies for top place in forensic settings.]

But unscrupulous, exploited, thoroughly self-interested tendencies are not restricted to convicted criminals. The majority of anti-social persons are not criminals. In public and private life, they use and abuse, outdo and outsmart other people and suffer little or no remorse. They can be extremely shrewd and lie and size up your weaknesses in no time. To get what they want, they will manipulate your conscience and compassion. Somewhere along the adventurous, anti-social continuum are people who commit professional ethics violations and think they are perfectly entitled, yet, who lie convincingly when caught or confronted. They'll charm and disarm you, telling you what you want to hear, or what will touch your tender heart strings.

An anti-social individual can con an elderly person out of his or her meager savings and feel thrilled with the victory. Obviously, individuals with anti-social disorder can rarely form deep, warm, close responsible relationships. Their ability to love and to empathize with others is so impaired that few of them can sustain a relationship with one person for as long as a year. They do have children since their sexual needs are powerful, and they rarely concern themselves with the consequences. Unfortunately, anti-social parents do not take care of their children or consider their future well-being. Child abuse, sexual and otherwise, runs rampant in these families.

Act Before You Think

Anti-social individuals can bear no frustrations. If thwarted or simply annoyed, they will often lash out violently against their own families or whoever else is around. They do not consider consequences. They do not plan ahead and they do not learn from experiences. In other words, anti-social individuals do not think before they act. Impulse rules them completely. Moreover, they are unafraid. They seem to suffer none of the anticipatory anxiety that would stop most of us in our ill-intended tracks. Again and again, their aggressiveness and impulsiveness and recklessness land anti-social individuals in court, jail, or hospital emergency rooms. People with anti-social personality disorder are more likely than others in the general population to die prematurely by violent means—suicide, accidents, and/or homicide.

Coping With Anti-Social People

While it may go against your own beliefs, do not assume that you can trust, help, or reform an anti-social person. Remember that these people can be very cunning and manipulative. Don't be conned. Protect your own interest and back out. If you can't pull yourself away from such a person, consider getting help for yourself.

10

The Idiosyncratic Style

I diosyncratic men and women are not like anyone else. They are dreamers, seekers of the spirit, visionaries, mystics. They march to a distinctive beat, different from the conventional rhythms that most people follow. They are true originals and often they stand out—sometimes as eccentrics, sometimes as geniuses.

The Six Characteristics

The following six traits and behaviors are clues to the presence of the idiosyncratic style. A person who reveals a strong idiosyncratic tendency will demonstrate more of these behaviors more intensely than someone with less of this style in his or her personality.

1. Inner life. Idiosyncratic individuals are tuned in to and sustained by their own feelings and belief systems regardless of whether or not others accept or understand their particular world view or approach to life.

2. Own world. They are self-directed and independent, requiring few close relationships.

3. Own thing. Oblivious to convention, idiosyncratic individuals create interesting, unusual, often eccentric life styles.

4. Expanded reality. Open to anything, they are interested in the occult, the extrasensory, and the supernatural.

5. Metaphysics. They are drawn to abstract and speculative thinking.

6. Outward view. Though they are inner directed and follow their own hearts and minds, idiosyncratic men and women are keen observers of others, particularly sensitive to how people react to them.

The Six Domains of
Idiosyncratic Functioning

The idiosyncratic is the only style for which the real world coupled with the self domain is the central determining domain of functioning.

Real World—Things Aren't Always...

Tonya, a writer of best-selling detective novels, lives in a 20-room Victorian mansion. She volunteered her house for the movie version of one of her murder mysteries. Three rooms and a closed-off wing of the house were refurbished for the film. After several days of preparation and setting up, the actors took their places and the camera men were poised to begin shooting the bedroom murder scene. No sooner had the director given the word than they heard a loud crashing noise from somewhere above their heads, then, another. "Cut!" yelled the director. He looked around for Tonya. "What's going on up there?" "I'll go see," she said. "Fred, go with her," the director ordered a young crew member. The two of them looked around the attic and found nothing out of place or unusual. After a 15-minute delay, the shooting resumed and nothing untoward happened for the rest of the day. The same noise recurred in different parts of the house on the second and again on the last day of shooting. No explanation was ever discovered although each time it happened, Tonya went off to look with Fred trailing close behind. "I can't explain it," Tonya said, shaking her head.

After the crew finished filming at the house and returned to California to complete the movie, Tonya's husband, Russell, came back from a business trip abroad. They talked about the strange incidence, "The Ghost," they both agreed. Tonya had refrained from telling the director what she believed was the cause of the peculiar noises. She had heard them before, always in that unused wing of the old New England house. She had no doubt that a ghost was there. Russell didn't really believe it, but he went along with that explanation for lack of any other. Besides, the idea of having one's own resident ghost amused him. The couple mentioned their ghost to very few others and certainly not to the film crew. They knew that people would think that Tonya, who believed thoroughly in such unearthly manifestations, was crazy.

Open Minds

Idiosyncratic individuals like Tonya are not crazy, but they often strike people that way because they perceive the real world so differently from everyone else. It's not that they all believe in ghosts, have a sixth sense, experience past lives, or hear the music of the spheres, it's that idiosyncratic individuals do not feel compelled to accept the customary explanations of what's going on in their world. Thus, in some settings, they may be viewed as weird or eccentric or even heretical, as were those Puritans in early Massachusetts who did not believe in witches.

The minds and imaginations of idiosyncratic types range far and wide. They are willing to consider anything as real. The open mindedness of this style is a boon to creative intellectual explanation and discovery. Idiosyncratic personality style frequently accompanies creative and intellectual genius. People such as Albert Einstein, Isaac Newton, Salvador Dali, and Lewis Carroll, to name a few, perceived something different out there because they were not locked in to the accepted explanations and interpretations that seemed to make sense to just about everybody else.

Genius or otherwise, idiosyncratic men and women are creatively curious. They are always asking "What if?" What if I represented reality with one black line down the center of this canvas? What if I played the Bach Partitas at twice the tempo? What if there really were a Santa Claus? "There's no Santa Claus. I put the keys to the new Pontiac under the Christmas tree and I paid for it. Here's the bill if you don't believe me." But if an individual's personality is sufficiently idiosyncratic, he may perceive a spirit of Christmas that you cannot begin to imagine.

Idiosyncratic individuals are by no means oblivious to what other people think and believe. They know that most people over the age of seven no longer believe in Santa Claus. Tonya is aware that few people believe in ghosts. It doesn't matter to them what other people think. Always their own understandings come from inside themselves, not from other people, books, and newspapers.

Idiosyncratic types are driven to live their lives according to the sensations, feelings, and ideas that spring from inside them. They are true nonconformists.

A New Age Personality Style?

By definition, idiosyncratic is an uncommon personality style. But you may find many people with this style involved in some way with the new age movement, for it provides them a forum and setting for their unconventional beliefs and their personal spiritual seeking. An idiosyncratic individual can attend a new age workshop on past lives or Shamanistic healing or spend months meditating on an ashram without fear of being thought of as peculiar.

Individuals with this personality style are very aware that other people may think them rather strange so they often seek the company of like-minded others in order to be more comfortable in life. This doesn't mean that everyone who identifies with the new age movement necessarily has an idiosyncratic personality style, or that all idiosyncratic people participate in new age activities. People come to new movements for many reasons—because the ideas or beliefs appeal to them, because their own belief systems no longer work for them, because they have a strong need to affiliate and to be accepted, because they need a person or a cause to lend new structure to their lives, and so on. However, idiosyncratic people are not "joiners." They do not affiliate or conform no matter who is in charge. They are not inclined to accept or espouse anyone else's principles and beliefs. Their quest is entirely personal and their beliefs, original.

Self—My World Is Real

The greatest reality for idiosyncratic types derives from their internal worlds from the domain of self. If they believe in something or their personal experience suggests for example, that they have ESP, then it exists and they don't need scientific proof. They heed their inner voices, not those of other people.

Unlike conscientious or sensitive style people, their self esteem is not based on following protocol or being correct from someone else's point of view. Thus, an idiosyncratic artist can break with tradition without worrying what the public or the dealers or the critics might think. With sufficient talent and genius, this artistic vision may be a huge ground breaker or it may offend throughout history. No matter, the artist with this personality style will follow his or her inclinations.

Whether You Like It Or Not

Somehow, many idiosyncratic people live and work and succeed, sometimes phenomenally well in the same world we live in, only they do it their way. [Individuals with schizotypal personality disorder, the extreme of the idiosyncratic style, do not manage to adapt to "our" world.] Still, predominately idiosyncratic people may find acceptance by others difficult. They are frequent subjects of ridicule.

The degree of their idiosyncracy will depend on the setting, the prevailing culture, on their successes or talents, and in the degree to which they need the warmth, support, and acceptance of other people. In the 60's, weird behavior and alternate lifestyles were "in." But neither then nor now could an idiosyncratic wife, military officer, or corporate executive get along well in the traditional corporate culture where proper form and procedure are everything. The fact is, the numbers of settings where highly idiosyncratic individuals can fit in are few. An idiosyncratic actor, writer, musician, intellectual, or psychic healer may be able to find his or her niche with great talent, achievement, or wealth. An extraordinary idiosyncratic individual [the late Howard Hughes comes to mind] will be courted by others no matter how bizarrely he or she behaves. But the quirky idiosyncratic individual who has nothing extraordinary to offer to mainstream society may find the going rough if he or she cannot locate a welcoming, or at least tolerant, environment. Moderately idiosyncratic people, especially if they have a more dominant conforming style [such as the conscientious] usually find it easier to accommodate the traditional external expectations by keeping their beliefs and ideas to themselves. Even so, in extremely "conventional" environments, they may seem a bit unusual, refreshingly original to some, a little "off" to others.

Stress and the Uncertainty Factor

Rethinking has it limitations. Idiosyncratics rejection of standard explanations and conventions plus their reliance on inner experience alone to assess the nature of the world can lead to doubt and uncertainty. It is characteristic of this personality style to question and to wonder. Among the "What if" questions that idiosyncratics may pose: "What if there is yet another way to explain things?"

Idiosyncratic types may experience anything from mild confusion to serious crisis of confidence when their personal systems begin to rearrange themselves into new world views. "I wish," sighed idiosyncratic Ben, "that I had been able to accept the Orthodox Judaism I was brought up in. My dad never had a doubt in his life. He never had to make up his mind. His father and the rabbis told him what to believe, what to do, what not to do, what to think, what to eat, who to marry." Ben is now in his late 30's, his spiritual quest is his reason for being. He has studied with mystics in South America, he has experienced his own personal god while on an acid trip, and he considered entering a Buddhist monastery. Ben, like many idiosyncratic people is constantly reinventing the universe in his search for reality and truth. He could no more accept an orthodox explanation of the real world than his father could have lived as a Buddhist. And in part, he envies his father, his lifetime consistency of faith, and his ability to accept conventional interpretations of things without wondering whether they are true for him personally. Ben wants a real world that can satisfy him intellectually, spiritually, and emotionally. But his self-styled system is in constant flux.

As a seeker, he will always be looking for something more, something else, something better. Usually that's fine with him. The quest itself is a source of joy and fulfillment for him. In times of difficulty, as when his marriage ended last year, it would have been easier for Ben to have an established set of beliefs to make sense of things. As it was, he found nothing in his understandings of the universe to explain what had happened to his wife. He lost faith and became deeply dispirited. Disillusionment often accompanies idiosyncratic seeking. This, along with having to conform to someone else's reality are this personality style's significant sources of stress. The inner strength is also characteristic of this style and idiosyncratic individuals will often find a suitable metaphysical explanation for their crises of confidence and then move on to embrace a new belief system or at least solace themselves with music or art.

Well-educated Ben was heard to say recently, "Maybe I'll take up East Coast intellectualism again." If, however, the stresses come from the pressures of a conformance society, idiosyncratic types may find it easier to cope by withdrawing from the mainstream.

Emotions and Self-Control
Testing the Limits

The idiosyncratic is a powerful thinking and feeling style. How these individuals feel within themselves is as important as what they think is going on out there. Like dramatic individuals, they seek emotional experience in life with the difference being that the dramatic emotional expression has much to do with other people. Not so for the idiosyncratic for whose emotions are felt in all their intensity for their own sake.

These individuals seek mind/emotional/spiritual expansion. They crave new experiences to send them to new peaks of feeling and awareness of their inner beings. To achieve this, many idiosyncratics will experiment with varieties of intensive experiences from primal scream therapy to fasting and long hours in meditation to psychedelic drugs to hours and hours of deep thinking or listening to music. Since they tend not to be constrained by convention, and will experiment with the forbidden, others may view them as out of control. Those who experiment heavily with drugs often suffer from extreme emotional and behavioral difficulties. These may have more to do with their drug use than with their personality styles, however.

Idiosyncratic types test the limits of emotional and spiritual experience. They seek rapture. They are also eager to explore their inner darkness. During a summer break in college, idiosyncratic Julie volunteered for a deep sleep study. For more than a month she lived in a room with no natural light, no clocks, no TV or radio, no cues to the external environment. She slept and woke when she felt like it. As the time went on, she became increasingly depressed. The more depressed she became, the more she felt she was approaching an important understanding. She began to write down her inner experiences and soon spent all her waking moments with pad and pencil sleeping less and less. When the study concluded, Julie, for all her depression, felt she had had a profoundly creative and insightful experience.

An objective observer might have concluded that Julie had experienced an emotional disorientation. That often occurs when a person's internal biological clock loses the external light/dark, day/night cues on which it depends for proper functioning. An idiosyncratic person, however, would consider that explanation as missing the point. To Julie, the experience was the point, not the manipulation of the environment that caused it.

Idiosyncratic people always give priority to their inner emotional experience over what others consider objective, external reality. No one is going to tell these people that what they feel isn't really happening. "I feel the presence of his spirit hovering over us," exclaimed Bethany at her husband's death bed. "Oh Mother, don't start this now," snapped her daughter Rachel. To which Bethany responded, "Rachel, who are you to say what's real?" at which Bethany's son, Dan, intervened to cut short the familiar mother/daughter go around. Similarly Tonya would declare to Russ, "Something terrible is going to happen. I know I can feel it." She'll walk around the house in a dark worried mood and nothing he can do or say will talk her out of it.

Emotional reactions by idiosyncratic types may be based more on their subjective experiences at a given moment than on what's happening around them, which may make their behavior at times seem strange and inappropriate. Extremely idiosyncratic individuals will often start to laugh in public because something inside them strikes them as funny. Sometimes they seem kind of "spaced out," because they are tuned inward, not outward toward others. They express their feelings and thoughts in their own way because conforming is no motivation for them. Still, they may become anxious and self-conscious when they have to be around others who dwell securely in the "regular" world. They know they are different and that people don't always respect or appreciate them for it. They can display quite a temper around rigid, narrow-minded people who insist that their idiosyncratic way of life is "wrong," and then try to make them mold themselves to "normal" behavior standards.

Work—Finding a Niche

Two key factors in the quality of idiosyncratic lives are as follows: first whether they can find an accepting environment and, second, how far they can go to adapt to other's expectations. Not many work settings tolerate eccentric behavior unless the idiosyncratic person has a great deal to offer through intelligence, talent, or skills. Still, the rent has to be paid. Like most people, idiosyncratic types have to work. Those who can keep their eccentricities to themselves, do best. Some idiosyncratics can do well with one ear tuned to their own little world and one outward to what the boss expects of them. Others, however, have a hard time understanding or accepting authority.

Idiosyncratic Pam, a word processor, could not figure out why her boss insisted that she work from nine to five when she could often concentrate best in the wee hours. She continued to ask that she be allowed to come into the office at midnight instead. Monica, her boss, at first was mildly amused by "Kookie" Pam's request and would repeat that the office opened at 9:00 and closed at 5:00. But she became increasingly annoyed by Pam's weirdness. Although Pam's work was better than average, when the firm needed to cut back on employees, Pam was the first to go.

Idiosyncratic types frequently are not ambitious or competitive in the conventional sense and can do well [if they can play by the rules] in routine work that does not interest or challenge them. They are often capable of intense concentration or can "tune out" and still accomplish a day's work well.

The Idiosyncratic Leader

Idiosyncratic people aren't often interested in leading others, certainly not in any traditional sense. They are not very efficient in the day-to-day requirements of a managerial role and they are not necessarily tuned in to others' feelings. With competent people to whom they can delegate the routine matters of running an office or department, and instituting discipline practices, however, they can often inspire creativity in others and bring a fresh view to the work.

Don't expect the usual sorts of meetings and process reports and overall concern for form though—this is something they are simply not capable of. I cannot say that I have ever seen an idiosyncratic leader at the senior levels of management in any organization.

Careers For the Idiosyncratic

Issues of security, benefits, and daily structure do not mean much to people with a predominance of this style. More important are freedom from rules and conformance expectations. If your personality self-portrait includes get-ahead, ambitious styles, such as the self-confident, the conscientious and the vigilant, in addition to the idiosyncratic, your prime requirement will be to seek out a challenging work environment in which your idiosyncracy will be accepted, or in which it is not too stressful to keep to yourself.

Even if you are very bright and talented, you will not be able to contribute in settings in which everyone is expected to behave similarly such as in the corporate world. Even if you do manage to produce, be aware that in traditional settings, including perhaps the family business, you may be an irritant to others and may not be politically successful no matter how much you can contribute.

Seek out creative work environments which are generally more tolerant of individual eccentricities provided the work gets done. In professions such as medicine and law, you may be able to find a niche for yourself in your own practice, or in partnership with others who are similarly free thinking. Consider, perhaps, a career associated with one of your personal concerns or hobbies. For example: you could sell new age publications or goods, or work in some capacity for an organization or cause that interests you.

For those of you who are not especially ambitious in the work domain or who need to earn money only to support your personal interests or endeavors, find a non-demanding job that provides stability and freedom from economic worry. With good concentration, idiosyncratic individuals often make skilled word processors, secretaries, baggage handlers, personal employees, work in which you can keep your mind to yourself while still performing. Idiosyncratic individuals often thrive as part-timers or temps, free of the pressures of performance evaluations and nine to five expectations. Consider freelance consulting work as well if you have a skill or talent you can market. Clients are often more tolerant of unusual personality styles as long as you can do the work and deliver it on time.

Zany Parents

Having idiosyncratic parents can be difficult. Children usually model themselves after their parents. At the same time, once they enter school, they tend to be conformers, needing the acceptance of their peers and a chance to do the "normal" thing. If a parent is highly unconventional and leading a lifestyle markably different from the parents of the other kids, the child may feel in conflict. He or she may begin to feel ashamed of the parent and guilty about harboring such "bad" feelings. And a highly idiosyncratic parent might pressure the child toward an unconventionality with which he or she is uncomfortable. Similarly, idiosyncratic parents often push their children to be more creative and expressive than they may be by nature.

The idiosyncratic parent needs to be sensitive to the child's own personality and tolerant of the real world in which the child must negotiate. He or she must be willing to bend a little for the sake of the child's world.

Ben's eleven-year old daughter, Ella, for example, told him recently that she wanted him to stop jogging. After his divorce from Ella's mother, on the two days a week that his daughter stayed with him, Ben liked to jog about five miles before he picked her up from her after-school activities. He'd arrive sweaty and smelly and Ella, it turned out, was embarrassed in front of her more "proper" friends. Ben launched into a little lecture about how she shouldn't let her friends' uptightness get to her, but he stopped himself in the middle of it. He looked at the child's sweet, unhappy face and said, sure, he'd go home and change first. Childhood is hard enough without dad trying to change all the rules, he realized. Now for the bright side. A mildly or moderately idiosyncratic parent may encourage creativity in a gifted child and provide a wide range of experiences for him or her. Most important, such parents may often teach their children to accept themselves and their individual uniqueness—a strength they can carry with them all their lives.

Tips on Dealing With the Idiosyncratic Person in Your Life

1. The idiosyncratic person is one of a kind. Accept, tolerate, and treasure this person for his or her uniqueness, not in spite of it. That is, do not assume that the idiosyncratic quirkiness is incidental to his or her personality. If you are looking for the "normal," conventional human being you think is lurking inside the idiosyncratic person, you will miss the point of who he or she really is.

2. Do not pressure the idiosyncratic person to conform to the real world and do not be pressured into conforming to his or her world either. Instead, recognize the ways in which your reality is different. Discuss the differences and prepare to compromise or to go your separate ways occasionally.

3. To widen your life together and to bring you closer, share the interests of the idiosyncratic person in your life. At least be willing to learn about his or her interest.

4. Help the idiosyncratic person to have more time for his or her spiritual or otherwise special interest. Most individuals with a moderate amount of this style are so bound up in conventional, real world responsibilities that they cannot indulge their special pursuits. As a result, they feel and act unhappy and unfulfilled.

5. To deal with a very idiosyncratic person, accept that you are the one who is more attached to conventional reality. Take charge of meeting the fundamental responsibilities of life. Many idiosyncratic individuals are "absent minded professors." They are so involved in their own inner world that they need to be reminded that it's time to pay the rent, buy the groceries, get the car serviced, buy new clothes for the kids, or turn off the light and go to sleep.

Making the Most of Your Idiosyncratic Style

You are interesting, original, spiritual, maybe highly creative and gifted. Because of your uniqueness, however, you may find that you pay a price in both your personal and professional relationships with others. You may not realize just how different you really are, so try the following exercises:

Exercise 1: Make a list of all the ways in which you differ in habits, beliefs, and feelings from the important people in your life. Your list might include for example: "I believe I have special spiritual gifts. My family believes that there's no such thing as special spiritual gifts." Or, "I think success in life can be sought only through spirit. I do not believe it is measurable in terms of money or possessions. My spouse, however, works hard for material possessions." Or, "I am an emotionally intense person. My spouse prefers to be more level headed."

Exercise 2: Look at your list and visualize a world in which everyone, including you, who is capable of accepting, tolerating, and living comfortably with all these differences in one another. Continue to go through your list and imagine yourself accepting each person's right to believe in whatever he or she pleases. Then imagine each person accepting you for all your differences and all of you living harmoniously.

Exercise 3: Make it easy on yourself, compromise. You can't always make your own rules and succeed in all important areas of life. For example: If your boss is a stickler for punctuality, make sure you get to work on time. If your spouse wants you to dress conventionally to attend a social event, do it to keep the peace.

Exercise 4: Very few people are like you, so to stay in touch with them, do something conventional. Pitch in with the dishes, help with the laundry, child care, household and garden chores, and so on. Give a conventional gift.

Exercise 5: Do something that someone else wants you to do. Your personality style is self-intense. You become consumed with your own desires, interests, and ideas. You may not realize that others do not share your enthusiasms. For example: While you may be excited about giving your mate an exotic gift you brought back from your travels, has it occurred to you that he or she might be happier with a bicycle, a comic book, a microwave, a pearl necklace, or something else from this person's own frame of reference. If you are in doubt about what others want for themselves, just ask.

If you suffer from social anxiety and terror around mainstream or more conventionally thinking people, refer to exercises one through five for the sensitive style.

Schizotypal Personality Disorder

Individuals who suffer from this very incapacitating personality disorder do not live in the same world as the rest of us. They experience little pleasure, they can't find a way to relate appropriately to other people, and they lose individual boundaries. The schizotypal personality disorder can be characterized by a pervasive pattern of social and interpersonal deficits marked by acute discomfort with and reduced capacity for close relationships as well by cognitive or perceptual distortions and eccentricities of behavior beginning by early adulthood and present in a variety of contexts as indicated by five or more of the following:

1. Ideas of reference [excluding delusions of reference]. For example: a belief that one is being talked about by others in the room.

2. Odd beliefs or magical thinking that influences behavior and is inconsistent with such cultural norms. For example: Suspiciousness, belief in clairvoyance, telepathy, or a sixth sense.

3. Unusual perceptual experiences including bodily illusions [for example: interpreting the feeling of a breeze on one's skin as being touched by someone.]

4. Odd thinking and speech. For example: vague, circumstantial, metaphorical, over elaborate or stereotype.

5. Suspiciousness or paranoid ideation.

6. Inappropriate or constricted affect.

7. Behavior or appearance that is odd, eccentric, or peculiar.

8. Lack of close friends or confidants other than first degree relatives.

9. Excessive social anxiety that does not diminish with familiarity and tends to be associated with paranoid fears rather than negative judgments about self.

Another World

The men and women who suffer from schizotypal personality disorder are estranged from the world of people, yet they are just as removed from a coherent, satisfying inner world. Outwardly, they are shy, aloof, withdrawn. They dress in a weird manner and they often appear disheveled. When they speak to you, they can't communicate effectively. They get lost in a tumble of irrelevancies and vague thoughts. They don't use or respond to the usual social gestures or cues such as smiling and nodding and their emotions are inappropriate to the situation. They just can't connect with other people. When they are faced with strangers, their anxiety may be extreme.

While they generally prefer to be alone, forming no close relationships, their inner life offers them little pleasure. A schizotypal person often feels disembodied, unreal, lost. These men and women need to believe that they have supernatural powers in order to give their impoverished, powerless, empty selves some meaning in this world. Thus, they often believe that they can predict the future, that if they eat some special substance, they will be immune to misfortune, that they can see, feel, and perhaps communicate with dead people, and that if they think of something, it will happen. Their special powers bring them a significance that is not always pleasant.

Schizotypal individuals often are certain that other people are aware of their dark inner feelings. That if they are angry, they will cause someone harm, unlike paranoid individuals, who believe other people are out to get them.

Coping With Schizotypal People

Schizotypal individuals maintain few or no relationships except possibly with family members. If you feel that someone in your family suffers from this disorder, encourage him or her to seek help. Try to avoid keeping these individuals dependent on you for everything. They can learn to take care of themselves. However, the transition can be stressful for everyone.

11

The Solitary Style

Solitary men and women need no one but themselves. They are unmoved by the maddening crowd as they are liberated from the drive to impress and to please. Solitary people are remarkably free of the emotional involvements that distract so many others. What they may give up in terms of sentiment and intimacy, however, they may gain in clarity of vision. Left to their own devices, solitary anthropologists, naturalists, mathematicians, physical scientists, film makers, writers, and poets can uncover the record of the facts of our existence to which our passions so often blind us.

The Six Characteristics

The following six traits and behaviors are clues to the presence of the solitary style. A person who reveals a strong solitary tendency will demonstrate more of these behaviors more intensely than someone with less of this style in his or her personality.

1. Solitude. Individuals with the solitary personality style have little need of companionship and are most comfortable alone.

2. Independence. They are self-contained and do not require interaction with others in order to enjoy their experiences or to get on in life.

3. Sangfroid. Solitary men and women are even tempered, calm, unsentimental, and unflappable.

4. Stoicism. They display an apparent indifference to pain and pleasure.

5. Sexual composure. They are not driven by sexual needs. They enjoy sex, but will not suffer in its absence.

6. Feet on the ground. They are unswayed by either praise or criticism and can confidently come to terms with their own behavior.

The Six Domains of
Solitary Functioning

The self and the emotions are key domains to the solitary personality style. For moderately solitary people with mixed personality patterns, each of these two domains may exert a more powerful influence. For clearly solitary patterns, self and emotions will merge to shape the solitary character.

Self—the Inner Sanctum

Solitary individuals are self contained. They are their own truest, most trusted companions providing the most important resources they need. They require no one else to guide them, to admire them, to provide emotional sustenance, to entertain them, or to share their experiences. Although they may marry or otherwise become involved with others, at heart, they remain separate and they find their greatest comfort, reassurance, and freedom alone with themselves. Their desire for solitude is not an apparent reaction or an avoidance. Sensitive people, for example, often avoid others because they just cannot be themselves around them. Some idiosyncratic types remove themselves from society because they cannot conform to conventional rules of behavior. Solitary types, however, simply prefer their own company. They like to be alone. Certainly they need no one to buttress their self-esteem or to rescue them from boredom. They can be remarkably free from loneliness.

Solitary Virginia cannot figure out why so many people seem incapable of doing things alone. Her young associate, Sally, invited her to go to a play. Virginia had already seen it. Sally was upset because she had phoned almost everyone she knew and she still couldn't find anyone to go with. Virginia asked, "Why don't you go by yourself?" Sally replied, "I just couldn't enjoy myself if I went alone." Virginia thought Sally was being ridiculous. What did anyone else have to do with her enjoyment of a play? If she needed to share the experience, why couldn't Sally just call someone up and tell him or her about it afterward? Sally gave up trying to explain. "Virginia, you just don't get it," she said.

Emotions—the Language of Dispassion

Virginia's personality is strongly dominated by the solitary style. She had never understood people who always have to have someone else around them. She met twenty-two year old, dramatic/sensitive Sally in Vietnam. They were on the same university sponsored travel tour. Sally, a graduate student in drama, joined the tour because she wanted to see that part of the world, but didn't want to travel alone. Virginia, fifty-three, a professor of botany, joined it only because she had limited time and was unable to make arrangements to get all the destinations on the tour's Southeast Asian itinerary by herself as she would have preferred.

On the tour, she kept to herself. At their destinations, she would walk off to explore on her own while the others clustered around the tour guide. At meals, she was friendly and responsive if seated with the group, but she was just as happy to dine alone. Sally frequently sought out the older woman and began to trail after her when they were sight seeing. She was fascinated with Virginia who knew so much and could look out over a seemingly barren site and point out details that chatty, emotional Sally would never have noticed. "Don't you just love this place," Sally once exclaimed when they arrived at a picturesque village. Virginia responded by pointing out to Sally how poor the village was. She drew the younger woman's attention to the tumbled down houses and the tattered clothes of some of the children. This time Sally seemed annoyed by the older woman's dry observations. "Sometimes, you're a real downer," she said, laughing uneasily. "Don't you have any romance in you at all?" Virginia looked at Sally physically rather like the way Star Trek's half human, half Vulcan Mr. Spock regarded Dr. McCoy when McCoy criticized Spock's lack of emotionality and sentimentality. The alien first officer on the Star Ship Enterprise, like others from the Planet Vulcan was all reason, no heart, or hardly any since he did have one earthling parent. Spock was an extraordinarily pure scientist and consummate observer. You could count on him never to be distracted by his feelings.

Virginia and her solitary style mates are not unlike such half Vulcans. They do not experience emotions as intensely as do most others on this planet. They are not feelers. Emotionally like Spock, they are imperturbable. Strongly solitary individuals, Virginia among them, have little emotional need of intimacy. Moderately solitary people, though, may feel frustrated by their inability to connect with anyone on a deep, feeling level.

But solitary people are not necessarily unhappy as long as others do not demand more of them than they can give. People often push solitary types to reveal themselves and express their feelings, trying to get a rise out of them as if they are keeping their feelings hidden and not sharing what is actually there. But for many solitary people who have no compensating emotional styles, their repertoire of emotions may truly be small. They do not speak the language of emotions, which is hard for many of us to comprehend.

Self-Control—Too Much of a Good Thing

It's hard to tempt a solitary person to over indulge his or her visceral appetites. Impulses, hungers, and delight in the pleasures of the flesh are all driven by spontaneous emotion, which is not this style's strong suit. Unless these individuals have a competing streak of an impulsive or pleasure seeking style in their personalities, or unless they experiment with dependency producing recreational drugs to help them relate or to intensify their emotional experience, they will be protected by their very nature from excessives of human passion.

They may also rediscover within themselves a stoic disregard of pain as well as passion. Virginia seemed to have an exceptional gift in this regard. More than 30 years ago when she was a graduate student, she took a bad fall on a rocky peak. For months afterward, the back pain was so debilitating that she could hardly turn or move. The doctors told her to abandon her hope for an active career. "Never," she told them. On her own, Virginia determined to get up and get on with it. Despite her agony, against doctors' orders, she began to get up and walk. Each time the pain attacked, by force of will, she began to ignore it. Eventually it receded and finally disappeared. She was back to her studies within two months of her decision to take control of her experience.

Relationships—Take Them or Leave Them

Without other directed personality styles to offset the solitary tendency, the individual will be more or less indifferent to the emotional ties that bind others together. Extremely solitary types will not be likely to pair up or involve themselves intensely with others, even friends. While they may have a rather detached interest in people, they will not naturally be responsive to many of them or wish to draw them intimately close. It is not that solitary people don't like people. They are not hostile or angry at anyone. They may enjoy the company of others in many of their activities. Some, those with a mixed personality pattern, may even marry. But in their relationships, they need much time to themselves and there will always be a wall of greater or lesser thickness between them and the people around them.

Stress

Even moderately solitary people may not intuitively comprehend others' feelings or respond to their emotional cues. "You don't love me!"is a common lament of partners of solitary people. This may be true as defined in the emotional language that most people speak. The more the partner pushes for emotional reactions and a depth of intimate feeling, the greater will be the stress on the solitary partner. To cope, the solitary person will retreat.

A solitary person who has other directive styles and a mixed personality pattern may feel frustrated and in conflict in his or her relationships. On one hand, he or she will be motivated toward people. On the other hand, the solitary person's need to protect solitude may be so strong as to prevent any deeply intimate relationship.

Richard, a brilliant chemist, is a case in point. He has a mixed solitary, conscientious, dramatic personality pattern. Forty-two years old, he has not been married nor has he lived with anyone for long, but he has dated a great many women. He has rarely gone without a companion. Typically, he sees the woman of the moment one, two, three times a week, meeting her late at night and staying over at her place, his apartment being off limits. The relationship can go on for many months with no increase in intensity. Richard becomes quite comfortable, but the woman starts expecting the relationship to grow. She begins to pressure him to spend more time with her and to tell her he loves her, to live together, to commit. At this point, Richard invariably realizes he'd rather be home by himself. The woman in question becomes hurt and outraged that Richard is withholding something from her, deliberately stringing her along, using her for his own purposes. But in fact, Richard is doing the best he can. "I mean it would be different if I loved her," he said recently to a friend as he was telling him about Joanne, the latest woman, who had thrown him out of her apartment. He has always clung to the notion that someday he would meet a woman whom he would love, a feeling he's never, in reality, experienced. He has always believed that when he met the woman he loved, then he would know what love was, they would marry, and have children. Richard's always hoped for a family. But now that he's crossed the forty barrier, it occasionally occurs to him that life may not afford him this opportunity. He feels stymied and sometimes depressed that he may never meet a woman whom he will love.

On the other hand, he's just met another woman, Sandy, and has begun his usual pattern with her. He will be comfortable as always until she begins to demand more from him than he can give. Maybe he will luck out this time though and find that Sandy wants no more of him than he wants of her. Then, possibly their relationship could go on indeterminately a few hours a day, two, three, four, even seven days a week. If he really wanted to change, Richard could probably change. But Richard likes his life and himself and he figures it's okay if things don't work out the way he has always dreamed that they would.

To the extent that society says a deeply committed, emotional relationship with one person is important, Richard is unequipped or maladapted. But our culture gives mixed messages. It's good to build a marriage and it's okay to be single. Richard lives in Chicago where single people of all ages abound. He has companionship when he wants it and he has numerous hobbies and interests and can entertain himself alone better than most people can. He buys single tickets to the movies or to the opera. He eats out alone, quite contentedly. He can and does find many rewards in his life.

Some predominately solitary people may commit to marriage because of family pressure, because they think they should, especially if they are women because of practical necessity. Although it may not prove easy for these individuals to feel emotionally connected to their mates, they may grow attached to their marital responsibilities and roles. As long as no one expects fire works from them or a social network outside the family, these nonemotional, non-sentimental, non-romantic individuals can survive in a marital union.

The Solitary Parent

The birth of a child is one of those extraordinary life experiences that can trigger the solitary person's unrealized genetic potential, especially for the mother once the bonding occurs, love comes, and she is forever changed. Without pairing up, of course, the solitary individual is not likely to have this experience. Moreover, many solitary individuals are not interested in having children. However, solitary individuals who do become parents discover a path to emotional experience and "togetherness" that they never perceived before. Not that they will cast off their lifetime personality patterns and be "reborn." They will continue to experience at least some difficulty in meeting and responding to some or many of the child's emotional needs. The other parent may be able to fill in what's missing. In any case, solitary individuals in their usual autonomous competence, will be reliable and be able to meet at least the nonemotional needs of their families.

Work—Going It Alone

Solitary types can function very well in the work domain. They get down to work, concentrate, don't waste time with personal calls or concerns, and are not easily bored. Characteristically self contained, they do not require a lot of feedback and can take criticism. The setting is the crucial factor for their performance, however. Extremely solitary individuals are not team players and do not relate well to the public. It's not that they are uncooperative. Rather, they can be clumsy and impatient with the give and take necessary to maintain most types of relationships. They tend not to be sensitive, diplomatic, or responsive to indirect and subtle forms of communication. They have little patience with office politics.

As leaders, they tend not to understand their direct reports' personalities and they usually cannot handle personnel problems. It is unusual for a solitary personality type to be an effective leader. Not only is it unusual for a solitary personality style person to be an effective leader, it is unusual for them to assume any leadership role whatsoever. But when left alone to their work, and this goes for leisure time activities as well, they can put their mind to it without distraction. They can fix a car, write poetry, deliver mail, design a bridge, or study for an exam with equanimity. Their previously mentioned ability to observe and collect information serves them well in many undertakings. And they can be sent far away to do their work, to repair an off shore oil rig, to man a remote light house, to watch for fires deep in the forest, to dig in the desert for ancient artifacts, all without feeling lonely, bored, or isolated. Or, they can retreat from society and work productively without much thought for recognition.

The poet, Emily Dickinson, was a great literary recluse who may have had some of this style in her personality. She withdrew into her Amherst, Massachusetts, home before she was thirty, [She lived from 1830 to 1886.] began to dress only in white, and eventually she never ventured out. She wrote well over a thousand poems, only a handful of which were published during her lifetime. It is said that "She became exhausted by emotional contact with others." Her mode of existence, although circumscribed, was evidently satisfying, even essential, to her.

Solitary Careers

Unless you also have other directed styles, such as the dramatic, in your pattern, steer clear of careers that involve you deeply with people to whom you must be responsive. You may be brilliant at your work, but success may be elusive because you do not deal comfortably or naturally within the political framework. Do not hesitate to remove yourself from that fray.

Reroute yourself toward autonomy, working from your own office, laboratory, or home. You may be able to work with clients who seek no more from you than the service you provide as an accountant, for instance. Freelance careers may also work for your style. Your ability to concentrate on solitude and to be completely comfortable in your inner sanctum may be a boon to you throughout your working life in creative, scientific exploration, in research, in technological and mechanical work, and security work in which you are paid to watch and to wait.

Be aware that the more you wish to take on in your career, the greater the number of people with whom you may have to be involved. It is that intense involvement with people that may well be the weakest link in your otherwise substantive personality style.

Real World—Privacy Please

The solitary individual like Star Trek's Mr. Spock, in a way has been transported away from his or her home planet. In their ideal solitary world, there are very few people and they go about their business without bothering one another. But the real world is arguably over populated with intrusive aliens who spend the majority of their time impeding each other's progress. The solitary folks do the best they can to create little pockets of solitude around themselves and try to spend as much time in them as they can.

Tips on Dealing With the Solitary Person in Your Life

1. Let this person be. The most common mistake people make in dealing with solitary types is trying to push them to be like everybody else. But solitary individuals are who they are. They may not mix much in the real world or react deeply to you. But they are competent and responsible and their inner worlds can be very interesting.

2. Do not assume that the solitary person is uncomfortable or unhappy because he or she is alone. For many solitary individuals, a life filled with people is hell. Indeed, they may pity you for your social and emotional needs.

3. Do not assume that the solitary person in your life is uncomfortable with you because he or she prefers to spend much time outside your presence or just sitting quietly instead of interacting with you. This person will be quite comfortable with you if you don't try to engage him or her, insist on filling up the silence with chatter, or try to smother the solitary person with togetherness.

4. Look for signs of caring that are different from the standard "I want you, I need you, I love you's." The fact that this person is in your life at all says a lot about his or her attachment to you considering that solitary individuals can do well without other people.

5. Ensure this person plenty of time to be alone. Anyone with even a small amount of solitary style requires time to him or herself to feel sane, well adjusted, and productive. Try not to consider a solitary person's private time your enemy. But if it is at variance with your own strong social and emotional needs, be honest with yourself and admit that this relationship isn't likely to work out.

6. Take up hobbies or find activities to occupy yourself while the solitary person is off on his or her own.

7. When you need to work out a problem with a nonemotional solitary person, appeal to logic instead of emotion. A solitary person may have a good head on his or her shoulders—speak to it.

Making the Most of Your Solitary Style

In your ability to entertain yourself and be comfortable alone, you have no peers. You may want to improve your relationships with people, however, if only to be able to go about your self-determined business more easily. You will need first to collect information about other people and then to learn to speak their language.

Exercise 1: Observe emotions. Watch how people express their feelings in their interactions with you and with one another. Look first for obvious emotions such as joy and misery. After you get good at spotting those, look for the more subtle, delicate expressions of feeling. Accept that feelings are very important to most people and that they are injured very easily.

Exercise 2: Search for your own feelings. In your comfortable privacy, stand in front of a mirror or sit with paper and pencil and search for what you feel at that moment. If you are at a loss for an emotion, think about what you felt the last time you had difficulty with someone. For example: if a companion pressured you to spend more time with him or her or a colleague gave you a hard time at work, did you feel frustrated? Angry? Sad? Hurt? Misunderstood? Annoyed?

Exercise 3: Practice endurance. Instead of retreating when you feel pressured by people, tolerate your discomfort a little longer. If you are in the city and want to escape to the country, just hang in there for one day longer. If you are with a companion and you want to be by yourself, wait another hour. If you are in a meeting and you just want to go off and do your own thing, stay until the meeting breaks. Be your stoic self and say to yourself, "I can handle this discomfort." The point of this exercise is not to make you do things you don't want to do, but to extend your flexibility and give you more freedom of choice.

Exercise 4: Negotiate with others to find a way for you to do things your way without affecting the cooperative effort. For example: make a deal with your spouse that Saturday is your day for yourself, but Sunday is for family. Try telling your boss that you don't function well in meetings and if he or she will excuse you, you'll contribute extra in some other way. That might not work, but it can't hurt to try. Keep in mind that the boss may not be able to grant you such flexibility because it is not in the best interest of the whole team.

Exercise 5: Talk about it. Don't expect other people automatically to understand you and don't expect yourself automatically to understand other people. Others may assume from your solitary behavior that you do not care for them or do not wish to cooperate. Tell them that your need to be alone has nothing to do with them. If you run into difficulty with others in your work, say frankly that you are used to working on your own. If others are not straight forward with you and seem to be sending emotional messages instead, ask them to explain what's on their minds. It will accelerate your ability to understand where other people are coming from.

Exercise 6: Learn to say things that please other people. Learn to be diplomatic. Even though you may be immune to compliments or praise, many people need to hear them. Tell whoever cooked dinner that it tastes good even if you are not used to expressing yourself in this manner. Tell your spouse that you care even if you don't customarily say it.

Exercise 7: Remove the blinders. If time after time, you refuse commitment because you think the right person hasn't come along, realize that your solitary personality style may have something to do with why you can't find happiness with another person. Think about how much you hold yourself back from other people. Consider getting a little more involved and being a little more open with the people you are interested in having a relationship with.

Schizoid Personality Disorder

The emotionally and often physically schizoid individuals are cut off from people. Neither happy or sad, they are careful to build lives that protect them from all human intimacy. The schizoid personality disorder can best be described as a pervasive pattern of detachment from social relationships and a restricted range of emotions in interpersonal settings beginning by early adulthood and present in a variety of contexts as indicated by four or more of the following:

1. Neither desires or enjoys close relationships including being part of a family.

2. Almost always chooses solitary activities.

3. Has little, if any, interest in having sexual experiences with another person.

4. Takes pleasure in few if any activities.

5. Lacks close friends or confidantes other than first degree relatives.

6. Appears indifferent to praise and criticism of others.

7. Shows emotional coldness, detachment, or flattened affectivity.

The Walled City

To others, individuals with schizoid personality disorder are impenetrable. They reside in a "walled city" deep inside themselves far away from other people. They're not anti-social, they're asocial. They want nothing to do with you. Even those mildly schizoid men and women who, on the surface, seem somewhat sociable, prove flat, empty, passive, unresponsive, or just indifferent when you try to get to know them.

Some mildly schizoid individuals may gravitate toward religious cults in which relationships among members are highly structured. There they can carry on the semblance of interpersonal relationships while managing to avoid close contact. More detached schizoid men and women may choose to live their entire adult lives alone in one room with no contact with friends or even family. Every day, they go to and from work where they can be very productive if left to work in isolation without sharing a warm moment with anyone except perhaps a pet. Or, they may live on the street.

A study of personality disorders among the homeless population in Baltimore, for example, showed a substantial prevalence of schizoid and paranoid personality disorders. Schizoid people are not without an inner life, however. Inside the "walled city" where no other person is admitted, they can have rich interests and fantasies, but almost no feelings.

Inwardly and outwardly, schizoid people are emotionally unmovable—no frills, no chills, no happiness nor unhappiness, no anger, no joy.

Coping With Schizoid People

Anyone, [including a professional counselor, a friend, or a helping family member] who can reach out in an accepting, friendly, respectful, and utterly non-intrusive manner to a schizoid individual can help improve his or her quality of life. Don't be put off by these people's apparent indifference to you and your feelings. And don't force them to interact with you. Show your friendship and interest and maintain a respectful distance. Some of the earlier tips on dealing with solitary people may also prove helpful.

12

The Mercurial Style

L ife is a roller coaster with a mercurial personality style and they will insist that you come along for the ride. From the peaks to the valleys, intensity fills their every breath. Mercurial women and men yearn for experience and they jump into a new job or lifestyle with both feet without even a glance backward. No other style, the dramatic included, is so ardent in its desire to connect with life and with other people. And no other style is quite so capable of enduring the changes in emotional weather that such a fervently lived life brings.

The Seven Characteristics

The following seven traits and behaviors are clues to the presence of the mercurial style. A person who reveals a strong mercurial tendency will demonstrate more of these behaviors more intensely than someone with less of this style in his or her personality.

1. Romantic attachment. Mercurial individuals must always be deeply involved in a romantic relationship with one person.

2. Intensity. They experience a passionate, focused attachment in all their relationships. Nothing that goes on between them and another person is trivial. Nothing is taken lightly.

3. Heart. They show what they feel. They are emotionally active and reactive. Mercurial types put their hearts into everything.

4. Unconstraint. They are uninhibited, spontaneous, fun-loving, and undaunted by risk.

5. Activity. Energy marks the mercurial style. These individuals are lively, creative, busy, and engaging. They show initiative and can stir others to activity.

6. Open mind. They are imaginative and curious, willing to experience and experiment with other cultures, roles, value systems, and to follow new paths.

7. Alternate stakes. People with mercurial style are skilled at distancing or distracting themselves from reality when it is painful or harsh.

The Six Domains of Mercurial Functioning

Take the relationship domain, add emotions and self-control, and you have the recipe for this tempestuous personality style.

Relationships—to Possess and be Possessed

Adam, a music critic, met Tabitha at a reception following her famous brother's cello recital. Speaking to her for less than ten minutes, this predominately mercurial and dramatic man told her he knew that they were meant to be involved in each other's lives. "I will fall in love with you," declared the tall, tuxedoed, well-spoken, middle-aged gentleman. Tabitha, a thirty-one year old music teacher and sometimes performer could only blush. The elegant man was coming on to her so strongly. Ordinarily, she would have made her polite excuses and moved on. But he seemed so genuine.

Uncharacteristically, this normally reticent woman took him at his word and gave him her telephone number at his request. Notwithstanding his cutting review of her brother's performance, Adam phoned Tabitha the next day. He had to attend an opera that evening and asked if she would grace him with her presence? Tabitha had other plans, but at Adam's urging, she agreed to go with him. Never previously married or even deeply involved with anyone, the sober woman had never experienced such attention. Adam was intense, emotional, insistent. He would not allow her to be slow, cautious, quiet, restrained. "This is meant to be," he continued to tell her. And although in the back of her mind, a voice said, "slow down," she loved being with this intensely romantic, changeable man. "You are the world to me," he would tell her.

Even after their love affair was over and his passion and fury were spent, and years after Adam had died, Tabitha knew that during the time they had been together, she really had been his entire world.

It's In the Stars

Mercurial individuals like Adam, are never casual about the people they care for. As between Adam and Tabitha, they immediately feel a magnetic involvement and a powerful sense that the relationship is destined. The relationship then becomes the center of their lives, the heart of their beings, and they pursue it with an intensity unlike any of the other personality styles.

A love affair, even a friendship with a mercurial individual is unforgettable. These individuals put their mates, friends, even colleagues on pedestals. They worship their perfection, they think the heavens are blessing them with such a person. They must talk to the other person every day, sometimes several times a day. They must know everything the other person thinks, does, and feels. They must fill themselves up with the other person. And if the other person resists, dark clouds gather. Mercurial feelings of hurt and fury mount as we will see later.

Adam drew Tabitha closer than anyone had ever before desired her to be. "We breathed life into each other," she says now with shy embarrassment about the early days of their relationship. He had to have her with him everywhere at every concert, at every meal, to visit friends, to shop for groceries. He introduced her to his vast circle of friends and insisted that they welcome her with open arms. He wanted to attend her music classes. He insisted on hearing her play her violin. He suggested new music to her. He urged her to perform at his weekly music salon, and he introduced her to new experiences at every opportunity.

Tabitha's famous brother disapproved. He thought Adam was arrogant, grandiose, and a poor judge of musical performance. The cellist believed that Adam's feelings for a performer got the better of his judgment of the performance. It was true that on occasion, Adam would be so taken with a performer that he would hear nothing short of perfection. Whereas, the audience and other critics might hear an off-register note, sloppy technique, or an ineffectual interpretation. Similarly, he could get a bad feeling about a performer [and, perhaps Tabitha's brother was among these,] and pan a performance that others considered accomplished.

While Adam was not the most universally respected music critic, and though he was rather poor at the business details of his life, he had a wide audience who enjoyed his critiques on music and musicians. On the radio program he hosted for nearly a decade, he was considered fascinating, out-spoken, controversial, and invariably interesting.

Giving All

Adam could be difficult, agreed virtually everyone of the hundreds of people who attended his funeral. But once he reached out and pulled you forcibly into his life, you were forever changed by his love. Despite his shifting moods, his incessant demands, and the ease with which he became disappointed in people, he created for himself a permanent place in the hearts of many throughout the world he lived in. One conductor known widely throughout Europe eulogized that one of Adam's greatest gifts was his encouragement and backing of talented, gifted, young musicians.

Many musicians who now have careers in classical and even popular music credit their success to Adam's ability to urge them to greater heights, to recommend them to gifted teachers, and to put in good reviews for them. There was nothing Adam would not do for the people he cared for. In his mercurial way, Adam was open to anyone. If someone struck him as belonging in his life, he did everything in his power to bring that person in. He could be sharply critical and unforgiving if the individual was not interested in being his friend and he would fight to hang on to someone he felt was slipping away from him.

A month after the emotional end of their year-long relationship, Tabitha retreated to her tiny mountain cabin, 150 miles away. The next day, she heard a car drive up and there was Adam with his three cats, his typewriter, suitcase full of cassettes, and a huge wicker basket filled with cheese, sausages, breads, smoked fish, and bottles of wine. Indulging his dramatic theatricality, he threw himself on her couch, sighed, and said, "It is simply that I cannot live without you." He said he had driven up only for the day, but he stayed the week. He cooked for her, tended her garden, read to her, filled the cabin with recorded music, and sipped wine. "All I ask of you is that you play for me," he would plead. Each time she played, Adam wept. Then, on the seventh day, he heatedly took issue with her interpretation of a sonata. His irritation grew to intense anger at her. "I don't want you, Tabitha," he shouted. He cast her a look of pure hatred and walked out.

Stay Close

Tabitha had loved Adam deeply, still she had been the one to end the relationship. It all just got too much for her. She had wanted to settle into a quieter, calmer life with Adam once the infatuation began to subside, into a more abiding love, but that wasn't Adam's style. His ceaseless activity, his pushing, his intensity, and not least, his changeable feelings began to drain her. For all his enthusiasm, Adam, like most mercurial people, was a brooder. He would go through more moods in a day than Tabitha would in a month. Tabitha was mature enough to allow him his moods, but they all seemed to involve her. If she was quiet and thoughtful, Adam would worry that she was withdrawing from him. If she played particularly well, Adam would be in ecstasy. If she played badly, he would snap at her as if she were a child who hadn't practiced her lessons. He seemed always to be watching her. She couldn't escape his eyes.

Adam needed to be involved in everything Tabitha felt and vice versa. If one day he felt that there was no meaning in his life, he insisted that she cling so closely to him that she experienced what he was experiencing. Many times, she tried to explain to him that she was a separate human being, with individual feelings, and if he didn't always pull so very close, she would not need to establish a distance from him. She had never experienced such ardent moments as when she and he truly connected with each other. But she found she could not sustain that intensity as a way of life.

Tabitha began to feel pulled in two directions—toward the man she most assuredly loved and admired and toward her own independent identity. Increasingly, Tabitha needed time away from Adam to marshal her inner resources for her teaching and for her own performances. Needless to say, Adam took her need for emotional distance badly. He became angry, critical, convinced that she was letting him down. Here he had given her his whole world, and she could only think of herself. "Tabitha, my Tabitha," he would sigh sadly, "you and I are among the very few people in this world who understand what life really is. It is music, it is love, it is knowledge, it is, after all, you and me. Why am I not the world for you? Why do you break my heart? What have I done to you that is so terrible? I love you."

Tabitha could not make him understand that she wasn't like him, that she had needs that have nothing to do with him, but that she still loved him. She could not get through to Adam that he demanded more than a "regular" person like herself could consistently give. "Don't put yourself down," he would insist. "You are a superior being, capable of more than you think." It caused her unbearable pain to end the most passionate and beautiful experience of her life, but emotionally Tabitha could not endure it any longer. Even as she broke off with him, she knew no one would ever give her the kind of love Adam had, that she would probably never care for anyone as much as she still cared for him.

Indeed, no one but a mercurial individual, like Adam, is quite so focused on you, so endowed with attention, totally filled up with you, and so generous. Adam gave Tabitha his entire being and he did it without a single reservation.

More

In an individual with a moderate amount of mercurial style among a balanced pattern, this focused attentiveness and generosity can contribute to a powerful, romantic, lasting love, the kind that songs are written about. However, Adam's personality was powerfully dominated by both the mercurial and the dramatic styles. Each of them, emotionally unrestrained and intensely needy. If this pattern had been balanced by more of the stop and think style such as the conscientious, he might have been more inclined to give Tabitha some breathing space and plan for a longer, more mutually fulfilling life together. But like other mercurial individuals, Adam's needs and expectations of others were enormous. His reactions to them, strong and immediate. He needed from others exactly what he gave to them—constant, intense passion and attention. But very few of his friends, although they loved him dearly, were able to give him back the intensity of emotion he required. Again, in mercurial fashion, he sometimes manipulated his friends and lovers to give him more. He would berate friends for not telephoning or visiting enough when he was ill, making them think that their occasional lapses had made his condition worse. One close friend, Eric, became angry at Adam for making him feel guilty. "You know Adam, if you needed me, you could call and ask me to come over. I never hear from you, yet you expect me always to know what you want." Adam was hurt by Eric's remarks and felt he did not deserve them. Mercurial individuals are not, as a rule, skilled at patching things up with other people. They tend to feel that they are the ones who give most and they have trouble recognizing the ways in which they contribute to difficulties within their relationships. If a relationship ends badly, mercurial individuals will often look back at their whole time together as dark and terrible. They may conclude that the other person was unworthy of them and that they themselves had been blind to this ultimate reality.

Stress

Relationship problems are the greatest sources of stress for mercurial individuals. Trouble comes when they feel they are not being recognized and treated as special. Like self-confident people, mercurial types feel entitled to more and when they don't get it or when the other person tries to establish distance, they feel threatened. They react to such stresses very intensely, of course. Often they'll throw themselves into a powerful, passionate experience to distract themselves from the abyss that is widening before them. Or, they'll step back and act as if it isn't happening, which can seem a little strange. But unless the stress itself diminishes, sooner or later, they'll react full force, often feeling that rejection is tantamount to the end of the world. If their outbursts of emotion fail to influence the other person, they cope by suddenly turning their backs on that person and becoming intensely involved with someone else. They hate being without love and they don't stay that way for long.

The Mercurial Versus the Dramatic

While in certain respects, the mercurial resembles the dramatic personality style in passion and feeling, and although the two styles often exist within the same personality, they differ in important ways. Dramatic men and women are outward directed. This means that they will be alert to you, to learn what you want in order to draw your love, and become the center of your attention. Dramatic men and women can be deeply sensitive and intuitive to the desires and needs of other people and they can orchestrate their own behavior to draw you to them. Mercurial individuals are much more intense and demanding. They are not content simply to dance in the light you shine on them, they need you to step in there with them. They want to fill up their whole world with you. They dream of being together with you as one throughout eternity. Their needs for such a relationship will dominate the picture. Generous and outgoing, they may be, mercurial individuals are less inclined to moderate their behavior for your sake or to adapt to anyone else's ways of looking at things.

The Mercurial Parent

Never stodgy, mercurial people can be wonderfully fun, entertaining, interesting, energetic, and involved parents when they are in the mood. As we will soon see, mercurial men and women have highly reactive moods and can be emotionally inconsistent in all their relationships. But they greatly enjoy the emotional intensity of parent/child relationships, especially in the child's earliest years. Dealing well with the child's emerging autonomy will be more difficult for them. Mercurial parents need to work hard to allow the youngster his or her independence and distance.

Also, as the child becomes contrary, they may need their spouse to help shore up their patience and forbearance. Since theirs is an impulsive style, they may also need some support in teaching their kids to control their own impulses and appetites. But a moderately mercurial parent can encourage emotional depth, generosity, creativity, courage, romance, and spirit in his or her offspring.

Emotions—Life in a Volcano

Emotions drive mercurial people and what moves them is what counts. Individuals with even moderate amounts of mercurial style experience all their emotions more intensely than do other people. They are all heart in that everything and everyone affects them on an emotional level. They laugh and they weep easily and openly. They can feel hot fury and ice cold rage and they experience profound excitement and passion encountering few inhibitions in this or any other emotional aspect of their lives.

Emotions drive even their thoughts. Listen to the strength of feeling with which a mercurial person possesses his or her convictions. Wishy-washy, they are not. Mercurial people let you know exactly where they stand. They are emotional reactors. They hold nothing back and they take nothing lightly, especially when it comes to other people.

As we noted earlier, relationships are the focus of the mercurial lives. All their relationships, from spouse to friends, to relatives, to co-workers, they react to everyone, finding emotional significance in everything another person says or does. As a result, they are easily flattered and pleased and they are just as easily devastated and disappointed. When you bring your lover a single red rose, you take him or her deep into your heart, but when you have nothing to offer or otherwise behave imperfectly, your romantic mercurial lover, who has so idealized you, becomes openly disappointed and deeply disillusioned with you.

A mercurial friend of Adam's, twenty-seven year old Marsha, an interior designer, told him how once she had fallen out of love with someone because he had worn an ugly tie. From then on, she felt a powerful revulsion to him. The tie had revealed something vulgar and tasteless about the man, she told Adam. "Yes," said Adam, "you are like me. We cannot settle for anything less than perfection."

Mercurial individuals idealize emotion. They seek perfect romantic love. They may find it too, but they cannot grasp it for long and perhaps no one can. For the idealized relationship exists only as long as no flaws, however minor, are seen. The strongly mercurial person prefers to remain infatuated in his or her personal relationship. Real human imperfections become a dreadful disappointment, and a calm, quiet life with a "regular" person spells boredom.

The Changing Tides of Feeling

Because their emotions are their primary source of experience and meaning, mercurial individuals who lack a solid anchor in the "head" style may be subject to rapid, sometimes unpredictable shifts in mood as they react to the unavoidable changes in their environments. Mercurial Terry, for example, went on a long awaited vacation to Puerto Rico with her husband, Jim. The first day, the weather was fabulous, the second and third day, it was stormy. Terry's mood crashed. She just couldn't help it, she told Jim. They had been looking forward so long to this vacation. Jim suggested they take their minds off the weather and try to have a good time anyway. Why not try some sightseeing? But unlike her part-conscientious husband, mercurial Terry could not reason with her emotions. She brooded and slept until the sun came out on the fourth day and the Puerto Rico of her dreams lay splendidly before her.

The greater the degree of the mercurial style in a person's pattern, the more frequent the mood shifts. With moderate mercurial style within a well-balanced pattern, a person may have a gift for experiencing the fullness of emotion. But as the style approaches borderline personality disorder, sufferers find that they lack a consistent emotional center. They can be hot for you one minute, cold to your approaches the next. Why the change? Like infants, they are at the mercy of their emotional reactions and like young children, they sometimes overreact to the most trivial incidents. They have no control over their emotional states and they suffer great torment as a result.

Self-Control—Acting on Impulse

Self-control is the last of the mercurial's three key domains. Appetites exert a huge force on the mercurial life. Propelled by their all-powerful emotions, mercurial men and women are hungry for and thoroughly responsive to pleasure, sensation, and experience, which also serve as all-encompassing distractions from hurt and pain that they may be unwilling to acknowledge. They are curious and interested. They love to taste and experiment. They are alive to the moment and they find it difficult to pass up any spontaneous gratification.

These men and women are intensely motivated to have a good time and experience new things. They will try anything. They are unafraid of risks and will head down a dark alley in a strange city while out partying with new friends without stopping to think what danger may lurk in the shadows. Often, they drive like demons and feast on food without a single thought about calories or cholesterol. When Tabitha and Adam traveled one summer, she never tired of commenting on the unhealthy way he indulged his appetite—the fat, the pastry, the size of the helpings, and she made sure to do all the driving after he passed a truck in a no-passing zone and nearly collided with a bus in the oncoming lane. Tabitha envied Adam's ability to act on his urges. She was a more plodding, planning type person. Alone, she had a hard time just dropping everything and indulging a whim. However, while she could learn to loosen up, Adam would not or could not be taught to stop and think.

Mercurial individuals are similar to dramatic and especially adventurous people in their reluctance to think things out and to plan for the future. Their skill is in living right now. Although he was relatively successful as a critic, Adam's business life was in shambles. His office was disorganized with paper strewn around his desk or heaped on the floor. Adam pleaded with Tabitha to help him straighten out his office, but as soon as she got started, he confessed that he preferred the chaos. He had not a cent in savings. He spent his money as soon as he had it, often on gifts for others. When he became ill, his friends and family paid for his care. For predominately mercurial types, their impulsiveness may reach the level of reckless self-indulgence and their distaste for goal-directed planning and their tendency to "go for it," instead of waiting for a more opportune time, may lead them to self-destruct, despite their talents and abilities. For even moderately mercurial people, the appetites are a strong force requiring continual conscious control. Many will have a hard time passing up the dessert tray, will have trouble moderating drug and alcohol use, or will find themselves repeatedly getting carried away with their credit cards. Many people are lucky enough to have mixtures of the mercurial and the nose to the grindstone common sense styles [including the conscientious, the leisurely, the vigilant, the self-confident, and the sensitive] which will keep them from venturing too far afield. A mate with these styles can also help to anchor the mercurial person.

Self and Real World
Fluid Identities

Their willingness to try anything affects even the self domain. Mercurial types tend to be extremely open minded and curious about other ways of being. Their sense of who they are rarely is concretely fixed to any particular identity or life style and sometimes not even to a culture.

Mercurial men and women have a talent for moving into new lifestyles and fitting right in. Whereas others with different personality styles seem out of place and uncomfortable.

I'm Not Exactly Sure Who I Am

The mercurial sense of self may also mean that the individual is not absolutely certain of his or her own identity. As a result, one mercurial person may have a hard time figuring out what to do in life, whereas another may feel somewhat empty inside. Some exceedingly mercurial people may resort to "borrowing" an identity—"I think I'll be like my sister," "I think I'll join a cult," as a way of achieving some self-certainty. In any case, the self or selves of the mercurial individual is likely to be painted in strongly contrasting colors. Mercurial people may be changeable, but they always stand out. To them, the real world is intense and powerful, often chaotic, often rather dark. This is a fire and ice type of personality style, inside and out.

Work

At work, mercurial types can be bright, outgoing, enthusiastic, energetic, original, and creative. Characteristically, they become intensely involved with their co-workers and take personally everything that happens in their work relationships. They can be passionately interested and involved in office intrigues. They often put their bosses on pedestals and expect them to behave with perfect judgment and compassion, which of course, can lead to disappointment. If the boss manages to maintain this ideal image, the mercurial individual will work extremely hard to make a good impression. But he or she will need to be recognized and rewarded for being so hard working for the "special" relationship with the boss is much of the motivation. Mercurial types will not become selfless drones. If all their intense efforts go unnoticed, or the boss acts as if the employee is just one among equals, the mercurial individual quickly loses interest in working so hard. Mercurial types rise to the occasion when they are admired, needed, depended upon, and idealized.

Mercurial men and women are as demanding at work as in the other areas of their lives, but their insistence on being treated well can serve them in this domain. Their sense of entitlement keeps them from being ill used and underpaid. Extreme mercurial people may have some trouble being realistic about entitlement though, and may insist on seeing themselves as more important to their employers than they really are. Some will also find that their tendency to react with strong emotion at work interferes with the progress of their careers.

In creative fields, however, this so-called creative temperament usually will not be a hindrance. Employers often expect creative people to be "difficult."

The Mercurial Leader

The mercurial personality style does not carry with it a gift for leadership, largely because mercurial types are loath to establish the necessary detachment from direct reports. They like to become intensely involved and they end up, as always, idealizing relationships. They expect extraordinary personal dedication and performance from those who work for them. When the direct reports do not meet these expectations, mercurial leaders tend to feel personally let down. They are moody and emotional, they often split those around them into an in-group and an out-group, although affiliation among the favored few is never guaranteed for long. Moreover, like dramatic leaders, they haven't much ability in planning, in dealing with money, or in organization. A bit of the mercurial style, however, may well aid a leader in inspiring reports to give their all. Mercurial individuals are sometimes capable of brilliant ideas and with a solidly conscientious, non-competitive second in command, such semi-mercurial leaders may be able both to fire up the spirit in the office and to make sure that the work gets done.

Careers for the Mercurial

To be happy and productive in your work life, you need a career preferably in a creative field where your emotive ability can work for you. You have good critical skills and enjoy sitting in judgment. Consider becoming a critic. You must always be involved with others in your work, steer clear of solitary, technical detail, and/or number related work, or work that requires rigorous, cerebral perseverance. You will need the discipline of a structured work setting in solo or independent work. You will have a tendency to lose focus or to get sidetracked by your personal whims. Consider acting professionally or simply as a hobby, which is natural for many mercurial individuals.

Tips on Dealing With the Mercurial Person in Your Life

1. Step up on your pedestal. The mercurial person wants and needs to idealize and overvalue you. Enjoy his or her admiration of the best, noblest, and most romantic aspects of your character. Let your relationship with this person bring out the best in you. It is inevitable that you will fall from grace by being human and fallible which will deeply disappoint the mercurial person in your life. Restore your image by going out of your way to do something extraordinarily loving, notable, or generous.

2. Step down from your pedestal. You may need to remind the mercurial person and yourself rather regularly that although you appreciate his or her feelings and expectations, you are, after all, a mere mortal. Ask for acceptance and understanding of all aspects of you. Remind the mercurial person that he or she views people as either all good or all

bad and that nobody is really that way. Tell this person that his or her acceptance of all sides of you is very important to you.

3. Don't be surprised or thrown by the mercurial person's change-able moods and try not to overreact to them. Realize that little things set off mercurial people. If you can remain steady and consistent, it will be easier for the mercurial person in your life to see the bright side again.

4. Mercurial individuals often expect you to understand what they are reacting to and are hurt when you don't figure it out. Save time and trouble—ask for an explanation.

5. Mercurial individuals can be impulsive and expressive and may let the necessary business of life slide. You be the responsible one if you're good at it, because the mercurial person will not.

6. Show your warmth, love, devotion, and dedication frequently. Hearing how much you love them and how special they are to you is important to mercurial people. The mercurial person in your life may be quite a handful for these people are tempestuous and what they want from you can be hard to provide. But they can be courageous, interesting, exciting, and can show you a deep and profound love unlike any you have experienced before. Openly appreciate them for all that.

Making the Most of Your Mercurial Style

Exercise 1: Try to imagine what it would be like not to experience emotions or to feel involved with people. Try to experience what it would be like to read a book, see a movie, listen to music, or be with a person without having an emotional reaction. Pretend that you are an actor and have to play a solitary role. Remember that this is just an exercise and a difficult one at that. We're not suggesting that you try to become solitary, only that you begin to experience the difference between thoroughly emotional and thoroughly nonemotional. If you cannot figure out how a solitary person would evaluate a person or a movie without depending on feelings, you may realize the extent to which you rely on and overreact to your feelings.

Exercise 2: Observe your feelings. As you go through your day, imagine that you are sitting in a movie theater watching yourself on the screen. Or imagine that there is another you, an observer inside your head who is watching everything that you are experiencing. As you become skilled at developing this dual sense of self, tell your observing self to watch especially for your feelings, keep an eye out for changes in feelings and emotions, keep track of how and when they change. If you like, keep a running list of each time you have a change in feelings, such as the moment you become disappointed with someone.

Exercise 3: When you have developed some skill in observing your feelings and their changes, try to disown your feelings. Every time you notice a feeling or change in feeling, say to yourself, "It's only a feeling." For example: if your mate does something stupid and you find yourself suddenly despising him or her for it, stand back from that feeling and do not claim it or any other feeling as your own. Let the moment pass without a feeling attached to it. Most important, do not react to that feeling. Again, this is just an exercise, not a suggestion that you no longer have feelings. If you practice it, you will find that you can develop unexpected control over what usually controls you. Try it when you get depressed. Insist to yourself that no matter how awful it feels, your depression is only a feeling, it is not the way the world is.

Exercise 4: Modulate your feelings. Every time you have a strong emotional reaction, imagine that you are turning a dial that lowers its intensity. Turn the reaction down ten percent, then another ten percent.

Exercise 5: Having observed and distanced yourself from your feelings and having conscientiously controlled them, try to observe your feelings about the people in your life and note exactly when they change for the worse. Each time you find yourself becoming angry or disappointed with someone, or suddenly beginning to hate that person, ask yourself whether you are reacting unfavorably to what you perceive as flaws in him or her. As soon as you catch yourself having this kind of negative reaction, immediately return to Exercise 3 and disown the feeling. Simply observe that you have a hard time accepting a person's fallibility, but do not act on your negative feelings in any way.

Exercise 6: Observe the degree to which you polarize people in the categories of all good individuals you love and adore and all bad persons whom you hate and revile. For each person you idealize, think of some of his or her traits that are not so wonderful. Similarly, for those whom you despise, force yourself to think of some of their acceptable or admirable qualities. Resist sudden shifts of feeling about any person when you do this exercise. If you find yourself suddenly beginning to hate a person whom you've been idealizing because you have thought of an unpleasant trait, try Exercises 3 and 4.

Exercise 7: To help prevent overindulging, time it. If you want one cookie or one sweater, but you usually eat the whole box or buy the whole store, carry a stop watch or other watch that has a timer. Take one cookie or purchase one sweater. Now set your timer to go off in one hour. You can have another cookie or make another purchase one hour from now. Usually, the urge would have passed by that time. If not, take one more cookie or make one more purchase and let the timer go off in another hour.

Exercise 8: Now take your attention off yourself and focus on the other people in your life. For each important person, concentrate on identifying his or her feelings, needs, and expectations from relationships. Look especially for ways in which each person's feelings, needs, and expectations are different from yours. If you find that you have negative or disappointed feelings when you think about these feelings, go back to Exercises 3 and 5.

Borderline Personality Disorder

Despondency, rage and fury, self-hatred, arrogance, anxiety, uncertainty, and emptiness, clinging, dependency, defiance, stubbornness, violent, self-damaging impulses, these are but some of the torments of the individuals who suffer from borderline personality disorder. They are desperate, intense, and unstable. They cannot make use of their abilities and talents, they are terrified of being alone, and they destroy the relationships that they can't live without.

To have this disorder is to exist in perpetual anguish and to be with people who suffer with it is to be trapped in an ongoing storm right along with them. Borderline personality disorder can be defined as a pervasive pattern of instability of interpersonal relationships, self-image, and affects, and marked impulsivity beginning by early adulthood and present in a variety of contexts as indicated by five or more of the following:

1. Frantic efforts to avoid real or imagined abandonment.

2. A pattern of unstable and intense interpersonal relationships characterized by alternating between extremes of over idealization and devaluation.

3. Identity disturbance, markedly and consistently unstable self-image or sense of self.

4. Impulsivity in at least two areas that are potentially self-damaging such as spending, sex, substance abuse, reckless driving, or binge eating.

5. Recurrent suicidal behavior, gestures or threats, or self-mutilating behavior.

6. Affective instability due to marked reactivity of mood such as intense episodic dysphoria, irritability or anxiety, usually lasting a few hours, only rarely more than a few days.

7. Chronic feelings of emptiness or boredom.

8. Inappropriate, intense anger, or difficulty controlling anger such as frequent displays of temper, constant anger, recurrent physical fights.

9. Transient, self-related paranoid ideation or severe dissociative symptoms.

Cycles of Despair

Life is nightmarish for those who suffer from this anguished personality disorder. Nothing ever stays the same. They fall desperately in love. No sooner done than their love turns into something hateful and supremely disappointing. When they are happy, they are certain there will never again be anything or anyone to be unhappy about. Just as quickly, the ecstasy is gone and the world, themselves, and everyone else turns to ashes, never to flower again. They live for love, yet they become stubborn, arrogant, and fly into a rage at the drop of a hat. They seek an identity such as a student, a member of a religious group, a cheerleader, a social worker, a political leader, but it doesn't feel right for long. They can't find themselves. They don't know what they believe anymore so they think they must become someone else. Who am I? What do I think? What am I going to do with myself? Their feelings, moods, sense of themselves, and their experiences with other people are supremely, tragically inconsistent. They can go nowhere, but in circles.

Coping With Borderline People

See the tips for dealing with the mercurial types in this chapter for help with individuals with mild borderline personality disorder. Otherwise, recognize the inner anguish that drives borderline people to behave as they do and try not to perpetuate a pattern of overreacting to their overreactions. In other words, try to stand back emotionally from the effects of their behavior on you. This will help you keep your own feelings under control and it will help you see manipulation for what it is.

Most important, you must understand your own limits. Tell borderline people that you love them, but you cannot be for them everything they need you to be and you cannot be responsible for everything they do to themselves. Encourage them to get help, insist if you can. If your family life is in chaos, seek help together.

13

The Self-Sacrificing Style

To live is to serve. To love is to give. These are axioms of individuals who have the self-sacrificing personality style. The way they see it, their needs can wait until others are well served. Knowing that they have given of themselves, they feel comfortable and at peace, secure with their place in the scheme of things. At its best and most noble, this is the selfless, magnanimous personality style of saints and good citizens.

The Seven Characteristics

The following seven traits and behaviors are clues to the presence of the self-sacrificing personality style. A person who reveals a strong self-sacrificing tendency will demonstrate more of these behaviors, more intensely than someone with less of this style in his or her personality.

1. Generosity. Individuals with self-sacrificing personality style will give you the shirts off their backs if you need them. They do not wait to be asked.

2. Service. The "prime directive" is to be helpful to others. Out of deference to others, they are noncompetitive and unambitious, comfortable coming in second, third, or even last.

3. Consideration. Self-sacrificing people are always considerate in their dealings with others. They are ethical, honest, and trustworthy.

4. Acceptance. They are nonjudgmental, tolerant of others' foibles, and never harshly reproving. They will stick with you through thick and thin.

5. Humility. They are neither boastful nor proud, and they are uncomfortable being fussed over. Self-sacrificing men and women do not like being the center of attention. They are uneasy in the limelight.

6. Endurance. They are long-suffering. They prefer to shoulder their own burdens in life. They have much patience and a high tolerance for discomfort.

7. Artlessness. Self-sacrificing individuals tend to be naive and innocent. They are unaware of the often deep impact they make on other people's lives and they tend never to suspect deviousness or underhanded motives in the people to whom they give so much of themselves.

The Six Domains of Self-Sacrificing Functioning

There is no question about it, relationship is the key domain for the self-sacrificing personality. Other people and how they can be served are at the center of their universe.

Relationships—For You Anything

Self-sacrificing individuals derive their meaning in life through giving to others. "I exist to serve," self-sacrificing Donna laughs with just a bit of self-mockery. Her husband, Bruce, has requested her homemade sourdough bread with dinner. It is late on a Sunday afternoon and Donna, a Nurse practitioner, has been trying to catch up on paperwork brought home from the office.

She pokes fun at Bruce for always getting his way, but it is she who generally anticipates his desires. Today, she's a little annoyed with herself for not having baked the bread that he always likes to have on cool spring evenings like this. But, of course, today she has all this work of her own, she reminds herself. And the reason she's behind on the paperwork is that she spends so much time, too much time, some of her colleagues tell her, with her patients. But that's Donna. Her patients come to her with individual needs and it simply is not in her character to turn anyone away before helping as much as she can.

Donna also has a streak of the devoted style in her personality pattern, but the self-sacrificing is stronger. Devoted types center their lives around their principal relationships—spouses, children, friends. Self-sacrificers do for and give to everyone they come in contact with. They are gentle, kind, doers of good deeds. It is their built-in value system, always to help others. They do for others, one way or another, in all their relationships. They don't seek rewards for their helpfulness. These men and women may sacrifice their own needs in the act of service. For example, Donna's willingness to put aside her work to bake the bread her husband loves. But the self-sacrificing personalities, such as Donna's, do not experience their action as self-renunciation. To do a good turn for another person makes them feel right with the world and that's what counts. They are altruists, in other words.

Anyone with a prominent streak of this style will find meaning in laboring to make others' lives better. Some self-sacrificers become great philanthropists, some missionaries. They are the people who take in ill or injured foster children, who work to help victims of one disaster or another, who lend their untiring support to charities and causes, and who sacrifice their own needs to those of the family.

They are drawn to creatures in pain and in need whose suffering and hardship they will do all they can to alleviate. Some individuals with self-sacrificing style are truly gifted healers. They labor long and hard, happy to lose sight of themselves in their helpfulness to a cause or a person. Sometimes Bruce will say to Donna, "Honey, it's almost midnight. Forget the ironing. I'll wear something else tomorrow. You look bushed. Think of yourself. Come to bed." But Donna doesn't mind the never-ending labors of her life. She will fall into bed with a calm, contented inner peace, her rest well earned.

"Don't Thank Me!"

Self-sacrificing men and women are active, vigorous, energetic, highly motivated, ever diligent. But unless they also have one or more of the "me" styles in their personalities, their efforts will always be for someone else.

They routinely deflect attention away from themselves. "It's nothing special," insisted conscientious, self-sacrificing Peter after he single-handedly organized and coordinated a fund raising dinner for a local theater company. He devoted three months of his off-work time to this task. On opening night, rather than relax with the guests even for a moment, he was continually overseeing the serving, the clearing, and the overall comfort of the 500 guests. "Don't thank me," he insisted with typical self-sacrificing modesty as the guests began to depart. "Why, Elizabeth baked these wonderful pies," he'd say or, "Raymond's firm donated the linens," or "Susan hand lettered every envelope."

Self-sacrificers do not like to take full credit for what they do. They do not enjoy the attention, it doesn't "feel right" to them. Indeed, some self-sacrificers so routinely take the attention off themselves that the important people in their lives may stop noticing their extraordinary efforts and begin to take them for granted, or even take advantage of their good natures.

After these self-sacrificers insist time and again that they don't want to be thanked, credited, or noticed, people begin to take them at their word and stop paying attention to their contributions and that hurts. They may not want to be lionized for their selfless efforts, but like most other people, self-sacrificers need to be loved and appreciated. They love to give and they hate appearing prideful or pushy. But to be treated as a nonperson can cause an under recognized sacrificer much pain and confusion.

After years of telling her husband, "Honey, don't make such a fuss over the sourdough bread. Really, it's no big deal." If Bruce ever stops fussing and begins to expect the bread there when he wants it, Donna will feel deeply let down. "Why," she will ask herself, "when I work so hard to make him happy does he seem not to notice or care?"

Guilty Pleasures

All self-sacrificers share, to some degree, this discomfort with positive attention. They don't feel right standing on a pedestal and they feel awkward when anyone says, "Let's concentrate on making you happy for a change." Self-sacrificers are in their element when they are giving pleasure or assistance to others, but they are not comfortable with themselves when the tables are turned. This discomfort may resemble guilt as if deep down they don't feel entitled to so much attention. For example, Lorraine's personality was dominated by the dramatic style with the self-sacrificing next in line. She had powerful dramatic needs to be on center stage, but her self-sacrificing streak made her feel embarrassed by her wishes. After a couple of years in therapy, she was able to throw herself a lavish thirty-fifth birthday party. She dressed exquisitely and was determined to be the star of the evening, as she was. But to keep up the show in front of her 75 guests, Lorraine needed to become intoxicated and thus not apparently responsible for her self-entitled show-off behavior. The next morning, she had a huge hangover and a miserable feeling of depression. She was later able to work out with her therapist that she had felt guilty for "wallowing" in all that "selfish" attention.

Secretly, Lorraine had always wanted and loved getting special attention. She realized that she had been taught to be humble, that "pride goeth before a fall."

A Fine Line

Obviously it can be very difficult for people with a lot of this personality style, who mean only the best for other people, to know where to draw a line. Moderately self-sacrificing individuals can balance their giving and doing for others and can, perhaps with some effort, ask more for themselves. As the style becomes extreme and approaches self-defeating personality disorder, however, the constant giving and doing puts an unwelcome burden of obligation on others.

Self-sacrificers always insist on going out of their way to help, generally oblivious to the fact that some people may not want their assistance. Unsolicited, "Let me do this for you," assistance often get on people's nerves.

When Bruce wants his nurse practitioner wife Donna, to stop ironing and come to bed before she begins to carry her personality style too far, perhaps she should ask herself whether he'd rather have her there by his side than her working herself to exhaustion for his sake. Since self-sacrificers work to achieve acceptance through their giving, some may find it hard to comprehend that those who love them may prefer that they give a little less or differently for a change.

The Self-Sacrificing Parent

Successful parenting requires the ability to sacrifice for one's children and to expect little for oneself in return, up to a point, that is. Individuals with moderate self-sacrificing style give of themselves naturally and happily, providing the child a strong sense of security in life. Extreme self-sacrificers, however, may become martyrs and lay a burden of guilt on their offspring. They work themselves to the bone for the children and suffer extreme disappointment when the children appear ungrateful when they grow up and go their self-determined way.

The very self-sacrificing parent who "went without so you could go to medical school," may not take kindly to the child's decision to pursue a career in rock music. "But mom, I never wanted to be a doctor. I never asked you to give up new clothes or a new car for my sake."

As for role models, self-sacrificing parents may have to remind themselves to set good examples of self-assertion for their children, to learn that it's okay to stand up for oneself and to ask that one's needs be met. They may also have to practice setting limits, expressing their anger directly, and saying no at appropriate times.

*Emotions, Self-Control, and Real World—
the Problem of Pleasure*

As we have seen, self-sacrificing men and women are pleasure givers, not pleasure takers. But they can be far more capable of the full range of satisfying emotions than they may seem. Emotionally, they can feel quite positive and full, especially when they have done something good for someone. As for their overt pleasure, their key is privacy. In the presence of others, they automatically give up their comfort in order to provide for another's comfort. They cook or serve rather than eat. They stand while others sit. They choose the uncomfortable chair in order to leave the soft chair for someone else. That is the way they are and they are good at it. But since they are other directed people pleasers, they will not find it easy to relax their strict controls over their own emotions and hungers in order to have a "let-loose" good time. Some extreme self-sacrificers may seem stiff, stern, uptight, and really no fun at all.

Stolen Moments

If there is no one else though, these same individuals may find relaxation and self-indulgence come easily. They can relax in the comfortable chair, dish out the ice cream, watch a movie, and enjoy themselves in private.

The stronger the self-sacrificing style, the more time self-sacrificers will spend in the company of others, worrying about what they need to do or might have overlooked for them. They'll indulge their own pleasures only when no one is looking as if they have something to feel guilty about. And in a sense, they do. They feel guilty for not being busy serving others. They feel guilty that they are taking some time for themselves.

The Dark Side

Still, self-sacrificing individuals are prone to sadness and depression for many reasons. They all see the world as a hard, tough place, painfully real in which their mission is to make things better for other people. Even those with balanced personality patterns may be more exposed than others to the pain, misery, and misfortunes of human existence through their efforts to help the needy. They will not see life as pleasant, just, or easy. Those who are more self-sacrificing may be weighed down by deep inner guilt and a sense of never ending, unfulfilled obligations to others.

For these and other reasons, self-sacrificing people often come across as long suffering, but always emotionally strong and capable of shouldering whatever burdens come their way in life. How they express their personal suffering will depend on the other styles in their profiles. With dramatic or mercurial streaks, a predominately self-sacrificing person may loudly fuss and complain about the number of ungrateful people in his or her life. With conscientious or some solitary influence, another may keep his or her resentment private leading to a chronically stiff upper lip. With considerable serious style, they will be cynical, pessimistic, critical, and resigned to what they see as the inevitable disappointments of life.

Stress

There are two principal sources of stress for self-sacrificing people. One, they take on too much, willingly giving up their leisure time to care for others. They don't kick back and put their feet up unless they dare to "steal" a moment. And they find it difficult to accept help from anyone else, thus, they may work themselves into poor health. Resentment, the other key stress for this style occurs when they begin to feel that others do not appreciate, understand, or love them despite all they do. But self-sacrificing types are strong. They can take on other people's burdens as well as their own. "Such is life whether I like it or not,

I can deal with it," say these stressed out individuals. Unless they are in a state of complete collapse, they will roll up their sleeves and restore their emotional equilibrium by doing someone a good turn.

The Undeserving Self

The extent to which they seek their identities through their acts of service may reveal some self-sacrificers' uncertainty about their self-worth. Would they still feel good about themselves if they were stranded alone on a desert island? Can they feel at peace with themselves if they are not trying to do something for someone else? Some self-sacrificers feel unworthy and undeserving of love, attention, and pleasure, therefore, they are always trying to earn it. Others may, deep down, have a very good sense of who they are and what they want for themselves, but they may feel that they should not indulge their "selfish" desires, but instead tend to the needs of others.

Work: Service Comes First

Work is a comfortable domain for their personality style for through their work, they perform their service to others. They resemble conscientious types in their competence, their loyalty, their reluctance to relax and enjoy themselves, and their giving their all to their work. Also, like conscientious types, self-sacrificers are respectful of those in authority. Give self-sacrificing individuals a task, and they will work all night and weekends, if need be, to complete it. They can handle drudgery and routine. They can adapt to many work situations and conditions. They don't complain that "it's not my job." If it is important to the boss, the spouse, the children, or the cause, they'll get it done. They might work exceedingly hard, but unless they have an ambitious personality style in their pattern, [the self-confident, for example] they will not be powerfully career minded. Neither will they be as demonstratively successful as you might imagine considering the amount and the quality of their work. Outward personal ambition, as we have said, does not mark this personality style. The value of the work itself or the person for whom they work is more important to a self-sacrificer than their own personal gain. A self-sacrificing individual may work tirelessly toward the candidate's victory, the patient's recovery, or housing for the homeless, but will not stop and think, "Hey, what's in this for me?" What counts most is the satisfaction that comes from serving others.

A Note to the Boss

Thank your self-sacrificing employees for all their untiring efforts on your behalf. You may forget these individuals are there because self-sacrificing types step off into the shadows and demand so little for themselves. Now that you have noticed these dedicated souls, give them a raise, give them a little praise. They may be reluctant to ask for what they deserve.

The Self-Sacrificing Leader

Generally, self-sacrificers avoid becoming leaders. They like to work for or on behalf of others rather than be responsible for overseeing others' work and behavior. They may end up in middle management positions, however, by their good work, loyalty, and devotion to their organizations or their bosses. They may have trouble delegating work, and insisting that it be done on time so they do it themselves and end up seriously overworked. They may be overly solicitous of a direct report's problems and go out of their way to help them. They may later feel that these individuals are not grateful and be angry when the employee continues to under perform.

Other self-sacrificing leaders may display a somewhat tyrannical side, expecting their direct reports to sacrifice themselves as completely to the job as they do.

Careers

Look for work in which you take care of or satisfy the needs of others. Consider any of the helping professions—medicine, psychology, nursing, social service, charitable institutions, volunteer work, and administrative—teaching, catering, interior design, production, library science, day care, homemaking, and custodial jobs. Avoid careers that involve public speaking or otherwise require you to be comfortable as the "front person," or the center of attention.

Unless you have a dramatic or mercurial side, avoid the performing arts. With a creative bent, consider writing, editing, song writing, or commercial art.

Tips on Dealing with the Self-Sacrificing Person in your Life

1. Remember to recognize and acknowledge this person's efforts, no matter how frequently he or she insists "It's nothing." Your self-sacrificer may be embarrassed by compliments, but inwardly needs to know you notice and appreciate.

2. Try to find a comfortable give and take formula. Self-sacrificing people must keep giving, helping, and doing, but they could use a little help from you in being able to relax and enjoy themselves. Don't hesitate to insist that the self-sacrificing person in your life stop building your bookcase or ironing your shirts and come and sit quietly with you.

3. Learn how to translate "self-sacrificing language." "Heavens, don't thank me," may mean "I don't feel right taking the credit, but thanks for the compliment." Similarly, "I really don't want to go out dancing," often means, "I really don't think I should go out and have a good time, so please drag me."

4. Try not to reject what this person has to give and don't be embarrassed by the constant attention. Self-sacrificers think of you first, they

love it, so relax and enjoy being cared for so well. In any case, don't get into a fight about it.

5. Be careful not to take advantage. Some extreme self-sacrificers may give away too much or move too far out of the way to please you. This person is not your slave no matter how he or she behaves. If the self-sacrificers won't draw the line, you do it. But when you refuse a favor, always explain why.

6. Insist on being more helpful. Take your own clothes to the dry cleaners even if the self-sacrificing person explains that it's no problem for him or her to do it. You wash the dishes or water the lawn, or otherwise find a way to relieve the person of the usual self-sacrificing overload. This will help you establish balance in your relationship and avoid taking advantage of this person's willingness to do everything.

7. Talk about it. Try to convey to the self-sacrificing person in your life that the way he or she can do something really nice for you is to share your leisure time with you. Unless you provide the feedback, this person may truly be unaware that you want something other than what he or she is giving to you.

Making the Most of Your Self-Sacrificing Style

You are a naturally unselfish, generous, helpful, giving human being. You work hard to please, even when no one asks or thanks you for it. You may deny your own needs and pleasures more than you realize. Work on establishing a firm or firmer balance of give and take by being more circumspect in the giving, more assertive in the taking.

Exercise 1: In your imagination, focus on your self for a change. Whenever you are with people, you automatically think about taking care of their needs. The next time you are with others, try to imagine what you would like for yourself in the same situation. For example, as you run to fix the drinks for your guests, imagine someone else making the drinks or even fixing one just for you. When you are listening to a friend's problems and trying to suggest solutions, imagine that you are the talker and your friend, the listener. This is just a thinking exercise and you may find yourself uncomfortable with these fantasies because they go against your nature. The point is to begin to recognize what you might really enjoy receiving from other people.

Exercise 2: Learn to ask. Make your desires and expectations known. For example, if you are the one who gets up to make the morning coffee, but you can imagine your spouse doing it for a change, ask. Say, "Honey, why don't you make the coffee tomorrow?" Won't he/ she be surprised! Don't worry if you feel uncomfortable making this request. You'll get use to it. But don't take it back. If your partner says, "Gosh, I would, but I don't know how to measure it out right." Don't give in. Say, "Here, I'll show you." There's a chance, of course, that your partner will be pleasantly surprised and say, "Sure, I never really thought you wanted that." People often report that they wished self-sacrificing individuals would let them know what they want for themselves. Others, particularly when they love you, are interested in pleasing you as well.

Exercise 3: Whenever anyone offers to do something for you or to help you out, say yes.

Exercise 4: If you feel that you are not being treated fairly, say so. Self-sacrificers usually expect the best from others and feel justifiably hurt and let down when people take advantage. You may be able to prevent or discourage this kind of behavior by speaking up sooner.

Exercise 5: Listen for the number of times and situations in which you say, "I'm sorry," on any given day. If the string beans come out too mushy or you are five minutes late or you forgot to put oil in the car although you promised, how big a deal do you make of it. If you find that you apologize frequently over relatively minor matters, ask yourself whether you worry too much about pleasing other people. Try to give yourself a break and catch yourself before an apology comes out.

Exercise 6: Every time you are about to offer to go out of your way for somebody, ask yourself, "Is this in my best interest?" There are times in life when you have to ask, "What's in it for me?" For example, if you volunteer to drive two hours to the airport to pick up a friend who can easily afford to rent a car, stop and think whether sacrificing your whole day makes sense. Or if you offer to throw a party for the out-of-town guests coming to the wedding of your friend's daughter, ask whether you really have the time, energy, and money, not to mention a genuine need for such an undertaking. In other words, do you really want to do this or do you think to be a good friend, you should make this gesture?

Exercise 7: Before you volunteer to do anything for anybody, ask yourself, "Does this person really want me to do this?" Your lasagna may be the world's best, but before you volunteer to bring the main course to your daughter's dinner, think first whether she is still on a diet. Be aware too, that people often like to do things for themselves or for you. Maybe your daughter would like to cook dinner for you, and that is why she invited you.

Exercise 8: Combat the guilt. Every time you find yourself feeling awkward or uncomfortable about having a good time, say to yourself, "It's good to feel good. What am I worrying about? I'm entitled to this."

Self-Defeating Personality Disorder

The men and women who suffer from this disorder are trapped in repetitive patterns of soured pleasure and missed opportunities. Happiness and fulfillment allude them no matter how hard they work toward those goals. Self-defeating personality disorder can best be described as a pervasive pattern of self-defeating behavior beginning by early adulthood and present in a variety of contexts. The person may often avoid or undermine pleasurable experiences, be drawn to situations or relationships in which he or she will suffer, and prevent others from helping him or her as indicated by at least five of the following:

1. Chooses people and situations that lead to disappointment, failure, or mistreatment even when better options are clearly available.

2. Rejects or renders ineffective, the attempts of others to help him or her.

3. Following positive personal events, [new achievement] responds with depression, guilt, or a behavior that produces pain.

4. Incites angry or rejecting responses from others and then feels hurt, defeated, or humiliated. [For example: making fun of spouse in public, provoking an angry retort, then feeling devastated.]

5. Rejects all opportunities for pleasure or is reluctant to acknowledge enjoying himself or herself [despite having adequate social skills and the capacity for pleasure].

6. Fails to accomplish tasks crucial to his or her personal objectives despite demonstrated ability to do so. [For example, helps fellow students write papers, but is unable to write his or her own paper.]

7. Is uninterested in or rejects people who constantly treat him or her well.

8. Engages in excessive self-sacrifice that is unsolicited by the intended recipients of the sacrifice.

Wrecked By Success

Individuals with this personality disorder cannot tolerate success or pleasure. Therefore, through their own actions they unconsciously undermine or sabotage all hopes of fulfillment. In 1916, Sigmund Freud used the phrase, "wrecked by success," to describe these people. Their behaviors, taking a low paying, unchallenging job when they are capable of far more, rejecting people who truly care for them, remaining in a personal or vocational relationship in which they are consistently mistreated are seemingly unavoidable. Yet, an individual with this disorder has no awareness that he or she is deliberately self-destructive.

Coping With Self-Defeating People

The tips for dealing with self-sacrificing individuals would be helpful for mildly self-defeating types. Assure these individuals that you care and try to encourage them to seek professional help. Resist feeling guilty about their unhappiness or suffering and while you are at it, do everything you can to avoid taking advantage of them. Very likely, if you are closely involved with a self-defeating person, you are in a troubled relationship that could use some help. Seek counseling as an individual or as a family, but seek help.

14

The Aggressive Style

Who's the boss? The aggressive type, of course. While others may aspire to leadership, aggressive men and women move instinctively to the helm. They are born to assume command as surely as is the top dog in the pack. Their strong, forceful personality style, is more inherently powerful than any of the others. They can undertake huge responsibilities without fear of failure. They weld power with ease. They never back away from a fight. They compete with the supreme confidence of champions. How these individuals use the power that seems always at their fingertips depends on other styles in their patterns. When put to the service of the greater good, the aggressive personality style can inspire a man or woman to great leadership, especially in times of crisis.

The Six Characteristics

The following six traits and behaviors are clues to the presence of the aggressive style. A person who reveals a strong, aggressive tendency will demonstrate more of these behaviors, more intensely than someone with less of this style in his or her personality.

1. Command. Aggressive individuals take charge. They are comfortable with power, authority, and responsibility.

2. Hierarchy. They operate best within the traditional power structure where everyone knows his or her place and the lines of authority are clear.

3. Tight ship. They are highly disciplined and impose rules of order that they may expect others in their charge to follow.

4. Expedience. Aggressive men and women are highly goal directed. They take a practical, pragmatic approach to accomplishing their objectives. They do what is necessary to get the job done.

5. Courage. They are neither squeamish nor faint hearted. They can function well and bravely in difficult and dangerous situations without being distracted by fear or horror.

6. The rough and tumble. Aggressive people like action and adventure. They are physically assertive and often participate in or enjoy playing competitive sports, especially contact sports.

The Six Domains of Aggressive Functioning

The key domains for this personality style are relationships and work.

Relationships—I Lead, You Follow

This personality style could well be subtitled "Top Dog." Because in their interactions with other people, aggressive individuals always move to the front. They have an instinctive gift for leadership and a driving need to dominate. This "organizing principle" is evident in all their relationships at home, in the social environment, on the football field, and most certainly in the workplace. Aggressive style men and women naturally vie for control of all the groups of which they become a part, often beginning very early in their lives.

This aggressive instinct to direct and to dominate need not be seen as hostile to others, however. Individuals who are strong, comfortable with power, and who can and want to bear the weight of immense responsibility for others are necessary and welcome in many organizations and families. In other words, like the rest of the dogs in the pack, the others are often glad to have someone else stepping forward to take responsibility, to make tough decisions, and to fight the battles. Many people find it comfortable indeed to have someone strong and competent to rely on. However, when the aggressive style grows extreme, the need to dominate becomes more important than any concern for the interest and feelings of others. Also, the end may become far more important than the means and these overwhelmingly aggressive individuals may disregard moral and ethical values on their way to grabbing the golden ring.

All aggressive types tend to be autocratic and tutorial. That goes with the territory. But with balancing features from other styles in their patterns, they may well be benevolent and protective, especially if no one from the ranks steps out of line.

Hail to the Chief

In their relationships throughout their lives, aggressive types reach their full potential when they are in charge. At home, they rule the roost. At work, they run the show. They prefer a pyramid type hierarchial structure with themselves at the top and everyone beneath them spread out in a well understood, fixed, pecking order. They like to give orders and to establish rules.

Sam [his family called him Chief] was "one macho guy," in the words of his twelve-year-old granddaughter. His father had come from an old world paternalistic tradition in which his power as head of the family was undisputed. Sam continued the tradition. He married May, a Southern belle with traditional views of a woman's place in regard to her husband. Dominated by the devoted style, May was content to let Sam make important decisions and determine family policy as long as he treated her with respect and took good care of her.

For his part, Sam liked the way May leaned on him. It made him feel right in the world—a man. He provided well for May and their four children. He even supported her widowed mother and her institutionalized retarded sister. May had a mind of her own, especially when it came to running her home and social clubs in which she took part. But if her views conflicted with Sam's, in front of him, she rarely voiced them. She almost never crossed her husband, at least not willfully. Since May always deferred to her husband and his will prevailed, in almost twenty years, they had not experienced a serious disruption.

Their family life seemed blessed. But when their youngest child and only son, Samuel Nathan, Jr., known as Nathan, in his adolescence began to rebel against his father, trouble festered at their doorstep. May found herself torn between her son and her husband. The issues between father and son were not huge—no criminal conduct, no drugs, no drinking, no unsafe, promiscuous behavior. They had become locked in an escalating battle of wills with Sam insisting that Nathan do everything his way and Nathan, defiantly setting his own course. For example, Sam ordered Nathan to work in the family business one summer during high school. Nathan said he had already gotten a job at a pizza parlor. Sam ordered Nathan to turn that job down or he would take his car away from him. Nathan refused to comply with his father's demands. Sam, true to his word, sold the car that he had helped his son buy the year before. Nathan began to stay out later than his midnight curfew. He'd come screeching up the driveway about one in the morning on the back of his friend's motorcycle. Sam grounded him. Nathan stopped talking to his father. It was war in the house. Nathan's sisters, all now living away from home, were on his side and called their mother several times a week to tell her so. But never their father. He'd been a strict disciplinarian and the girls, although they loved their father, had never dared to cross him. Instead, they waited until they left home to make their own decisions. Nathan had always been his sisters' treasured "Little Chief," as they liked to tease him. Now his sisters wanted their mother to intercede with their father on their brother's behalf. May thought they were right, but she had had no experience standing up to her husband. When she tried to, "Sam dear, can't you let up on Nathan?" He interrupted her abruptly, "Stay out of this, May." The harsh look he gave her was frightening to May. She retreated to their bedroom and began to cry. When Sam found her there, wiping her red eyes, he became furious with her and stormed out of the house.

May tried to tell Nathan to wait until he went away to college to assert his own personality. "Your father believes that he knows what is

best for all of us," she said, "and usually, he does. He works very hard
to give us a good life. But things have to be his way as long as he's head
of this family. When you go away to college, you can do what you
want. I trust you, Nathan." May added, "But your father thinks you
are being disloyal to him and he can't stand that. Please go along with
him for a short while longer for all of our sakes. But whatever you do,
don't do something foolish just to show your father he can't push you
around."

Nathan listened, but he didn't answer. Likely, he was hurt that his
mother wouldn't defend him more strongly in front of his father.
Nathan, president of his class, captain of the wrestling team, twice
voted most likely to succeed, was definitely his father's son. That was a
great part of their problem. The family had room for only one chief
and through his teen years, Nathan was jockeying to move up. Appropriate for his healthy development, Nathan was competing with his
father.

But aggressive style individuals often have difficulty tolerating challenges to their authority. They instinctively lash out to squash and to
punish the perceived disloyalty and to reassert their control. True to
the aggressive style, Sam mistook his son's essentially appropriate rebellion for a defection from the fold. Sam had never flinched at imposing
discipline and punishment when he felt it was necessary. When he
found out that Nathan had begun cutting classes at school, he hit him
so hard that Nathan's nose bled. Nathan, seemed stunned, like a boxer
about to keel over. After a moment, he wheeled around and punched
his father in the stomach. Sam fell to the floor. Nathan ran out of the
house. May managed to persuade Sam not to call the police. Eventually
Nathan wound up at his grandmother's house. He was scared to death
to go home. May, with Nathan's everlasting gratitude, was able to persuade Sam to let Nathan stay at her mother's house until everybody
calmed down. Nathan ended up living there for the remaining three
months of high school and through the summer until he left for col-

lege. This solution allowed him sufficient independence and distance from his father that he no longer needed to rebel so destructively.

Sam, for his part, in the absence of his son, could once more resume his role as the unrivaled chief. And May no longer felt torn between the two strong-willed, hot-tempered men in her life. She visited her son frequently at her mother's house where she could express support for his decisions without upsetting her husband.

Nathan did well in college. He distinguished himself in law school, practiced law for many years, and ran successfully for public office. He is now a third-term United States Congressman and he is planning to run for the Senate in the next election. He has never lost a race. He is ambitious, has a strong power base, and has let it be known that he wants to be President of the United States. He and Sam [now retired from the family business, which a son-in-law now runs] have never been close or comfortable with each other since the events of Nathan's adolescence. But May knows how much Sam respects his powerful son and she tells him so whenever Nathan comes back home for a visit or when he and his wife invite her to Washington. Nathan loves and respects the "Chief" equally and credits him for teaching him to be tough, courageous, and ambitious. But he may never be able to share these feelings with his father. For both, "sentimentality" goes against their aggressive grain.

The Next Generations

Nathan, as aggressive in personality style as his father, has managed to establish a well-structured, orderly disciplined family. His two children are still in grade school, so we have yet to know how he will deal with their adolescent assertiveness. His eighth grader, Sarah, will probably be tougher to deal with than his younger child, Sam, III. So far, Sarah seems to be a chip off her aggressive dad's block.

This style is not exclusive to men. Aggressive style women traditionally have assumed control of their families as powerful matriarchs. Girls now grow up believing themselves entitled to use power inherent in their personalities, to assert themselves, and to compete in a "man's world." If Sarah does go head-to-head with her dad in the coming years, one hopes that Nathan will be able to deal with it more creatively than his father did.

Nathan's wife, Kate, practices law part-time. She is bright and self-assertive, but she, like her mother-in-law, May, does not question her husband's authority in the family. She can imagine herself as first lady, strongly supporting her husband and participating in his presidency where possible. The bottom line is that when everyone is following the expected rules, Nathan, in his aggressive way, is a loving, giving, generous, often understanding, and unquestionably interesting and exciting husband. Life with Nathan is better than life without him, she has decided. As hard as Nathan is to live with, she preferred living with him.

More About the Aggressive Style Parent

Women with the aggressive style provide strong, capable, role models for their children. The kids know that they can count on them for protection from every threat from a dangerous world. They are often proud of such parents for their success and accomplishments in the world. As we have seen, these parents are strict disciplinarians and expect their kids to obey them without question. If the style is not extreme, but is tempered with flexibility and sensitivity, such a parent can help anchor the children to tradition and responsibility. Otherwise, they'll have extra tempestuous times with their teenagers for whom competition and rebellion against the parent are normal and healthy. If the aggressive parent nips the rebellion in the bud, the child who capitulates may have trouble with self-assertion, independence, and competition throughout life. The child who continues to rebel may overdo it and get into real trouble. Advice to aggressive style parents: bend a little so that your appropriately self-assertive children will be able to find more creative ways to cope with your authority. Try to understand your children's feelings. Also, if you are extremely involved in your work outside the home, as are many individuals of your style, recognize that your children may feel left out of your life. Work on listening to reason and compromising with your children and expressing more affection and spending more "quality time" with them, especially when they are young.

All's Fair

Pete, who legend has it, moved from stock boy to president and CEO without pausing anywhere in between, has been running a major corporation for more than a decade. He has consistently parried all takeovers, defended against all challenges to his base of power, and kept his corporation in the black despite changes in the economic climate. He holds complete control over the corporation, its finances, and its executives. Any of the principal executives to whom he allows some power must demonstrate total loyalty to Pete to remain in the inner circle. He rewards this loyalty lavishly with money and perks. He punishes disloyalty by withholding money and reducing power and recognition. Those who do not question Pete's right to run the show and who perform up to his high expectations are assured of good treatment. But should they fail to please him, despite years of service, out they go.

Recently, Pete summarily fired a senior vice president, Janet, who he felt was widening her base of power among the board members. The woman was extremely competent in the financial end of the business. To undercut her effectiveness and her support from the board, Pete leaked to the press her long affair with a powerful, well-known, and married director of a major brokerage firm. The newspapers gave the story all the play that Pete had hoped for. The board abhorred the unseemly publicity and fully supported Peter's decision to let this key executive go.

Some would consider Pete's action vicious, even vindictive. He saw it as justified—all's fair in love and war. And to the aggressive individual, work is strategic combat, a struggle to get and to keep power. He had known about Janet's affair for years, but it became his weapon when he found he needed one. He did what he had to do, he would tell you, and he would add that if you found his means so upsetting, you don't belong in the big time.

Ends and Means

Aggressive style individuals are strongly goal directed. They have a job to do and they get it done. Success, victory, power, and excellence are their objectives. But they are practical and pragmatic in their pursuit of them. They use the means that are at hand. If an aggressive individual has strength as well in the conscientious style, he or she will also be concerned about doing the right and honorable thing. Otherwise, there is a risk that individuals whose personalities are strongly aggressive, will act unscrupulously or vindictive without regard for morals or ethics, or the consequences that may come to others.

For aggressive style individuals, it is the objective that counts. The means tend to be expedient. For example, aggressive style Ilene was trying to sell the company car that has persistent transmission problems. A young man has seen her advertisement and calls to inquire about the car. He says he has never bought a car before, he doesn't ask about the car's problems, and Ilene doesn't tell him. If he did inquire, she would probably say something about it, downplaying the problem. It would be up to the potential buyer to have a mechanic check it out before coming to a decision. Ilene does not consider herself a criminal or a cheat. She wants to sell the car quickly at the best price, and like many people in a similar situation, she thinks it's not her problem if the buyer negotiates a bad deal.

As an aggressive person, Ilene, in most business situations, makes decisions in a similar style. She is less concerned with following the "right" or "honorable" course as with finding a practical, efficient, effective solution.

The accumulation of power, and the tendency to use expedient means can lead some aggressive types, like their adventurous cousins, to cross the line into outright criminal behavior. This becomes more probable if they have considerable adventurous style in their personalities. However, most aggressive styles will have in their profiles "mitigating" styles that will protect them from crossing moral and ethical boundaries. Or, they will have someone with a conscience, a conscientious second in command, sitting at a desk nearby to keep them honest [or to turn them in.]

The Aggressive Leader

Aggressive individuals make excellent, interesting leaders and administrators. With unflagging energy, they create structure and organization, perceive short and long-term goals, and plan effective strategies. They can see the big picture and can juggle numerous major responsibilities and projects at one time without becoming disorganized or distracted. They run a tight, disciplined ship and they demand loyalty and reward it generously.

Some aggressive leaders divide staffs into a loyal circle [those who share their dedication and sense of purpose] and an out group ["regular," less privileged others.] The most extremely aggressive leaders who attract a loyal cadre on their climb to the top may experience a mass defection of top lieutenants who become disillusioned with their unscrupulous behavior. For example, watch in times of government scandal how many of an agency leader's most trusted subordinates get disgusted, come to their senses, and abandon ship.

Aggressive leaders focus on results, not feelings. Their direct reports may think them hard-hearted or insensitive. They set high performance standards for themselves and for their direct reports, having little patience with inefficiency, error, and waste, and none with disloyalty. Aggressive leaders have little difficulty punishing or dismissing employees who do not meet their approval. Emotional appeals may hasten the execution.

Beside disloyalty, there's only one thing that aggressive leaders, indeed any aggressive style person in the workplace may not be able to deal with creatively—it's boredom. Work is strategic combat, accomplishment is winning. Like some military officers at the end of the war, once the battle is won, they don't know what to do with themselves. They must function at high stimulation levels at all times and may end up creating an internal political conflict just to keep the juices flowing.

Stress

Lack of power, serious competitive threat, and defeat or failure are the greatest sources of stress for aggressive types. They cope by establishing or strengthening their power base, planning a strategy, and fighting back, often with fury. Anyone with substantial aggressive personality style will not accept loss or failure and go quietly into the sunset. These folks are survivors, winners. They fight their way to the top, claw their way, if they have to.

Careers

Politics, government, the military, education, the corporation—look for a career in any area that offers a power structure you can climb. You may do equally as well as an entrepreneur in your own business where you create the structure yourself. You must, in all cases, be working with and around people so that you can aspire to being in charge of them.

Self and Real World
Aggressive versus Self-Confident

Individuals with these two styles reveal a fiercely competitive "me first" approach to life. But their differences can best be seen in the way each of them views the self and its relative position in the real world domain. The aggressive person, driven primarily by relationships and work domains, needs to dominate others to be in charge. Like vigilant types, their issue is control. It's a jungle out there and only those who can show their strength over others can survive. Aggressive men and women have tremendous faith in their own ability to win and to lead.

But perhaps unconscientiously they feel that unless they plunge in and take control, they will lose their power and have to give in. Submitting to a greater power is nothing short of humiliating for people with large amounts of aggressive personality style. They need to maintain and reinforce their sense of self by being the undisputed ruler of the kingdom.

Self-confident individuals, governed by the self domain, don't worry about other people. What other people? These types, as we have seen, are turned in toward their own wonderful possibilities and frequently must be reminded that other people exist. They hardly need to buttress their sense of self since they already feel secure in the center of the real world. They expect to be very successful, powerful, rich, famous—its their birthright. Nobody else presents a serious threat. Both self-confident and aggressive individuals compete easily and move up the power structure. Self-confident types are successful because they are so confident of their ability and their inherent personal stardom. Aggressive types succeed because they know so well how to take, use, manipulate, and keep power. They stand victorious, assured, skilled at the top of the dominance hierarchy.

Emotions and Self-Control
Strong in Both

Although aggressive men and women do not necessarily respond to other people's feelings, they have very strong feelings of their own. This is a powerful personality style in every domain, emotions included. Their feelings tend not to be of the soft "mushy," delicate, or otherwise sentimental variety, of course, although they can be very romantic once they are securely in control of a relationship.

Aggressive types can have a powerful sex drive. These personality types are very physical people. They need to express themselves with their bodies. Like adventurers, they need action and adventure, but whereas adventurers are turned on by physical risk in the present, aggressive types are motivated by the excitement of the "win" to come.

Thus, they often engage vigorously in competition and contact sports. Frequently, they are stimulated by combat and violence, if only on the pages of a book or on the movie screen.

Although failure may temporarily bring them down, aggressive individuals are not prone to depression or anxiety. Battling, competing, and winning are such a pleasure that for them "the cure" is the fight. Don't ask them to relax though. Aggressive individuals cannot let go of their sense of purpose. They will be glad to go on a cruise or participate in a conference, but not to relax in a deck chair.

The key to this style, as we have mentioned, is control. Aggressive types generally have extraordinary control over their emotions and their appetites for pleasure. These individuals will not let anything get in the way of their drive to the top. They generally do not react impulsively no matter how strongly they feel about something unless they're angry. In cases of anger, only the most extreme aggressive types as well as those with sadistic personality disorder will lose the all-important control and lash out violently. Their anger can be particularly powerful and can be used as a mighty weapon to keep others in line. Those on the receiving end will most likely be family and direct reports with whom these overly aggressive types may feel they have a right to do as they please.

Fortunately, most individuals with the aggressive style will avoid riding roughshod over those whom they wish to control. They will channel their aggressive energy into being crafty, strategic, shrewd. You will rarely find, even the most aggressive types, having a temper tantrum in the board room after they have been out maneuvered. Instead, they will convert the rage into a brilliant new plot to reestablish themselves and gain the day.

Tips on Dealing With the Aggressive Person in Your Life

1. Know yourself. In a personal relationship, this individual can be very easy to deal with if you understand and accept that he or she must

be the boss. Even if you are a very strong person yourself, although you might come close, you will never be equal in power if you pair up with an aggressive type. Is your personality style one that is comfortable coming second in your relationships? Does your self-esteem demand that you present yourself in all ways as an equal? These people can be wonderfully exciting, even charismatic, to be around and to share life with if you can be content with the hierarchal relationship. If you can't, you'll be miserable.

2. Be aware of competing with an aggressive person. Never try to undermine this person's authority or to unseat him or her unless you don't care about maintaining your relationship. If you expect to gain this person's respect by being more powerful than he or she is, think again. Aggressive people like to have strong, worthy, loyal individuals around them in positions lower in the hierarchy. If you do find yourself in competition with an aggressive person, allow him or her a way to save face in case you win. Otherwise, you may find yourself with a very powerful enemy.

3. Know the precise parameters of your job and/or your role so that you do not overstep the boundaries that the aggressive person may have set. In military terms, you need to know your orders and then carry them out—no more, no less.

4. Be strong and maintain your self-esteem. Just because you are in the presence of power doesn't mean you must fawn or fall back into a weak position. It is all too easy for an aggressive person to push people around and overwhelm them. But the aggressive person in your personal or business life doesn't have much use for "wimps" or "yes" types. To obtain an aggressive person's respect or love, show your natural metal. Present a worthy and self-assertive, but not competitive or defiant, front and negotiate strongly on your own behalf. If you allow an aggressive person to take advantage of you, you risk his or her contempt and a fall to the bottom of the heap.

5. To resolve conflicts that crop up in your personal life with an aggressive person, do not go after the win. Do not, in other words,

insist that he or she do it your way or admit guilt or error. The aggressive individual cannot tolerate losing, so don't seek all or nothing, I'm right, you're wrong solutions. Work toward compromises in which the aggressive person can maintain his or her top dog self-esteem. Try trading concessions. For example, "Okay, I'll change my plans and go to that convention with you next month, if you'll change your plans and come to the meeting at Jimmy's school." Should you find that winning the battle is as important to you as it is to your aggressive partner, ask yourself whether the victory is worth the sacrifice of this relationship when there may be other ways to accomplish what you need.

6. Appeal to reason, not to feelings. Aggressive people often give little weight to how a person feels. If you want to make your point, present a very reasonable case. With a show of emotion, you'll be up against a brick wall. Point out how your plan or approach directly benefits the aggressive person. Instead of saying, "You'll do this if you love me," put it this way, "If you come to the meeting at Jimmy's school on Tuesday, I think you'll find that his teachers would be very pleased to meet his father. You know Jimmy is very proud of you."

7. If the aggressive person in your life is your parent, look for ways to cope creatively with his or her possibly harsh rules and regulations. Don't take the bull by the horns. Instead of being defiant and demanding that your parent let you do what you want to do or openly and self-destructively rebelling, try to show respect and agree with his or her way of looking at things, and then quietly go about your business. This advice may come in handy for those who must deal with an aggressive person in the workplace as well.

8. Accept that the aggressive person in your life has a temper and avoid pushing the predictable buttons that will ignite it. Look for other ways to solve your problems and to deal with this person's anger. Don't fight back and don't blow off steam in his or her face. Back off and let the anger wind down.

Making the Most of Your Aggressive Style

Your personality style gives you enormous potential for success, especially in the work domain. The exercises that follow are designed to help smooth your sometimes over-bossy side and to make all parts of your life similarly rewarding. Being the boss in the workplace may work well for you, but the same authoritarian style may cause conflict for you at home.

Exercise 1: When you come home from the office, practice leaving your authoritarian style on the doorstep. Observe yourself interacting in a "boss-like" way to your family or friends. Realize that many people do not appreciate being ordered around. Try to experience yourself as an equal with others rather than as the commandant.

Exercise 2: Give people a chance to make their own decisions. You run a tight ship and get things done extremely well your way, but others, children in particular, need to gain experience and to learn for themselves. Give them some rope. You can always tug them back if they go seriously off the mark. Let your teenagers make some of their own decisions and mistakes so that they can forge a strong self-directed path through their lives and so that they don't have to go to extremes to prove they can do things for themselves.

Exercise 3: Learn to compromise and even to give in. Instead of insisting on your will being done, negotiate a solution that pleases everyone. In a conflict in your personal life, it's not a matter of win or lose; try to keep that in mind.

Exercise 4: Practice doing things someone else's way. Keep an ear open to disagreements over how things "should be done." Although you are used to getting things your way, try letting the other person take responsibility for a change. Get used to saying, "Fine, let's do it your way."

Exercise 5: At least once a week ask the people who are closest to you what you can do for them. Be open to all suggestions, including emotional ones such as, "I really wish you would show that you care for me a little more." Find a way to come through for each person and not to reject the request based on its merit. For example, suppose your teenager says, "Yeah, well now that you mentioned it, you could let me stay out all night on prom night." Instead of rejecting the request out of hand, perhaps you could extend the usual curfew a bit or otherwise find a way to lighten up on some of the rigid rules you impose on your child.

Exercise 6: Relax your control over your life and the lives of those around you and just have a good time for a while. Loosening your iron grip occasionally will prove advantageous to your health and may well prolong your vigor. It will also allow you to retake the reins of your powerful life with renewed strength. Relaxing with your family will strengthen the bonds among you all. That is, relax your control in all areas of your life except the control of your temper.

Exercise 7: Control your temper. Concentrate on holding back when you are about to explode and fight back. If necessary, turn around and walk out of the room. Punch a pillow, even leave the house until you have cooled down. Do not permit yourself to believe that anyone deserves your rage. Someone can make you angry, but no one except yourself can "cause" a ferocious, punitive reaction.

Exercise 8: Keep a list of what makes you really angry. Ask yourself whether your anger boils down to issues of dominance and control. Do you become angriest when someone close to you does something differently from the way you want it done or otherwise challenges your authority? Ask yourself whether you overreact to these issues. Run this through your mind. Other people will respect you even more if you accept that you have power and cease being quite so touchy about who is being defiant and who is trying to take it away.

Sadistic Personality Disorder

As the name implies, people with sadistic personality disorder are cruel, cold-hearted, and ruthlessly intimidating. They may be violent and will take pleasure in humiliating those around them. Sadistic personality disorder can best be defined by a pervasive pattern of cruel, demeaning, and aggressive behavior beginning by early childhood as indicated by the repeated occurrence of at least four or more of the following:

1. Has used physical cruelty or violence for the purpose of establishing dominance in a relationship [not merely to achieve some non-interpersonal goal, such as striking someone in order to rob him or her.]

2. Humiliates or demeans people in the presence of others.

3. Has treated or disciplined someone under his or her control unusually harshly. For example: a child, student, patient, or prisoner.

4. Is amused by or takes pleasure in the psychological or physical suffering of others [including animals.]

5. Has lied for the purpose of harming or inflicting pain on others [not merely to achieve some other goal.]

6. Gets other people to do what he or she wants by frightening them [through intimidation or even terror.]

7. Restricts the autonomy of people with whom he or she has a close relationship. For example, will not let spouse leave the house unaccompanied or permit teenage daughter to attend social functions.

8. Is fascinated by violence, weapons, martial arts, injury, and especially torture.

Dominance by Force

Sadistic individuals will hurt, humiliate, punish, bully, threaten, intimidate in order to control the members of the family and those who are subordinate or dependent on them in their work. Unlike antisocial individuals, they do not hurt just anyone. They may even show a benign, respectful face to those who are in authority over them. But where they feel they are entitled to be in charge, they establish their dominance through psychological and physical torture, especially when their victims prepare to fight back or to rebel against their cruel control.

They are disciplinarians, meting out harsh punishment to children, students, spouses, prisoners, or anyone else who is subordinate to them for the most minor indiscretions or errors. They are angry individuals. They turn violent when crossed or irritated by the people whom they feel are supposed to follow their orders. They often pick on people who suffer from self-defeating personality disorder who may all too easily be victims.

Coping with Sadistic People

Remember that interactions with sadistic individuals are no-win situations. You cannot work it out with them except by giving in completely. And even then, they may inflict pain gratuitously without a detectable reason. If the sadistic person you are trying to cope with is not so extreme or totally hard-hearted, try some of the tips for dealing with aggressive types. Rather than try to cope with the sadistic boss, quit or transfer. If you are the victim of sadistic behavior at home, move out. Should you lack resources and/or be fearful for your safety, move to a shelter for battered spouses, consult women's organizations in your area, or go to the police. If leaving is possible, but you find you cannot extricate yourself emotionally from a relationship with a sadistic person, ask yourself whether you may have an unconscious need to suffer. Either way, a relationship with a sadistic individual is doomed from the start.

15

The Serious Style

Serious men and women suffer no illusions. They don't hitch their wagons to a star, count their chickens before they hatch, sing that life is just a bowl of cherries, don rose colored glasses or paint their existence in a more beguiling hue. Even when things are not so pleasant, they see them as they are. Of course, since the current culture favors individuals who "think positive," look on the bright side, and attempt always to improve themselves, somebody with serious style may not exactly fit the image. But serious people don't expect to be popular.

What they sacrifice in silver linings, they gain in ability to carry on in even the worse of circumstances. No other personality style is quite so able to endure when a harsh climate seems to descend on the planet. This is a no frills, no nonsense, "just do it" personality style whose strength in hard times can help everyone to survive. Like many of the other personality styles, it is one in which a little goes a long way.

The Seven Characteristics

1. Straight face. Individuals with the serious personality style may maintain a sober demeanor. They are solemn and not given to emotional expression.

2. No pretensions. They are realistically aware of their own capabilities, but they are also aware of their own limitations. They are not tempted by vanity or self-importance.

3. Accountability. Serious people hold themselves responsible for their actions. They will not soft peddle their own faults and do not let themselves off the hook.

4. Cogitation. They are thinkers, analyzers, evaluators, ruminators. They'll always play things over in their minds before they act.

5. Nobody's fool. Men and women with a serious personality style are sharp appraisers of others. In their ability to critique other people, they are as unhesitatingly candid as in their own self-evaluation.

6. No surprises. They anticipate problems and when the worse happens, they are prepared to deal with it.

7. Contrition. Serious people suffer greatly when they realize they've been thoughtless or impolite to others.

The Six Domains of Serious Functioning

Work and emotions are the key domains for people with serious personality style.

Work—Life is Work

For predominately serious people, work truly is the metaphor for existence. Life is work—work is life. In the workplace or during personal time, everything is a series of chores. It's hard, it may even be a grind, but you do what you have to do to survive.

Serious people see no choice in this approach to life and they do not expect to find pleasure in it, or to achieve some hidden creative potential. In this way, they differ considerably from people with the two other personality styles in which work is a key domain—conscientious types who find a sense of themselves and a need for their lives through their efforts, and aggressive individuals who experience positive fulfillment from their welding of power.

To Toil and Travail

This is a personality style especially adapted to adversity. People with this style have the strength to keep on doing their duty, which can be a particular asset to their families and to the community.

April gets up at 4:30 in the morning in order to get to work as a cook's assistant. She has four children and she organizes the young one's clothing and meals before she wakes up the older two, who will feed their little siblings and take them to a day care on their own way to school. April's husband works the night shift which means they hardly see each other except on weekends. Although they live extremely frugally, both paychecks barely cover the bills; food stamps help. April lost her job because she couldn't afford the car fare. Although in her seemingly thankless travails, she is an inspiration to others around her, but she takes no pride in her achievement. She sees it as drudgery, not heroism. Typical of the serious personality, she feels that this is her lot. It's a sour one and she does not question it.

You're born, you work, you die. Although serious people like April press on where others might give up, they get no thrill from it, as with an adventurous person who survived a frightening challenge. Neither do they get particular gratification for doing things for others as would a self-sacrificing individual. Serious types are normally cautious, avoiding risks, but when their path is strewn with hardships, they'll keep on plodding.

In the Workplace

Life is hard work for serious people, whether or not their personal circumstances are extreme. They do their duty as they see it, but the doing of it may feel like toil on a treadmill. What it feels like is irrelevant to them. They persevere regardless of their like or dislike of a task or the presence or absence of rewards. No matter what, they will do the job responsibly. They may gripe about having too much work to do, but they will do it. Without any of the ambitious, self-promoting styles in their personalities, people who are dominated by the serious style will not map out their careers in a series of stepping stones toward the big prize. It is survival and for that, they will work single mindedly to stay in place rather than to conquer new challenges. They are not activists and do not assert their rights. Unlike the self-sacrificing person who works just as hard with similar humility, the serious individual doesn't long for the appreciation that he or she fails to insist on receiving. The ability of serious types to endure discomfort enables them to tolerate routine and tedium and prodigious amounts of work. They are steadfast, loyal, and trustworthy. They take their jobs extremely seriously and though they may lack the overt enthusiasm that some employers prefer, they can be counted on to complete the job.

The Serious Leader

Predominately serious people are not eager for authority and thus unlikely to seek management level positions. They may be promoted to lower or middle management because of their productivity and years of service, however. Someone with another predominate style and a moderate amount of the serious is more likely to rise to management level. The serious leader will expect others to take on a great deal of work, regardless of likes or dislikes of any particular assignment. The leader won't shirk his or her own responsibilities. The atmosphere will not be necessarily upbeat, personally encouraging, or even supportive. A lot can be learned from such a "doer" for this employee is self-motivated and does not require inspiration from on high. Serious leaders can be quite critical of those who work for them. However, usually they don't stress about others' mistakes since they don't expect things to go right.

Lacking political skills, the serious leader may not be able to fight for a direct report's rights when necessary or to stand up for them in other important ways. But whether they say so or not, they will appreciate the steady, reliable worker who shows up and does the job day after day.

Careers For the Serious

Because you are so responsible and hard working and can put up with routine, you will do well in virtually any kind of work that doesn't force you continually to demonstrate initiative, problem solving, or deal with people in an ever cheerful way. For many serious people, civil service, government, and union regulated employment offers the opportunity to work hard without having to compete to stay alive [although the competitive in these and all other settings will almost always go further.] A moderate amount of seriousness often enhances other styles to help you put your personality strengths to work in investigative journalism, research, law, accounting, secretarial work, and health care. Avoid sales and public relations which require that you manage the personal atmosphere more creatively than is your style. Consulting work is a possibility, but be careful that you don't under price yourself.

Emotions—the Glass is Half Empty

Emotions represent the second of the serious style's ruling domains. Mostly, these individuals emit a sober, unspontanious, emotional style. Their seeming joylessness is inherent, not a cover as it may be for self-sacrificing people whom they may often resemble. Self-sacrificing Sid and serious Doug sometimes play golf together. Both say they don't really enjoy the game all that much. But Sid tends to feel guilty about leaving his family at home and having a good time on his own. Whereas Doug, though he plays well, really doesn't get more than perhaps an occasional surge of pleasure for his efforts. The glass is invariably half empty to serious men and women. They see the dark side of life in sharp focus and are constitutionally incapable of coloring with a positive brush.

Pain and loss are impossible to avoid in life to be sure. To this reality, the fourteen personality styles all react differently. The mercurial person, for example, will try to escape into pleasure, while the dramatic type will want to shift his or her eyes immediately to the bright side. A highly solitary person may not feel much of anything very strongly. A serious person will stay with the dark side, even when the intensity of the emotion has faded. This style is incapable of the self-sustaining illusions that many others require to keep their chin up. "Things will work out," a self-confident person might say, which may or may not be true. "I'll believe it when I see it," is a more likely response for the serious person, whom we could very accurately say is "the realist."

Continually confronted with the harsh realities of life, serious types can't flip the channel, as it were, to take their minds off it. Irritability is, therefore, common and as the style becomes extreme, depression becomes a real possibility.

Serious Plus Outgoing Emotional Styles

Even though this is a characteristically dark style, it often co-exists along with normally outgoing, emotionally expressive personality styles. Its effects may be subtle. A mixed dramatic/serious person for instance, will often act more emotionally engaged than she or he really feels inside. And this person would not be as startled by misfortune as would a more predominately dramatic individual.

A person who was both serious and mercurial would be particularly vulnerable to depression and perhaps drawn to and frightened by risk.

Lighten Up

Reality is the best medicine for serious people. When they want to relax and take it easy, they read or watch the news, always finding their view of life affirmed by the latest unemployment statistics, reports of disasters, accusations of political corruption, and the like. Though these subjects may not be very relaxing or cheering to most people, serious individuals expect such events and find them interesting and curiously reassuring.

Relationships—Life in the Slow Lane

Predominately serious people bring the same virtues to their personal lives that they demonstrate in the workplace. They are dependable, trustworthy, steady, and predictable in their relationships. They are not socially outgoing, which might cause some difficulty in meeting potential partners. If they find a mate though, they'll invest sincerely in the long haul. They will provide for their families and perform all the responsibilities necessary for their daily lives. They'll remain faithful even if a partner is not. They do not expect the relationship to be perfect. If anything, they expect a rocky course and surrender in advance.

Olivia found out from a friend that her husband had been cheating on her. Rather than confronting him and insisting on better behavior, she told her friend sourly, "They all cheat, don't they," and resigned herself to this bitter pill. Still, although some people may think that the serious ability to accept the worse in others is harmful to themselves, Olivia and her husband did manage to weather the strains of their marriage and are now, after forty years together, clearly devoted to one another in their old age.

Whether or not they assert themselves in their relationships or face conflict creatively, serious types tend to be critical of their mates. This trait is a logical extension of their "half empty" approach to life. Like vigilant people, they see what is "off" or "not right" in any situation or person. Unlike vigilant types, however, they are not suspicious. What they see is real.

Even so, they do not see the whole picture since they are blind to the prettier realities. This can be quite stressful to their mates who may justifiably insist that their qualities and actions are not being weighed on a balanced scale.

Remorse

Accused of an unkindness, a serious person will suffer greatly. People with this style, though they may be unable to express positive feelings, are very dependent on their loved ones. They get no self-righteous pleasure in finding fault. When they recognize that they have caused pain, they become regretful and readily take the blame. They often chalk up others as well as their own shortcomings to the imperfections of the world and they trudge on.

Stress

Serious people can't stand the pressure that people often put on them to change. Loved ones commonly insist that they look at the bright side as if their point of view was not authentic. Others also may have higher expectations for them than they may have for themselves and, therefore, attempt to push them to be more assertive: "Be ambitious. You could get a promotion if you really tried."

In the face of increasing stress, their naturally serious pessimism may turn to gloom and eventually to true depression. But most of the time, their very cynicism helps them to cope, overcoming any unsettling wistfulness. As mentioned earlier, just because they are serious doesn't mean they are unhappy.

Serious Parents

They are responsible, cautious parents who try to make their children aware of life's unavoidable hard knocks. Whereas sensitive parents will try to control the child's world in order to make it safe [wear boots even if it's not snowing just in case it starts, you'll get chilled and God forbid, get pneumonia.] Serious parents teach them not to be surprised by misfortune [even if you wear boots, scarfs, parkas, you can't avoid getting sick in winter.] Like sensitive parents, they will not encourage their children to take risks, but they will not overprotect them either. They won't fight the children's battles for them. Their children will not expect easy street and they'll have a role model on how to endure adversity. But they'll need one non-serious parent from whom to learn that a person can change things for the better as well as how to overcome difficulty.

Like conscientious and aggressive parents, serious mothers and fathers will inculcate the value of work, but they must take care to allow kids time for activities other than homework and chores. The non-serious parent, one hopes, will impart the benefits of fun and the joy of life.

Self, Real World, and Self-Control
Watch Out, Some Things Never Change

Serious people have a clear sense of who they are. They are limited people in an imperfect world. They work extremely hard since they see the world as harsh and hard work as a necessity to stay in place. Their self-critical humility, and moderation can be appealing. These people do not struggle to present a better face, to pull the wool over anybody's eyes, to improve themselves, or to fit an image. Their sense of self becomes vulnerable, however, when they are under stress or when the serious style becomes extreme. In such cases, their self-esteem can hit bottom and require some shoring up.

The real world of the serious person is a forbidding place. One way these individuals come to terms with it is to dwell on their past failures or their helplessness in the face of forces beyond their control. "If only I hadn't sold that stock fourteen years ago, I'd be well off today." "My life would have taken a different course if I had been born with a different temperament." Often these thoughts run through their mind repeatedly, acting very much like a broken record.

The other, more adaptive way they come to terms with the harsh real world is to continually prepare for the worst, and in so doing, prevent other potential calamities. In this, they take great satisfaction.

Finally, serious people prepare for the worst of the real world by removing any potential for surprise. Through sheer self-control, they keep their noses to the grindstone, adhere to routine, and remain undistracted by impulse or passion. Serious types think everything through before acting. They do not take risks or challenge fate and they don't escape into pleasure or appetites. Extremely serious people may take too little initiative, however, which may give them good cause to feel limited in life.

In a moderately serious person, however, this sober, dour approach to life may provide a literal survival advantage. There is even some evidence that those who have been somewhat cheerless, dutiful, and dependable since childhood tend to live longer than the happy-go-lucky optimists.

Tips on Dealing With the Serious Person in Your Life

1. Acceptance is key. Refrain from trying to get the serious person in your life to see the bright side of every situation or to be more outgoing, to show more enthusiasm, or to set higher goals. Whatever might be bothering you about this person, trying to change him or her is as fruitless as it is with most personality styles.

2. Look on the bright side yourself. This person is steady, responsible, loyal, hard-working, and caring. You can count on the serious person through thick and thin. These traits are extremely positive indicators for a long-term relationship.

3. Don't assume that the serious person's dark view means he or she is miserable. Although your own pessimism may result from your occasional bad moods, the attitude is utterly normal for the serious person. But if the serious "bah humbug" outlook influences your own moods, think twice about getting involved with the serious personality type.

4. You are allowed to be happy. Don't inhibit your own natural emotions just because the serious person doesn't respond as you would like. If he or she doesn't exactly jump for joy over your promotion, there's no reason to curb your own excitement.

5. Compliment the serious person for what he or she adds to your life. Expressions of caring are very important to people with this personality style, although they themselves often have trouble sharing positive feelings with you. If you praise him or her, the habit may rub off.

6. The serious person will usually comment first on what is not right in any situation. Such criticism is par for the course. For example, when you've just had an exceptional haircut, expect the serious person to comment first on your muddy raincoat or unshined shoes. Let the person get this stuff off his or her chest and then you can get on to what's right about things. In any case, don't assume that the serious person in your life hates how you look. Do you like your own haircut? Then say so and move on.

7. Be honest without being manipulative, punitive, or indeed, critical yourself. Tell the serious person in your life that being complimented and directly appreciated is very important to you. Say that you realize these sorts of comments don't come easy for him or her. Pay attention in the days that follow for at least some subtle signs that he or she heard you.

8. Don't be put off by the serious person's apparent lack of enthusiasm for you in the beginning of a relationship. Remember that this style is very, very slow to lighten up. Just because he or she fails to rave about the wonderful time being had by all doesn't mean you should not ask this person to accompany you in the future. Often a serious person's ability to show satisfaction or levity has little relation to how important being with you really is. Serious people have needs like everybody else.

9. Don't wait for a serious person to be spontaneous. Do it for both of you. Show initiative in all aspects of your life together. You'll enlarge your mutual scope of experience.

Making the Most of Your Serious Style

You are a hard worker. You persevere in all your tasks and you feel the weight of the world on your shoulders. In order to protect yourself from stress, to enhance your relationship, and to preserve your strength for truly difficult times, you need to develop some flexibility. Approach the following exercises as tasks like others you do throughout your day.

Exercise 1: Make one list of ten things you would like to have happen to you in your relationships and another one concerning your work life. Avoid expressing your wishes as negatives. For example, instead of saying, "I would like not to always do the dirty work at the office." Phrase it as, "I would like to do more responsible, enjoyable work," or name specific tasks you would prefer to be doing.

Exercise 2: For each item on your two lists, write down at least one practical action that you could take in order to make it happen. This is just an exercise, remember, not something you are going to have to do if you don't want to. The only point is to think up a way to achieve the goal, if in imagination only. For example, to use the example from Exercise 1, one action might be to request a transfer to another site or department.

Exercise 3: Again, consult your two lists. Now, sit back, close your eyes, and item-by-item, step-by-step imagine first that you are taking the action and achieving your goal. If you get used to rehearsing it in your mind, you may find it easier to approach in real life.

Exercise 4: After completing the previous exercise, again relax and close your eyes. Now, one-by-one, imagine that you have achieved each of these goals. What does it feel like? Try to visualize as many details as you can.

Exercise 5: Keep a confidential daily journal for at least one month. Each day, after recording what occurred that day, and anything else you might wish to say, sum up with a positive comment about the day. What good of any kind came out of this day? This requirement may seem an artificial constraint, and it is. But remember, it's only an exercise.

Exercise 6: If you have difficulty putting yourself forward in social situations, when seeking employment, or on the job, consider taking an assertiveness training course to learn the necessary skills.

Exercise 7: To relax, practice not thinking. For serious style, clear your mind immediately when you find yourself thinking and rethinking the same point or issue.

Exercise 8: Think of or better yet, write down [perhaps in your daily journal] ten things you like about yourself.

Exercise 9: Think or write down ten things you like about the significant other in your life.

Exercise 10: Everyday, try to compliment the important people in your life and do something just to please them. You care about them, but they may not always realize it.

Exercise 11: Every time you are about to criticize somebody, think of something favorable to say first. This will make the substance of your criticism easier to take since the person will not immediately be on the defensive. You could use this same exercise when you are about to criticize yourself.

Depressive Personality Disorder

They think there's no hope now or ever. They seem incapable of pleasure. They can't relax. They're critical and angry, while heaping abuse on themselves. All told, sadness and gloom dominate the perceptions of people with depressive personality disorder.

Depressive personality disorder can best be described as a pervasive pattern of depressive cognitions and behaviors beginning by early childhood and present in a variety of contexts as indicated by five or more of the following:

1. Usual mood is dominated by dejection, gloominess, cheerlessness, joylessness, and unhappiness.

2. Self-concept centers around beliefs of inadequacies, worthlessness, and low self-esteem.

3. Is critical, blaming, and derogatory toward self.

4. Is brooding and given to worry.

5. Is negative, critical, and judgmental toward others.

6. Is pessimistic.

7. Is prone to feeling guilty or remorseful.

8. These behaviors do not occur exclusively during major depressive episodes and are not caused by dysthymic disorder.

When the Sun Never Shines

It is a dreary world that people with depressive personality disorder inhabit and there's no escape hatch for them. They look inward and find themselves inadequate and worthy of reproach. Outwardly, they perceive an existence without hope. In others, they find cause for complaint. They are passive, helpless, hopeless. They attend to what must be done in their unhappy lives, which feels like pushing a huge weight up a steep incline. If they let go, they'll be crushed, so they have no choice but to keep up the terrible task.

Clearly, individuals with this personality disorder are in pain. They dwell on their thoughts and the unhappiness they perceive everywhere. They find no relief outside themselves, no letting down and getting away from it all. They don't even have the "luxury" of blaming others for all their misery as do those with paranoid and passive aggressive personality disorders. To people with depressive personality disorder, they only have themselves to blame. Not that their self-censure leads to an objective appraisal of their attitudes and behaviors, for most do not see that the gloom comes from inside them and colors their every perception and behavior. Even if they do, they believe there is no hope at all for change.

Coping With People With
Depressive Personality Disorder

People who are constantly unhappy and who think that nothing will ever change are difficult to deal with because nothing you say or do helps. Becoming angry may help you vent your feelings, but it will accomplish little that is constructive since a person with this personality disorder may react to your anger with such guilt that you'll end up feeling guilty yourself. You will also end up driving this person deeper into their depression.

Tips on dealing with the serious person may help. In any case, keep in mind that relationships with others are very important to people with depressive personality disorder, although their sourness may make you think otherwise. If you have been a significant person in his or her life, be compassionate, but firm about going for help. Consider going together if you are a couple.

16

Making the Most of Your Personality Style

N ow you see it. Your personality style is a kind of map of both inner geography and the outward direction of your life. You follow its pathway every day of your life. You seek and react to experiences and people according to your own style. You change or stay the same according to your own style.

As we said in Chapter I, temperament is what you are born with and character is the result of what you learn and experience. Temperament is the hand you are dealt at conception which sets the stage for all later experiences. The development of your personality style depends on what you bring to your environment and what it brings to you—nature and nurture, heredity and environment.

Not long ago, child development specialists believed that life experiences alone shaped an individual's personality. Now, thanks to the work of psychiatrists, Sibylle Escalona, Alexander Thomas, Stella Chess, and Daniel Stern, among others, researchers have taken a renewed interest in the biologic "givens" of individual personality. In the words of some researchers in this field, "What IQ has been to our understanding of cognition, temperament is becoming to our understanding of personality development."

Parents who have more than one child know that each child is undeniably unique and that the differences among their children are apparent almost from the first moments of life. Some infants cry a lot, some don't. Some are easily soothed, some aren't. Some quickly develop regular eating and sleeping patterns, whereas others are difficult to train to any schedule. Some have powerful, intense emotional reactions, whereas others are calm and easy going.

Children are born with these differences. Every individual enters the world with his or her own particular constitution and reaction patterns, at least some of which can be traced to his or her genes. These are the inborn, biologically determined differences among all individuals that set the stage for the differences in personality.

The Four Humors

The ancient Greeks believed that nature consisted of four elements—air, earth, fire, and water. Each of these cosmic elements was represented in the human body by a corresponding humor or bodily fluid—blood, black bile, yellow bile, phlegm. Based on these humors, Hippocrates, considered the father of western medicine, formulated the first scientific typology of personality in the fifth century BC. He postulated four temperament styles, each of which corresponded to a predominance of one humor: sanguine; [hopeful, enthusiastic, optimistic, energetic] melancholic; [sad, moody, withdrawn] choleric; [irascible, irritable, impulsive] and phlegmatic; [apathetic, slow.]

Every person's personality could be classified into one of the four categories which also predicted everyone's vulnerability to mental and physical disease. This is a simple scientific classification that anticipated modern understanding of temperament and personality in many ways. "The ancient Greeks had an uncanny knack for intuiting the nature of things thousands of years before the available instrumentation could confirm and refine these hypotheses," Psychiatrist Alan J. Francis and psychologist, Thomas Widiger, have noted.

"Their concept that behavior arises at least in part from the state of the body's chemistry is as an impressive a biological intuition as was the inspired physical intuition that matter consisted of atoms." Even though, it strikes us today as naive, the "humorist" recognized simple fundamental dimensions along which all humor behavior can be measured. Hippocrates and his followers recognized also that these dimensions of personality are biologically determined. We know today that inborn, biological style strongly shapes an individual's ultimate personality style.

The Three Temperaments

In 1956 some twenty-five hundred years after Hippocrates, husband and wife psychiatrists, Alexander Thomas and Stella Chess began an ongoing study following 133 individuals from their infancy onward. In their decades of research, they identified nine categories of inborn temperamental variables and three broad basic normal temperamental styles, into which the majority of infants seemed to fit. Their work was the first in recent history to show scientifically that temperament and behavior by the age of three powerfully predict personality in adulthood.

The Variables of Temperament

1. Activity level. Every infant has a characteristic activity level from slow to speedy.

2. Regularity. Some are regular in their eating and other biological functions, others, unpredictable.

3. Approach/withdrawal. When presented with a new toy, food, person, or other stimulus, does the baby respond positively and with interest [approach] or negatively and fearfully [withdrawal]?

4. Adaptability. Does the child learn and adjust to new situations and tasks easily or does he or she have difficulty adjusting to change?

5. Threshold of responsiveness. What does it usually take to get a "rise" out of the baby, a strong sensory stimulation, such as a loud noise or a mild one such as a soft voice? Does the child become over-stimulated easily by sensory experiences?

6. Reaction intensity. Some react loudly to everything, whereas others typically are less intense in their positive and negative reactions.

7. Mood. Even babies have characteristic mood patterns, varying from predominately cheerful to frequently unhappy.

8. Distractibility. Does the child tend to focus on tasks at hand or is he or she easily distracted?

9. Attention span and persistence. How long does the baby typically stick with an activity and will he or she persist despite difficulties?

About forty percent of all children fit into what Thomas and Chess called the "Easy Child Category." These children adapt easily, are regular in their habits, are quick to adapt to new situations, are happy most of the time, and usually quiet. Overall, they are easy to deal with.

Fifteen percent of children fall into the "Slow to Warm Up Group." They don't find new situations or people easy and they react in a mildly negative manner. But they take to them eventually in their own time. They are not intense in their reactions and are fairly happy most of the time after they get used to new things.

Thomas and Chess identified the "difficult temperament" among ten percent of the children in their studies. These kids are harder for parents to deal with because their reactions are intense and often negative. They don't adapt easily and they don't adjust well to regular schedules. They are more demanding of parents, less easy to please. While difficult children display a wide variety of additional temperaments, according to Thomas and Chess, there are three main categories in which most children seem to fall by reason of innate biology regardless of culture. The temperaments represent normal styles of response with which children are born. Thomas and Chess have shown that the parents' attitudes and actions have little influence on their children's basic temperamental patterns.

Interestingly enough, almost any industrial psychologist, [that is the psychologist who specializes in the workplace,] will tell you that the workforce generally falls into the same broad categories fairly predictably. Just about forty percent of all employees in almost any organization are fairly easy to deal with. They do their job. They deal with each other in responsible ways. They are often cheerful and pleasant. They will also tell you that about fifteen percent of the people in any given organization tend to be kind of slow to "warm up" to the group, slow to become part of the team, and a little slow to engage or to adopt the culture of the organization they have been hired into. And, almost any industrial psychologist will tell you that about ten percent of any workforce creates about ninety percent of the problems in the workplace.

These patterns which appear by age three continue throughout life in a reasonably predictable pattern.

Strategies for Change

Sometimes life changes you. Many young men and women have gone to war and come back different. Their values and attitudes were rearranged for them the hard way. Sometimes education will provide the impetus for change. Many women began efforts to reshape their personalities as the women's movement taught them to question traditional views of women's roles.

Changes in personality do not come about overnight. For the Vietnam vets who were changed by their experience, for example, it took months of war horrors to set them on a changed life path. Women who are attempting to learn new roles and personality patterns must struggle with the attitudes and expectations that were set in motion when the doctor uttered "It's a girl." The work of psychotherapy may continue for months or years. Personality is an automatic pilot that guides us through our lives. To try to change it, one must learn the complex components of the system and learn to modify their arrangement, which is no small challenge.

Fine Tuning the System

Your personality self-portrait [provided you have taken the self-portrait instrument] has given you a map of your own component styles and the individual chapters have provided their descriptions and bases. This material, combined with practical exercises, may be sufficient for you to make adjustments to your personality, or at least to smooth

some of your rough edges. For example, if you know that you sometimes go too far out of your way for other people in your self-sacrificing
manner, you can learn to catch yourself as you are about to offer too
much. If your self-confident style sometimes makes you insensitive to
other people's needs, you can practice paying more attention to the
needs of others.

Having become aware of your style's characteristic trouble spots,
you may now be able to learn better habits. Day in, day out habits are a
big part of personality styles and fortunately, with sufficient motivation, habits can be changed. If you are dramatically disorganized, for
example, you might learn from a book how to get and stay organized.
If you are a leisurely procrastinator, you could sign up for a workshop
on overcoming procrastination. Assess your troublesome habits on a
style-by-style basis and look for a practical way of dealing with them as
we have done in our exercises for "making the most" of each style.

Love and Work

After you have assessed your key domains, consider the effect your
personality patterns have had on the two key domains of human
life—love [relationships] and work. Are you continually frustrated,
unhappy, unfulfilled, operating far below your potential or unable to
function at all in these essential areas? Are you sad and lonely, frightened of asserting yourself, unable to express or experience appropriate
feelings? Are you creative? Are your creative powers trapped inside you
unable to come forth? Most important, do you find yourself repeating
the same patterns time after time, the same old miseries in your love
life, the same old miseries and problems at work?

If your personality style is not working for you and you want to
make adjustments, it is important to keep in mind that it requires time
and discipline. Like any other life change, it is necessary to decide what
kind of person you want to be and what adjustments you can make,
then establish a set of goals and action steps to get you to where you
would like to be.

But for healthy personalities, there is no way to overstate the importance of discipline and time. Decide what changes you want to make and stick to it. Even if you find yourself lapsing into old behaviors, [falling off the horse] it's important to get up, dust yourself off, and get started again. Don't give up. Remember, people, that includes you, change slowly. It will take some time.

Then Again,
Maybe You are Fine the Way You Are

So many people want to change themselves. Before you consider psychiatric or psychological intervention to alter the essential shape of your personality pattern, you might ask yourself your reasons for wanting to change it. Take a look at your personality self-portrait. Compare it with those of others in your life. The personality self-portrait shows you that you resemble other people in fundamental human ways and differ from them along the same dimensions. Notice that in overall shape, each self-portrait you observe is different. The intensity and configuration of the fourteen personality styles in your self-portrait are yours alone. Throughout these pages, we have recommended ways you can make changes in your personality in order to make the most of yourself. We have also said that individual personality is a kind of fate, changes or no changes, you are fated to be yourself, short of the ideal, full of your own peculiarities and blemishes. You are not the perfect companion or parent or leader or helper, and not the worse either. You do things the way you do them. He does things the way he does them. She does them still another way. Most of the time, that's just fine. Your brain cells and your psyche are at all times capable of learning to accept and appreciate yourself and others for the differences in the ways we all think, feel, and behave. For many people, that is the single greatest adjustment their personality needs.

It is often true that at home or at work, what we sometimes refer to as a "difficult personality" or even a personality disfunction, is in fact a given individual's failure to recognize the legitimate differences between people. Differences which, in and of themselves, are not right or wrong. So before you work on yourself too hard, ask yourself to what degree you have integrated the following three statements into your understanding of the world around you:

1. People are more alike than they are different. That's right. There are things that everyone shares, no matter where they are from. It doesn't matter if they are from South America or Asia. It doesn't matter if they are from Australia or South Africa. Everyone shares the same basic needs. Everyone wants food to eat when they are hungry. Everyone wants water to drink when they are thirsty. Everyone wants to be warm when it is cold outside. Everyone wants to feel valued and appreciated by somebody. Everybody wants an opportunity to realize their potential to achieve. And, everybody wants to be happy.

2. While people are more alike than they are different, they are different. Although it is true that we all want food to eat when we are hungry, the variety of foods that a given individual might choose to eat are almost unlimited. One person would simply prefer to have meat and potatoes, nothing more, nothing less. Another person might prefer a meal of pizza or kimchi. One might want to be warm when it is cold outside, but how warm we might want our homes to be might vary dramatically. We might all like sports to one degree or another, but one person might have a great preference for football, while another person can't imagine why anyone would spend their time watching football rather than gymnastics. We might all like to travel at one time or another in our lives. However, one person might define travel as going just a few hundred miles from their place of birth and always staying in the country that they are familiar with. On the other hand, another person might define travel as visiting some strange, exotic country thousands of miles from where they have lived most of their life.

We all want to be happy, but how one person defines "happy" could be different from how another person defines "happy." Some people find wonderful contentment in staying close to home, close to family, and close to friends, and find life very fulfilling in the most simple experiences. Then again, there are those people who find happiness and fulfillment only by being on the stage, that is becoming famous or perhaps even infamous. They need the spotlight to be happy. They may find that they are happy only when they are performing on a stage or when they are giving a campaign speech.

3. Everybody wants to feel that they matter. Perhaps the most consistent characteristic of all healthy personality styles is that all emotionally healthy individuals want to be valued. They want to live lives of meaning and purpose. Therefore, the wisest possible strategy, both at home and at work, is to develop ways of relating to others in a win-win manner. Helping others fulfill their need to be happy and valued is the best way to gain their cooperation in your efforts to be happy and valued.

The bottom line, learn to speak the language of each of the fourteen personality styles and you'll find you can get through to others much more easily, perhaps even develop compassion for those you never thought you could tolerate. And to your surprise, you may discover that your openness, your willingness to create win-win relationships gets others vested in your success.

It may sound trite or over simplistic to say that everybody just wants to be happy, but the truth is that they do. And if you can find a way to help them achieve that goal, you will often discover that they will help you achieve your goal of becoming happy and fulfilled as well.

0-595-22239-0

www.ingramcontent.com/pod-product-compliance
Lightning Source LLC
Chambersburg PA
CBHW061338280526
45784CB00001B/54